Time flows on, and if it did not, it would be a bad prospect for those who do not sit at golden tables. Methods become exhausted; stimuli no longer work. New problems appear and demand new methods. Reality changes; in order to represent it, modes of representation must also change. Nothing comes from nothing; the new comes from the old, but that is why it is new. *Bertolt Brecht*

Thinking with elsewhere   Comparative urbanism   Located theory
Terminology   Everyday observation   Urban ecology
Site-writing   Site-reading   Critical spatial practice
Action-orientation   Participatory design   Relational urban design
Worlding   Visual ethnography   Iterative design
Collaborative workshops   Participatory film-making   Re-enactment
Visual palimpsest   Experimental photography   In situ modelling
Hacking data   Community co-design   Making accessible
In situ editing   Hacking knowledge   Crowd production
Undercover journalism   Performance   Immersion
Performative photography   Investigative photojournalism   Alter ego
Experimental documentation   Visual ethnography   Infrastructure narratives
Systematic photography   3D laser scanning   Survey
Repeat photography   Documenting inscriptions   Surface analysis
Participatory photography   Workshops   Visual lobbying
Documentary   Collaborative photography   Assisted self-portraiture
Image interview   Visual interaction   Public conversation
Photo biography   Visual analysis   Archival interpretation
Computer modelling   Mapping   Morphology
Diary writing   Public reading   Mobile performance
Open-ended ethnography   Listening   Embodied practice
Walking   Wayfinding   Getting lost
Constructing situations   Autobiography   Intuition
Smell mapping   Chemical analysis   Olfactory design
Cross-continental performance   Music exchange   Live-stream
Multi-media installation   Bordering practices   Swapping
Visual comparison   Sand sculpture   Watercolour
Migration visualisation   Sculptural installation   Film
Negotiation   Social building   Assembling
Spatial appropriation   Photo matrixes   Documenting demolition
Temporary installation   Documenting immateriality   Memory transmission
Collaboration with materials   Salvage   Story-telling
Speculation   Poetics   Fire

ENGAGED URBANISM

Cities & Methodologies

Edited by Ben Campkin
& Ger Duijzings

I.B.TAURIS
LONDON · NEW YORK

CONTENTS

PREFACE AND ACKNOWLEDGEMENTS

This compendium of projects and texts presents innovative and experimental methodologies designed by academics, artists, activists and others to produce new knowledge about cities. The contributors work in, and across, an array of academic disciplines and practices, including anthropology, architecture, architectural history, fine art, live art, engineering, film-making, geography, graphic design, photography and urban planning. What binds them together is a commitment, expressed in varied ways, to understanding the social, cultural and material realities of the contemporary metropolis. Through the creative juxtaposition of methodological statements and experiments, the volume as a whole captures something of the dynamic experiences, discourses and other realities that constitute today's cities worldwide.

The work featured has been selected from University College London's (UCL's) Cities Methodologies programme: a rolling series of exhibitions and events.[1] Since 2009, Cities Methodologies has, in eight instalments, provided space for informal exchange and the sharing of innovative methodologies across a wide range of disciplines. In various iterations, it has consisted of a walk-through exhibition, emulating the form of a street, or a grid of streets, enlivened by talks, workshops, readings, dialogues, interviews, informal conversations, seminars, screenings and performances, all designed to familiarise visitors with the methodological choices, challenges and findings of participant researchers. At best, streets are the setting for public expressions and unpredictable encounters, with the potential to produce creative friction as well as to accommodate diversity. This form has been adopted as the appropriate one for the Cities Methodologies programme, so as to accommodate an eclectic range of researchers, methods and cities worldwide. Although it is hard for a book to emulate a street, this compendium is conceived in the same spirit, and is therefore open to being read and used in multiple ways. As a public site of everyday interactions and mundane practices, the street can be tactically appropriated to contest assumed conditions.[2] In this vein we hope that this book will provide inspiration for those who seek to produce new knowledge with a view to making better cities.

Cities Methodologies was initiated to provide space to foster new ideas and inventions. Led by UCL's Urban Laboratory, the initiative reflects a desire to ground research locally, within specific cities, and to compare and exchange experiences across a growing network of urban laboratories — broadly conceived, and not just those based within conventional academic settings — across the globe. As a curated project, this open and flexible format accommodates a plurality of distinctive curatorial and collaborative research practices and formal and informal networks that have emerged in diverse places and institutions. As a compendium that includes many strong collaborative projects, as well as outstanding work by sole researchers, the book points to a rapidly evolving and eclectic field of critically engaged urban research. The geographical scope is wide and includes glimpses of Bangkok, Beirut, Belfast, Belgrade, Berlin, Bucharest, Cairo, Chester, Chicago, Halden, Hong Kong, Johannesburg, Kaohsiung, Kisumu, London, Mainz, Manchester, Mexico City, Mumbai, New York City, Petra, Phnom Penh, Prishtina, Rio de Janeiro, Rome, San Lorenzo de Tarapacá, Salford, Sarajevo, Shanghai, Tunis, Vienna, Visaginas and Windsor.

The Cities Methodologies initiative began in 2008 with a grant received by Ger Duijzings from the UCL Arts and Humanities Faculty towards a faculty-wide event around a 'cities' theme. In conversation with John Aiken (then Director of the UCL Slade School of Fine Art), the idea emerged to focus on 'urban research methodologies' as the only common denominator, rather than try to identify an overarching theme. Whether working in the social sciences or arts, for example, the premise was that all researchers of cities have, consciously and explicitly or not, a 'methodology': that is, a way of perceiving and exploring urban environments and phenomena. Cities Methodologies was settled upon as the title, with both terms rendered plural, reflecting the idea that every city, every urban site, every emerging condition or issue, needs its own distinctive method of exploration. This concept found wide resonance and has proved productive as new editions of the programme have been realised.

The first exhibition, in 2009, was jointly hosted by UCL's Slade School of Fine Art Research Centre and the UCL Urban Laboratory and was organised by Ger Duijzings (UCL School of Slavonic and East European Studies) and John Aiken (UCL Slade School of Fine Art), with curatorial assistance from artist and activist Rastko Novaković and a selected group of invited participants. Since 2010, seven further events have been produced in London, led by Ben Campkin (Bartlett School of Architecture, Director of the UCL Urban Laboratory and a contributor to the inaugural 2009 exhibition), with curators drawn from the Urban Laboratory's Steering Group and the Slade, and participants selected through public calls and a curatorial review process. An offshoot programme was produced in Bucharest, Romania, in 2010, curated by Aurora Király, Simona Dumitriu and Ger Duijzings.

The curators and editors would like to thank all those who have committed time and energy to the Cities Methodologies initiative, in particular the individuals and groups who have produced and exhibited work and who have organised and run events. Special thanks also, of course, to the many contributors to this book who have generously shared their work in the spirit of Cities Methodologies as a collaborative endeavour. It has only been possible to include a small selection to represent the hundreds of participants from Cities Methodologies, but nonetheless an excellent indicative sample.

We are also grateful to the UCL units and departments that have, on more than one occasion, supported Cities Methodologies with financial and in-kind contributions towards running costs, including the Faculties of Arts and Humanities, Engineering, Social and Historical Sciences, the Bartlett Faculty of the Built Environment, including the Bartlett School of Planning and the Bartlett School of Architecture, UCL Grand Challenges, the School of Slavonic and East European Studies, the Slade School of Fine Art, the Department of English and the Department of Geography.

We would particularly like to thank the following colleagues who have provided curatorial, administrative, technical and other kinds of support: Wes Aelbrecht, John Aiken, Adriana Allen, Sabina Andron, Pushpa Arabindoo, Matthew Beaumont, Sarah Bell, Camillo Boano, Rohan Bolton, Matthew Bowles, John Bremner, Susan Collins, Max Colson, Julio Davila, Adam Drazin, Michael Duffy, Simona Dumitriu, Mary Fulbrook, Nick Gallent, Matthew Gandy, Andrew Harris, Laura Hirst, Liz Hudson, Aurora Király, Vera Marin, Clare Melhuish, Caroline Newton, Rastko Novaković, James Paskins, Alan Penn, Hilary Powell, David Price, Peg Rawes, Kieren Reed, Jane Rendell, Jennifer Robinson, Rebecca Ross, Rafael Schacter, Ian Scott, Bob Sheil, Claire Thomson, Nigel Titchener-Hooker and Jo Wolff.

We also wish to express our gratitude to the Polish Cultural Institute (London and Bucharest), the Embassy of the Kingdom of the Netherlands in Bucharest, the Romanian National Cultural Fund (AFCN) and the Goethe Institute in Bucharest.

We are immensely grateful to all those who have contributed to the book's production. At I.B.Tauris, thanks to David Stonestreet, David Campbell and colleagues for their professionalism and help to realise the vision behind the project. As Editorial Assistants, Rodrigo Cardoso did an excellent job of patiently and professionally coordinating the editorial process; and Jordan Rowe provided invaluable support in managing the final stages. Finally, massive thanks to Guglielmo Rossi who, as the book's designer, has captured the spirit of Cities Methodologies by crafting each page intelligently to communicate not only the content and qualities of varied research, but also the journeys and encounters from which it derives.

UCL Cities *Methodologies* 2011
Exhibition and events showcasing
innovative methods in urban research
4 to 7 May 2011
UCL
Venue:
Slade Research Centre
UCL, Woburn Square
London WC1H 0AB
4 May, 18:30 - 21:30
Exhibition launch
Full events programme and opening hours
available at www.ucl.ac.uk/urbanlab
For general enquiries please email Füsun Türetken
at fusun.turetken.09@ucl.ac.uk with the subject CM 2011.
Design Füsun Türetken
Image courtesy of subREAL, 'Framing Bucharest', 2002
UCL Urban Laboratory
UCL Bartlett Faculty of the Built Environment
UCL School of Slavonic and Eastern European Studies
UCL Slade School of Fine Art
urbanlab

CITIES *METHODOLOGIES*
Exhibition and events showcasing innovative urban research methodologies, **4-7 July 2012**
Launch, 4 July, 18.30, all welcome
UCL Slade Research Centre, Woburn Square, London, WC1H 0NS
Open Thurs to Fri 10.00-20.00, Sat 10.00-13.00
Programme and updates: www.ucl.ac.uk/urbanlab
Adriana Allen-Rachel Alliston-Sarah Bayliss-Megan Bradshaw-Otto von Busch-Ben Campkin-Caterina Carola-Vanesa Castán Broto-Alejandra Celedon-Paul Charman-Julian Cheyne-Steven Chodoriwsky-Philip Comerford-Steve Dowding-Andreas Eriksson-Ismail Farouk-Gynna Franco-Hayley Gewer-Mohamad Hafeda-Hanna Hilbrandt-Steven Hobbs-Sandra Jasper-Sebastian Juhnke-David Kroll-Angela Last-Matteo Melioli-Rebecca Merrill-Ignacia Mesa-Agnieszka Mlicka-City as Interface module from MSc Adaptive Architecture and Computation-MSc Building and Urban Design in Development-MSc Urban Studies-Azzurra Muzzonigro-Marcus Neustetter-Benny Nilsen-Farid Noufaily-Fiacha O Dubhda-Alexandra Parry-Brent Pilkey-Hilary Powell-Liz Rideal-David Roberts-Mireille Roddier-Rebecca Ross-Troy Schaum-Rachel Scicluna-Ariel Shepherd-Rosalyne Shieh-Simson&Volley-Martin Slavin-Carolyn Smith-Anna Subirats-Johan Thom-Evren Uzer-Mike Wells-Peter R.H. Wood-Laura Weatherly-Daniele Zacchi
Curatorial committee
Dr Pushpa Arabindoo, UCL Urban Laboratory/Geography
Dr Camillo Boano, UCL Development Planning Unit
Dr Ben Campkin, UCL Urban Laboratory/Bartlett School of Architecture (Chair)
Dr Ger Duijzings, UCL School of Slavonic & EastEuropean Studies
Dr Andrew Harris, UCL Urban Laboratory/Geography
Laura Hirst (Secretary), UCL Urban Laboratory
Kieren Reed, Slade School of Fine Art

UCL
UCL Cities Methodologies 2010
Exhibition and events programme 5-7th May 2010
Venue: Slade Research Centre, UCL, Woburn Square, London WC1H 0AB
5th May, 6.30 pm, exhibition launch
6th May, 10am to 8pm; 7th May, 10am to 6pm
Full events programme available at www.ucl.ac.uk/urbanlab
SILENT CITY
BETTER CITY
Recent innovations in urban research methods from the UCL community including distinctive perspectives and interdisciplinary collaborations from the built environment, the arts and humanities and the social and historical sciences
urbanlab

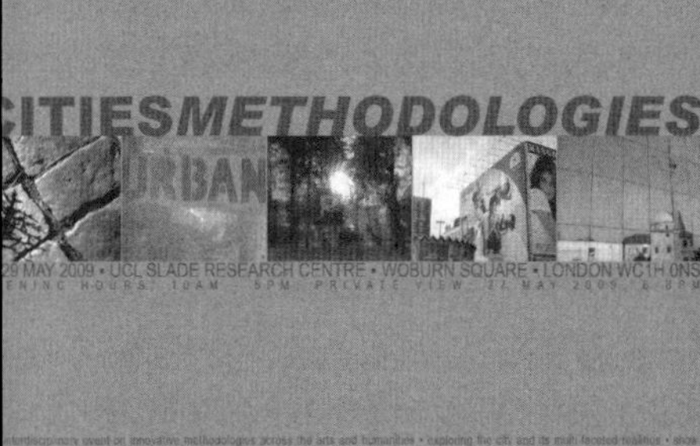

Cities Methodologies publicity, 2009–2014.

Engaged urbanism: situated and experimental methodologies for fairer cities

Ben Campkin and Ger Duijzings

The purpose of this book is to encourage methodological innovation and exchange in the formation of new knowledge about cities. It presents a selection of experimental strategies and tactics devised to critically explore cities and urbanization. Rather than being confined only to the built-environment professions, or to the social science terrain of 'urban studies', the contributors work within and between a wide variety of disciplines and practices. What new methods are being developed to explore the changing realities of contemporary cities and urban life, and how are established methods being updated and transformed? Where is urbanisation taking place? What forms does it take? As cities transform, how do researchers and practitioners gather information about the new issues and phenomena emerging across the globe? With whom do they collaborate and how? How do they gather data, and what protocols do they apply? What challenges arise in what are often intuitive, in situ and 'trial-and-error' processes? What goes wrong and how are lessons learned? These are some of the questions that prompt and frame this compendium. Going beyond the immediate research context, we also question which methods of presentation and communication are being used to disseminate research findings, and who the findings of the research are being shared with.

Ongoing conversations about method are crucial in urban scholarship, where theorisation can easily lose touch with newly emerging empirical realities. The urban field will benefit from fine-grained empirical research and a renewed search for sophisticated and situated methods, sensitive to diverse local contexts, and adaptive to the new questions arising from changing conditions. This stance resonates with sociologists Barney G. Glaser and Anselm L. Strauss's classic call for more 'grounded' theory.[1]

In this collection's opening two chapters, in 'Cities methodologies matter: comparative urbanism and global urban theory' (Chapter 1), Jennifer Robinson synthesises her plea for a post-colonial, decentred and empirically based comparative urbanism, while in 'Methods, metaphors and the interdisciplinary terrain of urban research' (Chapter 2), Matthew Gandy calls for an expansion of the imaginative and methodological scope of urban writing and the inclusion of dimensions of everyday experience as an important focus.[2] We align ourselves with these two positions, and the volume as a whole actively and creatively addresses the challenges these writers present.

Gandy cautions that grand theories and terminologies can limit or impoverish the analysis of concrete cases by overriding nuances of meaning, and by prioritising hegemonic (albeit parochial) 'circuits of knowledge'. The result can be an aestheticisation of scientific models and metaphors, which are mobilised and coopted within a capitalist logic that divorces them from specific locations. He cites the recent scholarship on 'planetary urbanisation' that contends that thinking of 'the city', and individual cities for that matter, as distinctive entities and analytical categories, is obsolete.[3] Although we can no longer rely on the traditional opposition between 'the urban' and 'non-urban', we concur with Gandy that it is still possible — and desirable — to talk meaningfully of individual cities in terms of their geographical and historical specificities and/or bio-physical, cultural, and political characteristics.

It is a fundamental acknowledgement underpinning this anthology that urban sites are diverse, specific, unique and changeable, and that this requires methodological flexibility. We need to be prepared to adapt or fine-tune our methods to respond to new issues and questions and to capture the variety and dynamism of urban sites and experiences across time and space. This means investment in methodologically innovative work that is sensitive to empirical complexity and malleable in its analytical and theoretical framing. Emphasizing the importance of open-ended or hybrid approaches, the research presented here also stresses the need for methodologies to be anchored in concrete places at specific points in time. This need for both openness and specificity is emphasised by both Gandy and Robinson. As Robinson argues in 'Cities methodologies matter', new evidence and ideas are most likely to be forthcoming if we look beyond existing centres of scholarship in 'global cities', such as New York and London, to those places and contexts where contemporary urbanisation is happening most rapidly and dramatically. She places emphasis on the locatedness of all theoretical endeavours and the need to constantly adapt and situate our concepts and methods within the local contexts in which we work. Most importantly, we should start thinking with variation, in Robinson's words, 'thinking with elsewhere' across different cases, rather than trying to 'control for difference'.

Each city, each urban site, and each urban phenomenon may need its own methodological toolbox, validating the special ontological status of individual cities and places in different parts of the world, each with their characteristics and histories. Following Robinson's post-colonial approach, as a compendium the book paves the way for a comparative urbanism that critiques and destabilises the dominant sites of urban theorizing and foregrounds case studies from a much wider range of cities. We have been keen to feature cases from many parts of the world, such as post-socialist Central and Eastern Europe, the Middle East, Asia, Africa, and Latin America. Furthermore, numerous individual contributions are themselves comparative in approach, and they invite theoretical and methodological exchange and adaptation.

We define the content of the book, and the scholarship and projects it features, as engaged urbanism. By this we mean work that critically and purposefully responds to the concrete problems and issues that are important to improving quality of life for city dwellers. That involves, first of all, collaboration across disciplines and other knowledge silos, and dynamic uses of bodies of historical and theoretical knowledge, bringing theory and practice into productive interaction. Most projects included here are interdisciplinary (transforming conventional methods through new alignments across disciplines) or transdisciplinary (with diverse researchers focusing collaboratively on questions or challenges salient within multiple disciplines, and resonant for a wide range of urban practitioners). As a field of research, the urban, as the contributors demonstrate, necessitates bridging across the conventional divides of the social and historical sciences, the arts and humanities, the built environment and the engineering and physical sciences.

Secondly, engaged urbanism increasingly takes place outside of traditional academic environments, featuring strong collaborations between academic, professional groups, community-based organisations, artists, activists and others. Most contributors to the book support, implicitly or explicitly, an engaged, hands-on urbanism that is sensitive to local contexts and employs collaborative, interactive and participatory methods that work to secure the interests of vulnerable categories of people — who suffer dislocation, eviction, loss of community and housing as a consequence of war, destruction of livelihoods and habitat and processes of segregation, gentrification and ghettoisation.

In an engaged urbanism that is practical in orientation, scholarship and theorisation work in tandem with other forms of intervention, with the goal of improving cities and urban conditions in the present and future. This focus on contemporary and future cities does not preclude historical work. On the contrary, it necessitates a heightened historical awareness of, for example, previous processes and phases of urbanization, or of the colonial structuring of disciplines and professions, all of which continue to shape conditions and practices in the present.

In privileging methods that are interventionist, we align with — and feature — examples of 'critical spatial practice', a term coined by Jane Rendell and exemplified in the book in a selection of texts and projects that have been inspired by her method of 'site-writing'.[4] Common to these is an explicit acknowledgement of the authors' own positionality, as well as their commitment to designing reflexive and situated methodologies, being critical of processes through which knowledge is constructed, and open to the questioning and renegotiation of established disciplinary procedures.[5]

Given our scepticism of rigid generalised models, this anthology does not offer a simplistic blueprint for others to reproduce, or a textbook or manual that describes methods to be emulated. The work presented here is embedded in, and has emerged from, a close engagement with specific cities and their material conditions, and this would undermine any attempt at generic application. In showcasing work that is highly diverse and inventive of new methods and practices, or that repurposes established ones, our intention is to inspire further experimentation and collaboration.

The volume is organised into six cross-cutting sections, discussed in more detail below:

- I Frames
- II Site-Specific Collaborations
- III Performance and Participation
- IV Situating Images and Imaginaries
- V Embodied Cartographies
- VI Fabric and Fabrication

These can be read consecutively or otherwise, as the reader chooses. No matter which pathways are taken, using the book will involve encounters with:

- × diverse conceptual frameworks and collaborative and curatorial strategies underpinning urban research;
- × projects situated in the distinctive qualities of particular cities and periods;
- × methods and practices that help to elicit and underscore the performative, imagined, experiential and everyday dimensions of urban space;
- × reflections on the materiality of cities, broadly conceived, and the varied fabric of urban space.

The book includes a cross-referencing system, echoing city maps such as the old *A–Z: London Street Atlas*, with arrows and page references to point readers from one chapter to related and comparable ones, as from one neighbourhood to another. This play on cartography reflects the idea of the book (and the exhibitions from which it derives) as an arrangement of streets.

Following the two framing essays by Gandy and Robinson, in Part II, 'Site-Specific Collaborations', the next three contributions foreground our interest in featuring modes of practice-led research that are particularly attentive to context. These authors offer examples of experimental research-led teaching, developed through careful pedagogic practices and a self-reflexive attitude to the position of the researcher, as well as a critical and flexible response to the site of research. Jane Rendell's 'Site-writing' (Chapter 3) is a mode of performative intervention, an approach to urbanistic and architectural criticism where the positionality of the writer and researcher, the specifics of particular places or artworks, and the spatiality of text are all emphasised and seen to be in dynamic relation. As critical spatial practice, this method seeks to bridge the gap between critical and creative work and to 'write sites', rather than 'write about sites'.[6] The project Site-Writing/Site-Reading, presented here by Rendell's postgraduate students, shows how the method has been adopted in a range of different contexts. Site-writing gives a powerful capacity to criticism as a mode of intervention rather than as detached commentary.

In studio-based architecture and urban-planning education, taking a post-colonial approach means changing established design practices to include peripheral and hidden perspectives and silenced voices. In Chapter 4, 'Towards an architecture of engagement: researching contested urbanism and informalities', Camillo Boano, Caroline Newton and Giorgio Talocci argue that architects and urban designers must reform their practices in ways that makes them 'active, relational, collective, embedded, reflexive and transdisciplinary'. Their project is collaborative and works across teaching, research and built-environment practice so as to create an action-oriented approach to architecture, using participatory design methods to engage with activists and community organisations, and providing a framework for contestation of planning decisions in the context of informal urban settlements.

Suzanne Hall and Juliet Davis make a similar call for a critical reorientation of design practices in '"Worlding" the studio: methodological experiments and the art of being social' (Chapter 5), drawing inspiration from Aihwa Ong's concept of 'worlding', meaning engaging critically and creatively with local and global forces that impact on particular localities as part of the design process, in order to reimagine urban futures and provide alternatives to the injustices associated with the logic of neoliberal urbanization in its variegated forms.[7] Pitched against commercial architectural design approaches that fetishise form and architecture-as-object, their approach mixes methods, employing, for example, visual ethnographies and defining the research and design process as an iterative one.

Given its origins in the Cities Methodologies project (see preface), London figures prominently in the book, and Part III, 'Performance and Participation', is wholly dedicated to research being done on and in this global city. Here, all of the contributions pertain to the redevelopment of London and reveal this as an ongoing and contested negotiation. They connect in different ways with the themes of participation and performance, both in terms of research and built-environment practices, and urbanisation processes at large.

Several projects, such as those of David Roberts and his collaborators (Chapter 6), Felipe Lanuza Rilling (Chapter 7) and Kate Crawford and her collaborators (Chapter 8), engage with 'estate redevelopment' in contemporary London, which, it should be noted, mostly refers to the demolition of social housing and the redevelopment of new housing, with private ownership increasing and the numbers of affordable rented homes decreasing.[8] As showcased in 'From "heroin" to heroines' (Chapter 6), as an artist and architectural researcher, Roberts collaborated with a group of tenants of a London estate using site-specific workshops, architectural history, performance and film-making to critique housing policies and practices and to counter hegemonic dystopian 'sink estate' narratives.

Felipe Lanuza Rilling's work 'Four palimpsests on the erasure of the Heygate Estate' (Chapter 7) uses experimental photography, moving images and local archives to engage in the debates around the demolition of a high-profile estate in South London. His palimpsests are spatially and visually evocative reimaginings of the Heygate Estate's past. They are large-scale and immersive, evoking serene atmospheres through the digital and manual layering of images from different periods, suggesting 'both the memory of what it [the Heygate] was and the dream of what it could have been'. They are reminiscent of the English Romantic painter J. M. W. Turner's nineteenth-century scenes and ambiences of ruins, landscapes, seascapes and industrializing cities. Although Lanuza Rilling's work is distinctly individual and not participatory or collaborative in its production, like that of Roberts, both these projects mobilise history as a critique of the scorched earth or tabula rasa approach that is a dominant form of development in many contexts globally. A shared theme that emerges in these and other contributions in the book is, therefore, a plea for commemorating pasts, critically mobilising history in the present and simultaneously reimagining futures. This can include documenting historical layers of change in contemporary cities, starting from 'absences' and 'erasures' left behind after urban interventions, man-made or natural disasters, or forms of 'spatial cleansing'.[9]

If Lanuza Rilling repurposes archival survey photographs to produce new readings of a contested space, the project presented by Kate Crawford and her collaborators reveals the deeply politicised nature of data as it is produced and used to justify development strategies. The production and dissemination of knowledge is intimately connected with issues of power, which is another theme that runs through the volume as a whole.

In 'Hacking London's demolition decisions' (Chapter 8), a team of researchers and community representatives (including engineers, community organisers and housing-estate residents) report on a project where research is designed collaboratively by mobilizing different kinds of technical and other expertise to enable the residential community to respond better to demolition plans. Community leaders, often excluded through the inaccessibility of technical language and specialist resources needed to access and interpret the evidence for or against the demolition or refurbishment of estates, here co-designed the research and benefitted from the specialist know-how of engineers, reversing the usual imbalances in access to knowledge. In the process, marginalised 'dissenting' opinions and perspectives (for example, of local residents and activists) were brought to the surface, shaping the research agenda from the community's perspective, challenging the narratives about the dystopian character of social housing estates and the misuse of evidence by elites.[10]

These researchers highlight power imbalances in access to data and in the availability of specialist skills and resources required to interpret and mobilise evidence. The project shows that key documents, figures and analyses supporting decisions are not consistently in the public domain. It also speaks to a trend towards commercial confidentiality in urbanisation, whereby public bodies are no longer accountable, the evidence on which they base development plans is obfuscated by labyrinthine networks of contractors and subcontractors, complex financial accounting schemes, impenetrable technical data sets and specialist vocabularies. In this context, evidence provided by community groups is given little weight or is discredited altogether.

In this book we are particularly interested in the socio-political aspects of urban knowledge production and the social life of this knowledge. Through the employment of alternative and unconventional methods, we try to insert 'local', 'subjective', 'phenomenological', 'psychogeographic', 'idiosyncratic' or 'quirky' bits of knowledge into the vestiges of 'objective' hegemonic knowledge, or to create situations, frames, platforms or archives, either ephemeral or open-ended in their interpretation and analysis, highlighting the multiplicity, dynamism and unknowability of cities, as well as suggesting more equitable scenarios.

In a context where a large developer was dominating the production of narratives about an area undergoing massive regeneration, in 'Authoring the neighbourhood in Wikipedia' (Chapter 9), Rebecca Ross and Chi Nguyen come up with another kind of 'hacking' strategy: of performative rewriting or overwriting, showing how evidence and knowledge of cities can and should be thought about as a question of power, ideology and context. They carried out an intervention online, rewriting the Wikipedia entry for the King's Cross area in London, that is, 'King's Cross Central' — a new name coined by the developers. They subverted the corporate description of the area, rewriting the entry to change its tone and content and to reflect the diversity of voices from the local community, redefining it as a 'place of community' rather than a 'corporate development project'. Undertaking the editing in situ, in King's Cross, this was a public act of exposing the processes through which urban knowledge is produced and disseminated. Such artistic counter-geographical strategies connect with those described by Stephen Graham in his book *Cities Under Siege* (2010), an analysis of the militarisation of urban environments.[11]

Urban securitisation, a key theme for Graham, is at the core of Henrietta Williams' project 'The secret security guard' (Chapter 10) and Max Colson's 'Hide and seek: the dubious nature of plant life in high security spaces' (Chapter 11). Both connect with an investigative 'undercover' tradition in urban research and commentary: Williams took a job as a security guard. Her report on the security arrangements surrounding the London 2012 Olympics was published anonymously in the *Guardian* newspaper. This undercover method mirrored — and was necessary to unveil — G4S's own deception of the public as the company employed people with little actual training, dressed up as security guards and performing 'security' as a spectacle. William's 'acting as if' exposed and disclosed G4S's 'doing as if'. Her project confirms Erving Goffman's point, made long ago (in 1959) that in urban contexts 'performing roles' and 'managing impressions' are key strategies of getting by for researchers and other urbanites.[12]

Williams' immersive and undercover investigative approach, where the researcher's identity is hidden, raises ethical questions, of course. As a radical tactic, because of the commitment and risk involved, it also highlights that critical and independent research require a certain degree of suspicion or even paranoia on the part of the researcher in the quest for knowledge.[13] This is made apparent in Max Colson's performative photography project, 'Hide and seek' (Chapter 11), where he operates under the alter ego of the photojournalist Adam Walker-Smith, employing a paranoid mode of observation to underscore the insidious way in which security is embedded in built environments in ever more subtle, yet pervasive, ways. Walker-Smith's paranoid images direct us to what Benjamin has called 'the optical unconscious', making us see certain things which we would not normally consciously notice.[14] They alert our senses to the paranoid atmospheres of new, privatised and highly-regulated business parks and the flows of capital and power that govern them.

The authors we have been discussing focus on London, but they view the city in relation to common phenomena elsewhere. Other contributions to this volume insert experiences of distant and 'peripheral' urban sites into London, such as in Ger Duijzings and Rastko Novaković's performance piece and experimental film *Lebensraum / Living Space* (Chapter 20), where Duijzings, an anthropologist, walks the streets of London reading extracts from his diary recording war events in the former Yugoslavia. Another example is Leah Lovett's project *Contra Band* (Chapter 25), which describes a musical live-art intervention in which musicians in London and Rio de Janeiro are hooked up through a video link — a cross-continental inter-urban connection — playing political songs and exploring experiences of censorship in both countries between 1964 and 1985. Both of these projects are discussed in more detail below.

Part IV of the book, 'Situating Images and Imaginaries', focuses on research conducted on or with the visual. These essays emphasise both the complexity of visuality, and the potential of visual methodologies and situated image analyses in comprehending the production of urban imaginaries. Taking a city that has been subject to concerted and multiple efforts in global imagineering, Mumbai, Andrew Harris opens this section with a rich example of methodological adaptation to local circumstances. His essay 'The ups and downs of visualising contemporary Mumbai' (Chapter 12) offers a frank and lucid account of how he developed a set of visual and ethnographic methods to explore the social spaces emerging at flyovers that have recently become characteristic to the city. This account charts not only the physical heights and undercrofts of the city, but also the highs and lows experienced as one iteratively conceives a methodology and tests it out in practice. As with later chapters (see Chapters 31 and 32) Harris' methods allow alternative narratives about infrastructure to emerge, alongside arguments about their practical and symbolic functions in contemporary developer-led urbanisation in Mumbai.

Two further contributions demonstrate creative and sophisticated uses of visual methods, all featuring systematic surveys that bring otherwise invisible phenomena to the fore. In 'Creating systematic records through time' (Chapter 13), Bernadette Devilat shows how the use of systematic photography and 3D laser scanning has enabled insights into the processes of destruction and reconstruction of heritage areas affected by earthquakes in Chile. In 'Paint. Buff. Shoot. Repeat: rephotographing graffiti in London' (Chapter 14), Sabina Andron presents her own systematic survey tuned to the visual and material qualities of local inscriptions and overwritings (graffiti, street art and tags) changing over time. Andron reflects on her application of repeat photography to analyse changes in particular sites. Diverging from digital photographic archives of street art, her emphasis is on examining inscriptions and visual tags in situ rather than in isolation, as images that interact with the physical conditions of place. This facilitates an appreciation of the mutability of street art as part of the environment, through the observation of change in visuals marked upon surfaces, as well as modifications in the surfaces themselves. In both of these cases, photography is used to 'pause' for a moment in order to make sense of ongoing developments in a transient situation.

Coming from an engaged and ethical position, as with earlier essays in the collection, when using visual methods some authors in this section make a principled choice for participatory research as a collaborative effort between academics, practitioners and artists, on the one hand, and (otherwise marginalised) communities and individuals on the other.[15] In 'Critical urban learning through participatory photography' (Chapter 15), Alexandre Apsan Frediani and Laura Hirst describe such a collaboration in Kisumu, Kenya. Here participatory photography is used as a heuristic tool enabling researchers and community members to question urban governance and cast doubt on the mechanisms through which knowledge and policies are formulated. Photographic methods are designed and deployed to enhance community groups' and members' capacities to have their voices heard. Working with a local NGO, the two researchers gave cameras to community members in order to help them visualise the neighbourhood's issues and their priorities.

Whereas Frediani and Hirst highlight the practical possibilities of participatory photography as a heuristic tool, in their artists' conversation, 'Assisted self-portraits and GUESTures: excerpts from a discussion on photography and participation' (Chapter 16), artists Margareta Kern and Anthony Luvera reflect on the ethics of control and authorship in collaborative and participatory photographic practices, giving us a sense of how they set up the 'contract' between photographer and subject. Representing the fringes of urban existence is not without ethical challenges, especially when it is a priority for researchers to give marginalised people (such as the homeless) agency and a means of expressing themselves in their own terms.

Other contributors also deal explicitly with how knowledge (and power) reside in images and their production and application. In 'Picturing place: the agency of images in urban change' (Chapter 17), Ben Campkin, Mariana Mogilevich and Rebecca Ross discuss the method they have developed for close, relational and situated analyses of images to understand their roles in urban change; and to ascertain their articulation of imaginaries with strong social, physical, economic and other impacts. Their method is aimed at eliciting and understanding images as triggers for urban change — working comparatively across genres, periods and geographical contexts — as well as stimulating critical discussion of these images' positive and negative effects. They use three examples — different image archetypes — demonstrating how they embody specific kinds of expertise and how, in the negotiation of projected futures, they interact with sites and people within embodied transactions. Other contributors share this concern with the detailed analysis of urban images. For instance, Wes Aelbrecht, in '"Seeing is believing": the social life of urban decay and rebirth' (Chapter 18), undertakes a 'biography' of one photo, showing the potential of an in-depth and meticulous study of an iconic photograph and the crucial role it played in mediating exchanges between city authorities and citizens within Chicago's 1950s' 'renewal'.

In the final contribution to this section, 'We thought we were making the car but it was the other way around' (Chapter 19), Sophia Psarra uses computer modelling and digital mapping — Depthmap software as used in Space Syntax research and GIS — in combination with documentary evidence to understand the historical development and current condition of Detroit. This adds nuance to the otherwise abstract grand narratives of Fordism and post-Fordism through which the city's emergence and decline are understood. It highlights that these conditions result from a complex interplay between structural conditions and the city's morphology, with the street network being seen to mobilise people and resources in particular ways and continuing to provide an interface to services and enterprise.

In this volume, it is our concern to foster an experimental turn in urban studies, showcasing projects that push methodological boundaries and produce original insights and types of data that hitherto have not been captured. Such an approach means questioning established methodological habits, loosening up intellectual and conceptual grids and inverting the relationships we may have with our 'subjects' and 'objects' of study. In Part V, 'Embodied Cartographies', this is creatively exemplified in Andrew Stevenson's contribution. In his essay 'Abdication and arrival: using an open-ended, collaborator-led ethnography to explore constructions of newly encountered cities' (Chapter 21), Stevenson explores how new arrivals or immigrants to Manchester and Salford navigate the city: how do they access and generate knowledge about their new location and how do they begin to identify with it? Declining Stevenson's initial suggestion to use photography to document this process, the participants were then prompted to choose the medium they felt most comfortable with. The result is a rich mosaic of experiences, actively constructed by the migrants themselves, which goes far beyond the visual to evoke taste, smell and the kinetic.

Even where dealing with the visual, many authors in this volume aim to break the hegemony of visual representations and to embark upon the study of embodied experiences, that is, the multi-sensory, phenomenological and tactile experiences of the city: how ordinary inhabitants and transient visitors traverse, inhabit, or occupy urban spaces in a personal and subjective manner. In Duijzings and Novaković's film *Lebensraum / Living Space* (Chapter 20), London's streets, and the tactile and physical experience of walking them, forms the canvas for a retelling of the war-related experiences of an anthropologist working in the former Yugoslavia during the early 1990s: representational conventions are disrupted by omitting the usual images of war suffering and embedding the retelling of war in a dislocated environment.

Walking as an embodied spatial practice and as a research strategy is brought out in a number of other contributions too, such as in Stevenson's 'Abdication and arrival' (Chapter 21), and Boano et al's 'Towards an architecture of engagement' (Chapter 4). It is reflected upon most directly and extensively in ThienVinh Nguyen's 'Learning to walk: on curating a walking methodologies programme' (Chapter 22), a commentary on a curated set of works that use various walking methodologies across disciplines. Building upon her own experience of getting to know a new city on foot, Nguyen engages with a range of theorists and writers on walking. She shows how walking — at different speeds, in varying modes of attention or distraction, as an individual or in a group — can be an important tool, documented and mapped in diverse ways. This is followed by a number of vignettes, by photographer David Kendall, and architect and urban and architectural theorists Jonathan Hill, Gabriela García de Cortázar and Amy Thomas, in which they reflect, respectively, on the picturesque tradition of walking through landscapes, on city guidebooks and wayfinding, and on walking as a pedagogic practice.

Various contributors try to overcome the objectifying and distancing effects of mainstream academia by directly engaging with and intervening in urban contexts through performance and other situated art practices. Following, implicitly or explicitly, Situationist principles, some of the contributors use acting, adopting roles and alter egos, constructing 'situations', actively inserting ideas and practices into the urban fabric so as to provoke a public response.[16] These performance strategies trigger interesting reactions that are ethnographically revealing, in the fashion of Augusto Boal's 'invisible theatre', in which public space is transformed into stage, drawing in bystanders and forcing them to act or respond.

An interesting example of performative interventions in urban public spaces is exemplified in Joanna Rajkowska's work. In 'I hear sounds inside my head' (Chapter 23), she begins with an autobiographical reflection on her part-deafness and blindness and the hyper-alertness to spaces which she developed during her childhood. This was in part nurtured by her mother's progressive psychoses and set the scene for her subsequent preoccupation, as an artist, with burdened places, and with creating public art interventions and objects that aim to process and alleviate the traumatic experiences that haunt individuals, societies and communities. Not unlike Lanuza Rilling, Rajkowska works intuitively, aiming to open up troubled sites, characterised by a sense of loss or absence and counter to a sense of belonging, so people can finally interact and start to relate to each other, more often than not non-verbally.[17]

Mădălina Diaconu's project 'Charting smellscapes' (Chapter 24) again takes us beyond the visual, focusing on smells and charting the olfactory profiles of cities such as Vienna and Bucharest. She describes the ways in which smell impacts on our experience of environments, arguing for a more conscious and sophisticated consideration of olfactory aspects in urban design. As an object of research, smells present us with challenges, eluding attempts at precise textual or visual representation, and it is difficult to recreate them, in particular, for cities of the past.

Other contributors also use performance as a path towards urban knowledge, such as Lovett, who, at the time of the 2014 World Cup, carried out an experimental musical live-art performance in which musicians in London and Rio de Janeiro hooked up to perform a set of political songs previously censored in their respective countries. While they accompanied one another, they sang the songs in their counterpart's mother tongue. The moments of disconnection that occurred at unpredictable moments when the technology broke down duly emphasised the distance between the two cities and across political regimes, national boundaries and continents. The unintentional 'dropping out' of connections, however, added to the intrigue of the performance, reminiscent as it was of processes of censorship, leaving the work 'incomplete' but also stimulating in the musicians and audiences a desire for a closer link.[18] This project shows that one method can be experimentally applied to two cities simultaneously, in tandem, in a comparative and interactive manner, watching what the differential responses and effects will be.

The final section of the book, Part VI 'Fabric and Fabrication', contains eight contributions by artists who have developed distinctive and experimental methodologies for engaging with the materiality of cities and who all use physical installations in their repertoire. These authors are also interested in the non-verbal and embodied dimensions of urban experience, and in the power of material installations as a method of constructing and disseminating new knowledge. As these and other works in *Engaged Urbanism* suggest, we are keen to prioritise more intuitive, subjective and phenomenological explorations of cities, often dealt with most effectively in the work of artists, yet whose work is used merely illustratively in many academic contexts. The collection as a whole features work by several artists whose practices lead to outcomes that constitute important contributions to knowledge. A precedent for such cross-fertilisation between the arts and conventional social-science approaches to urban studies is the rapprochement between art and ethnography.[19] Indeed, many of our contributors work at the intersection of conceptual art and ethnography, bringing to mind recent debates about 'ethnographic conceptualism' where fieldwork is considered as a performance and the researcher adopts different positions or what Michał Murawski calls 'chameleonic positionality'.[20] As Nikolai Ssorin-Chaikov writes, 'ethnographic conceptualism', that is, conducting fieldwork as, or as if, a form of conceptual art, means experimentation and provocation. The 'happenings' and 'situations' created in such research encounters pay off not only in terms of triggering responses that may be revealing ethnographically, but also in stimulating new forms of public engagement.[21]

As is evident throughout the book, experimentation can mean allowing research practices that in conventional social-science or humanities research contexts may be considered 'unscientific' or 'undisciplined' to be tried and tested, and hopefully to flourish, helping to push the traditional boundaries of disciplines. An example is Mohamad Hafeda's essay 'The twin sisters are "about to" swap houses: displacement and the bordering practice of matching' (Chapter 26). In this practice-led architectural research, theoretical shifts (moving from representation of a physical 'border' to everyday practices of 'bordering') in tandem with geopolitical changes (the rise of sectarian politics and processes of spatial segregation in Beirut) led Hafeda to develop a bespoke and situated methodology. He uses multimedia installations to interrogate both the material and immaterial dimensions of borders in Beirut, and he also shows how boundaries in a divided city are made manifest physically and spatially and how they are experienced — and subverted — in unexpected ways.

Echoing Hafeda's concern with bordering practices and the constitution and transgression of city boundaries, in 'City shapes and urban metaphor' (Chapter 27), artist John Aiken discusses a number of his own works — watercolour drawings and sand sculptures — that respond to the designation of city walls, questioning the ways that knowledge of them is produced, represented and disseminated. In one pair of images he compares the nineteenth-century contours of Amsterdam and Stockholm, which, even rendered as abstract 'shades', show the differential development of these two cities. Alongside this he provides maps and drawings of the Nga Tsin Wai walled village, one of the historical, clan-based, walled villages prevalent in Hong Kong before British colonisation, and sand installations based on patterns found there, bringing home the transient quality of urban walls and perimeters. Narrating these projects, Aiken highlights the ephemerality of city forms, the sometimes arbitrary but always consequential nature of boundaries, and the tensions between static representations and the continuous flows and transactions of which they are comprised.

Through their practice, Aiken and Hafeda examine the dynamic relations between the material and immaterial city. This is true also of South African artist and curator Johan Thom, who, in his contribution '(In)visible bodies: migrants in the city of gold' (Chapter 28), comments on three art and installation projects that use embodied strategies, including sculpture and film, to prompt reflections on mobility and migration, touching upon the experience, movement and visibility of migrant workers in Johannesburg's gold-mining industry. Connected through the different artists' deployment of collaborative methods in working with various communities, each work evokes the traces of the material acts of moving into, away from, or through the city, providing new insights into migration — a core thematic for urban researchers today, across different locations.

We are less concerned with actual empirical findings in this volume than with the methodological and practical decisions, improvisations, negotiations, protocols, processes and practices through which insights are arrived at and knowledge is produced. Linking to some of the participatory aspects of the work discussed by Thom, Kieren Reed's essay 'Negotiating space: the artist working as a creator and enabler of spaces for working, thinking and meeting' (Chapter 29) discusses site-specific art practices through an explicit contemplation of his own position as an artist arranging permission to construct inhabitable sculptural spaces and then collaborating with art-going audiences to build them. Resonating with Rendell's practice of 'site-writing', Reed thinks through some of the dilemmas of such practices in connection to recent writing in art theory, and he poses fundamental questions regarding collaborative or participatory art, architectural and urban practice. What do these terms mean? How do the relationships between researcher-practitioners and audiences unfold in particular places at certain points in time, and how are they constrained by resources? How can one build, organise or curate spaces for effective interaction and learning?

Artist Mircea Nicolae also uses his text to present a critical and self-reflexive commentary on his project *25 Demolished Houses*, a site-specific installation (Chapter 30). Linking back to the contributions on demolition and renewal in London, his work explores this theme in the context of socialist and post-socialist Eastern Europe. The project focuses on the brutality of the successive modernist (and post-modern) demolition campaigns of the 1980s and 2000s in Bucharest and the lack of respect for the city's architectural heritage. Nicolae brings the sheer materiality of these cycles of large-scale demolition and construction to the centre of our attention, and, like Lanuza Rilling, he is interested in the specifics of this dynamic of effacement and new beginnings and in questioning how heritage values are constructed. His work also connects, in this section, with Simson&Volley's temporary installation, *The Bridge of Sighs* (Chapter 31), an installation that uses spatial, material and poetic strategies to examine the ephemeral relations between memory and place. This artwork points to the immaterial, fleeting experience of beauty in the city through drawing our attention to monumental and infrastructural urban form as well as to the possibilities of critical art interventions to constructively shape experiences of the public realm.

London-based artist Hilary Powell further reinforces the critical possibilities inherent in art practice in her long-term, practice-based and multimedia research into demolition as a continuous feature of urbanisation. In 'Materials. Stories' (Chapter 32), Powell examines the material components of demolition sites (from zinc, copper, steel, concrete, brick, asbestos, lime mortar, cement, to lead and slate), and, in collaboration with the materials — as non-human agents that contribute to the production of urban space — she tells stories and creates images, salvaging the physical remnants of industrial decline and putting them to artistic use. Exploring the lifecycles and micro- and macro-economics of such material components in post-industrial landscapes, Powell questions the way we value, consume and waste materials. Her radically multimedia work, which draws us into the affective qualities of places in transition, reinforces the queer theorist Laurent Berlant's remark that 'experimental work always forces us to imagine analogous genres around it'.[22]

Also crossing genres and media, in the group contribution that concludes this compendium, 'Buildings on fire: towards a new approach to urban memory' (Chapter 33), curated by Stamatis Zografos, a number of scholars, artists and other practitioners offer a multifarious series of provocations and experiments exploring the role of fire in constructing or disrupting urban memory, again examining issues of heritage and destruction. By playfully using fire as a methodological tool and conceptual springboard, these authors investigate fundamental issues in architecture, politics and heritage. Together, these works reconfigure our understanding of fire as a primeval force by combining a variety of media such as drawing, photography, film, text, computer programming and sound installation. As a set of provocations that flicker around fire as a playful methodological trope, in concluding the book these works can be read in multiple ways, prompting us to connect our methodological experiments with the performance of ancient rites that emerge, adapt or die at particular moments. The collection demonstrates, overall, that urban knowledge emerges along iterative yet non-linear trajectories and is actually embedded in the materiality and spatiality of cities and their institutions.

1 Barney G. Glaser and Anselm L. Strauss, *The Discovery of Grounded Theory: Strategies for Qualitative Research* (New York: Aldine Publishing Company, 1967).
2 Jennifer Robinson, 'Cities in a World of Cities: The Comparative Gesture', *International Journal of Urban and Regional Research*, 35 (1) (2011): 1–23.
3 See, for example, Neil Brenner and Christian Schmid, 'Towards a New Epistemology of the Urban?', *City: Analysis of Urban Trends, Culture, Theory, Policy, Action*, 19 (2–3) (2015): 151–82.
4 Jane Rendell, *Site-Writing: The Architecture of Art Criticism* (London: I.B.Tauris, 2006).
5 Jane Rendell, 'Architectural Research and Disciplinarity', *ARQ: Architectural Research Quarterly*, 8 (2) (2004): 141–7; Ben Campkin, 'The "Postmodern Mindset" or Critical Pluralism? Architectural Doctoral Research Today', in *Doctoral Education in Schools of Architecture across Europe*, edited by Maria Voyatzaki (Thessaloniki: European Network of Heads of Schools of Architecture, 2014), 49–58.
6 See also Jane Rendell, *Site-Writing*; 'Critical Spatial Practice', essay written for Art Incorporated, Kunstmuseet Koge Skitsesamling, Denmark (2008). http://www.janerendell.co.uk/wp-content/uploads/2009/06/critical-spatial-practice.pdf (accessed 20 January 2016).
7 Aihwa Ong, 'Introduction: Worlding Cities, or the Art of Being Global', in *Worlding Cities: Asian Experiments and the Art of Being Global*, edited by Ananya Roy and Aihwa Ong (Oxford: Blackwell, 2011), 1–26.
8 Ben Campkin, *Remaking London: Decline and Regeneration in Urban Culture* (London and New York: I.B.Tauris, 2013).
9 Michael Herzfeld, 'Spatial Cleansing: Monumental Vacuity and the Idea of the West', *Journal of Material Culture*, 11 (1–2) (2006): 127–49.
10 Campkin, *Remaking London*, 77–104.
11 Stephen Graham, *Cities Under Seige: The New Military Urbanism* (London: Verso, 2010).
12 Erving Goffmann, *The Presentation of Self in Everyday Life* (New York: Anchor Books, 1959).
13 For a relevant discussion of the role of critical paranoia and other possibilities for modes of critical engagement, see Eve Kosofsky Sedgwick, *Paranoid Reading and Reparative Reading; or, You're So Paranoid, You Probably Think This Introduction Is About You* (Durham, NC: Duke University Press, 1997).
14 Walter Benjamin, 'A Small History of Photography', in *One-Way Street and Other Writings* (London: New Left Books, 1979), 240–57. First published 1931.
15 See also, for example, Luke Eric Lassiter, *The Chicago Guide to Collaborative Ethnography* (Chicago, IL: University of Chicago Press, 2005).
16 Tom McDonough (ed.), *The Situationists and the City* (London: Verso, 2009).
17 See also Joanna Rajkowska, *Where the Beast Is Buried* (Winchester: Zero Books, 2013).
18 See also Matthew Gandy and B. J. Nilsen (eds.), *The Acoustic City* (Berlin: Jovis, 2014).
19 Alex Coles (ed.), *Site-Specificity: The Ethnographic Turn, vol. IV: De, Dis-, Ex-* (London: Black Dog Publishing, 2000); Hal Foster, 'The Artist as Ethnographer?' in *The Return of the Real: The Avant-Garde at the End of the Century* (Cambridge, MA: MIT Press, 1996), 171–204; G. Marcus and F. Myers (eds.), *The Traffic in Culture: Refiguring Art and Anthropology* (Berkeley, CA: University of California Press, 1995); Arnd Schneider and Christopher Wright (eds.), *Contemporary Art and Anthropology* (Oxford: Berg, 2006); Nikolai Ssorin-Chaikov, 'Ethnographic Conceptualism: An Introduction', *Laboratorium*, 5 (2) (2013): 5–18; Kiven Strohm, 'When Anthropology Meets Contemporary Art', *Collaborative Anthropologies*, 5 (2012): 98–124.
20 Michał Murawski, 'Palaceology, or Palace-as-Methodology: Ethnographic Conceptualism, Total Urbanism, and a Stalinist Skyscraper in Warsaw', *Laboratorium*, 5 (2) (2013): 56–83.
21 Ssorin-Chaikov, 'Ethnographic Conceptualism'.
22 Laurent Berlant, 'Claudia Rankine', *BOMB*, 129 (fall 2014). http://bombmagazine.org/article/10096/claudia-rankine (accessed 20 January 2016).

I

Frames

1

CITIES METHODOLOGIES MATTER

Comparative urbanism and global urban theory

Thinking with elsewhere

Comparative urbanism

Located theory

Jennifer Robinson

How researchers approach cities methodologically has important consequences for wider conceptual understandings of the urban. Concerning the potential for generating a more global urban studies, for example, open to including insights from any city rather than only the conventional Euro-American heartlands of theorisation, there are significant theoretical consequences of the ways in which we frame enquiries methodologically. Inventive methodological assumptions and tactics could enable the transformation of urban theorisations, opening up the possibility to expand the range of conceptual insights relevant to the diverse, shifting and uneven world of cities.

Indeed, in any enquiry, methodological choices actively frame what it is possible to see. As multiplicities of both outcome (urban territories assemble many different entities and activities) and process (many flows and connections with elsewhere produce the urban), these methodological choices matter greatly. It is the multiplicity of cities which for Henri Lefebvre provided the grounds for revolutionary hope, that even the most power-laden spaces might be appropriated and lived differently, or imagined as part of an alternative future.[1] In terms of methodology, for example, assessing only the lines of governmental power rather than excavating the diversity of engagements around specific urban outcomes and experiences might lead to some 'false' pessimism — a too early declaration of the end of politics.[2] Building knowledge from the often precarious mobilisations of residents, new arrivals and marginalised groups is an essential methodological choice for opening up insights into alternative urban futures.

The urban is also a multiplicity in a global sense. Given the great diversity of urban forms and processes across the world, the opportunity to draw on investigations in a wide range of different contexts to inform the broadest interpretations of urbanisation and the urban therefore matters. Building theoretical insights which are intended to travel widely based on a narrow range of urban experiences can be very disabling for thinking the multiple forms of the urban. And this is especially so when there is a great mismatch between the sites of theorisation and those of dynamic urbanisation, as is the case at the current moment. With expansive urbanisation in Asia and rapid urban population growth across Africa, the demands of conceptualising the urban are out of geographical phase with the historical concentration of English language global urban studies in wealthier Northern contexts.[3]

In the search for new methodologies for a more global urban studies, at stake are the scope and starting points of enquiries as well as the cultures of theorising. While there is general agreement that new evidence and ideas might arrive from different contexts and disturb wider theorisations, it is essential that the terms of theorisation are not pre-set. The suggestion that we can theorise only using already given concepts long ago drew a derisory response from Partha Chatterjee who wondered what, then, would be left to think?[4] There are also important issues to debate concerning the cultures

5 → 53 12 → 109 17 → 147 25 → 211

of theorising which could facilitate a more global urban analysis: we need theory cultures that are alert to their own locatedness and sources of inspiration, open to learning from elsewhere, respectful of different scholarly traditions, and committed to the radical revisability of theories.

At stake too are the geographies of theorising. Being open to ideas from elsewhere while attending to the locatedness of all conceptualisation raises challenging questions about the specificity or limited scope of some concepts and about the extent to which it is productive to think with ideas across many different experiences — at the limit, to propose a universal theory of urbanisation. Conversely, we need to be alert to the ways in which the differentiated grounds for speaking into wider theoretical conversations are framed and delimited. Theorising from distinctive locations can certainly be productive and engender novel conceptualisations but might also potentially reinstate incommensurabilities between different kinds of contexts.[5] Whether the different sites from which new urban concepts might emerge are imagined as 'regions', continents or the invented geopolitical concept of the Global South, the imagined geographies of new subjects of theorisation demand our critical attention.[6]

Methodology therefore matters immensely, and numerous questions need to be addressed in order to imagine how a more global urban studies might be grounded, methodologically and conceptually. How can we think cities in a world of diverse cities? Or, how can we think 'the urban' in the face of its determinate multiplicity? How might we work productively with existing (often parochial) theories while keeping conceptualisation open to inspiration from any city? Can we encourage a culture of theoretical practice commensurate with the need for revisable concepts, respectful of divergences and differences? How might we provide a rigorous foundation for the possibility of beginning conceptualisation anywhere, in any urban context?

I take methodological inspiration for addressing these issues from comparative urbanism, especially the openness of comparative enquiry to conceptual revision. I propose some methodological and philosophical grounds for a new repertoire of comparative methods committed to 'thinking with elsewhere'.[7] Such an approach would start from the premise that conceptualisation can begin from any city while also acknowledging the locatedness of all theoretical endeavour. New concepts might then be initiated from anywhere and inherited conversations about the nature of the urban refined or refused. To achieve this, there is a need to reconfigure the conventions surrounding the determination of the 'third term' of comparison, which provides the grounds for thinking across different cases and justifies bringing different urban outcomes together for critical reflection.[8]

Based on vernacular comparative practice — what good urban comparativists actually do — rather than formal methodological requirements which have often seemed very restrictive, grounds for comparability can be found in shared features across cases (for example, fiscal crises, or popular mobilisation, or governance coalitions for growth).[9] We can compose studies across different contexts in order to stimulate thinking with the variety of outcomes. Comparability can also be found through more natural experiments, exploring the 'repeated instances' that make up the urban landscapes of many very different urban contexts. Distinctive outcomes are found in different contexts which are produced within shared and interconnected processes; think of gated communities or high-rise residential developments or business parks, or pavements.[10] In developing some new repertoires of comparison we can build on the specific spatiality of the urban, notably the overlapping interconnections (such as economic links or policy flows) among cities that shape both distinctive but often shared and repeated outcomes. The 'case' drawn into comparison, then, is no longer a territorialised entity known as a 'city' but any number of phenomena, outcomes, processes, buildings and activities, and in their repetition or ubiquity they draw us to invent new kinds of comparative trajectories across different cities which are often kept apart analytically.

Thus, with methodologies fine-tuned to thinking with wide variation and prolific repetition, rather than trying to 'control for difference' in a traditional comparative idiom, we can take inspiration from the comparative commitment to creative theoretical practice focused on the revisability of inherited (and always located) understandings. Theory-building tactics seeking to compose comparisons across diverse outcomes, or designing 'natural experiments' by following the numerous interconnections and repeated instances across and among cities, hold out much promise for creating new methodologies, which could help with the work of generating a more global urban studies. In the array of experimental and inventive comparative practices for conceptual innovation which increasingly characterise the field of urban studies, as well as in the archives of vernacular comparative urban practices, there is much potential to craft a more global urban studies.

In some ways, then, we are invited to reformat comparison for twenty-first century urban studies. Paring comparison back to its minimalist components, I suggest we can think of comparison as a wide-ranging set of practices for 'thinking (cities) through elsewhere', bringing different cases together in either 'composed' (researcher-designed to explore a variety of urban outcomes) or 'natural' experiments (following the connections amongst cities) to inspire conceptualisation. New taxonomies of urban comparisons become visible which can be (and have been) put to work for a more global urban studies: building comparisons through putting *case studies* into wider conversations where case studies do not need to be defined territorially but might be any kind of urban process or outcome, such as projects or events or flows and connections among cities; *composing* bespoke comparisons across shared features or 'repeated instances'; *tracing* connections among cities to inform understandings of interconnected repeated instances or to compare the wider interconnections and extended urbanisation processes themselves; and *launching* distinctive analyses from specific urban contexts or regions into wider theoretical conversations.[11] Such methodological practices can bring cities together for analytical reflection from many different parts of the world and indicate something of the potential for a reformatted comparative imagination to support a more global urban studies.[12]

Some difficulties remain with ensuring theory is treated as light and revisable rather than as saturated with weighty and ambitious authorising voices which tends to reinforce the power of existing centres of scholarship. Solutions to this are both philosophical and cultural. On the one hand, we need to reflect on the ontology of comparative methods. How we understand 'cases' and 'theories' and their relationship requires engagement with some long-standing philosophical puzzles, such as the relation between the concrete and the abstract, or the particular and the universal, which bear on the potential of cases (in fact perhaps better considered as singularities) to inform and transform, and not simply reproduce, existing conceptualisations.[13]

But a vital and urgent requirement for any new geography of theorising — comparative or otherwise — is that the mode and style of urban theorisation itself is transformed from an authoritative voice emanating from some putative centre of urban scholarship to a celebration of the conversations opened up among the many subjects of urban theoretical endeavour in cities around the world, valorising more provisional, modest and revisable claims about the nature of the urban. To achieve this requires not only methodological innovation but also a change of theoretical culture in urban studies and strong efforts to work against the consequences of the very uneven distribution of institutional resources for global knowledge production.

5 → 53 12 → 109 17 → 147 25 → 211

1 Henri Lefebvre, *The Urban Revolution* (Minneapolis, MN: University of Minnesota Press). First published 1974. Christian Schmid, 'Henri Lefebvre, the Right to the City and the New Metropolitan Mainstream', in *Cities for People, Not for Profit,* edited by Neil Brenner, Peter Marcuse and Margit Mayer (London and New York: Routledge), 42–62.
2 See, for example, Eric Swyngedouw, 'Governance Innovation and the Citizen: The Janus Face of Governance-Beyond-the State', *Urban Studies,* 42 (11) (2005): 1991–2006.
3 You-tien Hsing, *The Great Urban Transformation: The Politics of Land and Property in China* (Oxford: Oxford University Press, 2010). Susan Parnell and Edgar Pieterse (eds.), *Africa's Urban Revolution* (London and New York: Zed Books, 2014).
4 Partha Chatterjee, *The Nation and Its Fragments: Colonial and Postcolonial Histories* (Princeton, NJ: Princeton University Press, 1993).
5 Although see Tariq Jazeel, 'Subaltern Geographies: Geographical Knowledge and Postcolonial Strategy', *Singapore Journal of Tropical Geography,* 35 (1) (2014): 88–103, for some important comments on the limits of translatability.
6 For a critique of regions, see Ananya Roy, 'Conclusion: Postcolonial Urbanism: Speed, Hysteria, Mass Dreams', in *Worlding Cities,* edited by Ananya Roy and Aihwa Ong (Oxford: Wiley-Blackwell, 2011), 307–35; and Tim Bunnell, 'City Networks as Alternative Geographies of Southeast Asia', *TRaNS: Trans-Regional and-National Studies,* 1 (1) (2013): 27–43. See also Achille Mbembe and Sarah Nuttall, 'Writing the World from an African Metropolis', *Public Culture,* 16 (3) (2004): 347–72; Vanessa Watson, 'Seeing from the South: Refocusing Urban Planning on the Globe's Central Urban Issues', *Urban Studies,* 46 (11) (2009): 2259–75; Jennifer Robinson, 'New Geographies of Theorising the Urban: Putting Comparison to Work for Global Urban Studies', in *The Routledge Handbook for Cities of the Global South,* edited by Susan Parnell and Sophie Oldfield (London and New York: Routledge, 2014), 57–70.
7 Jennifer Robinson, 'Thinking Cities through Elsewhere: Comparative Tactics for a More Global Urban Studies', *Progress in Human Geography,* 40 (1) (2016): 3–29.
8 Jane M. Jacobs, 'Commentary: Comparing Comparative Urbanisms', *Urban Geography,* 33 (6) (2012): 904–14.
9 Jennifer Robinson, 'Cities in a World of Cities: The Comparative Gesture', *International Journal of Urban and Regional Research,* 35 (1) (2011): 1–23.
10 Jane M. Jacobs, 'A Geography of Big Things', *Cultural Geographies,* 13 (1) (2006): 1–27.
11 See also Jamie Peck and Nick Theodore, 'Follow the Policy: A Distended Case Approach', *Environment and Planning A,* 44 (1) (2012): 21–30; and Ola Söderström, *Cities in Relations: Trajectories of Urban Development in Hanoi and Ougadougou* (Oxford: Wiley-Blackwell, 2014).
12 For a fuller discussion, see Robinson, 'Thinking Cities through Elsewhere'. See also Abdou Maliq Simone, *City Life: From Dakar to Jakarta* (London and New York: Routledge, 2011).
13 See Robinson, 'Thinking Cities Through Elsewhere'; and Łukasz Stanek, 'Space as Concrete Abstraction: Hegel, Marx, and Modern Urbanism in Henri Lefebvre', in *Space, Difference, Everyday Life: Reading Henri Lefebvre,* edited by Kanishka Goonewardena, Stefan Kipfer, Richard Milgrom and Christian Schmid (London and New York: Routledge, 2008), 62–79, for a useful discussion of these terms.

2

METHODS, METAPHORS AND THE INTERDISCIPLINARY TERRAIN OF URBAN RESEARCH

Terminology Everyday observation Urban ecology

Matthew Gandy

Just as the city itself is not a discrete object of analysis or critical reflection, we also find that urban research cannot be contained within the intellectual domain of just one or even a few academic disciplines. In this sense, 'the city' can be conceived as an interdisciplinary focus for research par excellence ranging from the successive material manifestations of capital circulation to the fleeting and multiple sensory realms of urban consciousness. Urban space is simultaneously fixed and mutable, measurable and indefinable. Faced with the dizzying complexity of urban space, a common reaction is to seek ways of reducing uncertainty through forms of intellectual filtering and refinement so that an initial cloudburst of ideas can be reduced to a more precise set of interrelated themes or research questions. Without this process of simplification, most types of research could not proceed although there are more experimental forms of cultural expression that attempt to retain ambivalence, complexity and the haunting presence of an ill-defined elsewhere. A critically reflective epistemological strategy must contend with the unknowability of urban space in its entirety and the sense that all our insights must of necessity be both provisional and transitory.

If urban research requires a combination of methods or ideas drawn from different disciplinary fields, then what kind of interdisciplinary approaches have emerged? Can we identify methodological and theoretical frameworks that are not merely additive but comprise more than the sum of their parts? Are there transdisciplinary conceptual vocabularies that enable disparate bodies of work to be brought into an effective dialogue? We could argue that David Harvey's *Limits to Capital*, first published in 1982, marks the acme of a neo-Marxian approach to urban studies that sought to bring a vast range of phenomena under a unified explanatory framework.[1] The investigations of other Marxist scholars in art history and related fields during the 1970s and 1980s also added to a sense in which neo-Marxian scholarship could be extended to incorporate disparate realms of social and cultural analysis. T. J. Clark's study of Édouard Manet, for example, provides a vivid counterpart to Harvey's own account of the transformation of nineteenth-century Paris, while Marshall Berman articulated a compelling synthesis between literature, politics and urban history.[2] And earlier works of Marxist cultural criticism such as Walter Benjamin proved increasingly influential within an expanded realm of critical urban writing. A radical extension of what constituted 'the political' served to dispel earlier formalist modes of cultural scholarship and place cultural artefacts within a wider nexus of developments and relationships.

Some of the most trenchant early critiques of what we might term 'theoretical over extension' emerged from within these radical traditions, especially through emerging feminist and post-colonial insights in the writing of critics and scholars such as Dipesh Chakrabarty, Rosalyn Deutsche and Gyan Prakash.[3] Yet the gathering critique of 'grand theory' since the 1980s has not entirely dispelled the search for similarly complete or expansive modes of interpretation. A characteristic feature of contemporary writing on cities is the deployment of 'grand terminologies' in the sense of rhetorical rather than analytical claims to novelty: the accelerated emphasis on new forms of intellectual innovation has put immense pressure on the vocabularies that we rely on to convey our thoughts and ideas. Urban lexicons have expanded, but the nuances of meaning are often overlooked, especially where words hide complex etymologies or have been borrowed from different cultural contexts.

Although the contemporary impetus of urban research is leading towards novel forms

8 → 77 32 → 259 33 → 267

of comparative analysis, the Anglo-American dominance of urban discourse has advanced unabated. This linguistic juggernaut is producing a flattening of cultural expression that extends to many different modes of writing, driven in part by the changes within publishing itself as well as reader expectations. The subtle complexities of translation have been displaced by an emphasis on linguistic simplification at variance with attempts to provincialise Eurocentric circuits of knowledge.

The circulation of ideas derived from different contexts is especially significant in the use of approaches derived from the bio-physical sciences in the urban arena. If we consider the term 'ecology', for example, the difficulties of conceptual translation between the bio-physical and social sciences become immediately apparent. The Chicago School of Sociology developed a variant of 'urban ecology' that simply transposed elements of 'plant sociology' to an urban context. Models derived from ecological succession were used to explore the competitive dynamics of capitalist urbanisation. From the 1970s onwards, a conceptual movement in the opposite direction is discernible as ecologists sought to bring cities into their frame of analysis to produce an 'urban ecology' based on detailed empirical analysis of the complex bio-physical characteristics of the built environment. Urban ecologists such as Paul Duvigneaud or Herbert Sukopp drew on the idea of ecological zones or distinctive biotopes to capture elements of the material transition between a city and its rural hinterland.[4] These intricate representations of the bio-physical characteristics of urban space, including botanical or microclimatic variations, mark an elaboration of the earlier cartographic investigations of figures such as Alexander von Humboldt and the nineteenth-century emergence of the natural sciences. The emphasis here was very much on urban nature rather than the nature of the urban since the historical dynamics of capitalist urbanisation remained outside the epistemological frame. More recently, the zonal model of urban space has resurfaced as a means to investigate the dynamic transition between the city and its hinterland. The environmental historian William Cronon, for example, has drawn on the agricultural geography of von Thünen to interpret the relationship between the growth of Chicago and the transformation of its vast environmental hinterland.[5] Or, in other cases, the idea of zones has been deployed as an ironic heuristic device as in the diagrammatic representation of Los Angeles offered by Mike Davis with its 'medfly quarantine zone', 'gulag rim' and proliferation of carceral archipelagos.[6]

The allure of science remains powerful within urban discourse. In architecture, for example, we find frequent references to 'morphogenetic pathways' or other types of spatial algorithms derived from the biological sciences. The increasingly molecular emphasis of the bio-physical sciences has been reworked in an urban context as an aesthetic or rhetorical accoutrement to design discourse. The allure of science, emboldened by new advances in digital imaging, raises questions about the use and production of knowledge. The question, to paraphrase François Lyotard's report on knowledge, is not whether a particular analytical framework is 'true' or even simply coherent in an epistemological sense but rather its potential worth: the issue at stake, therefore, is how the borrowing of models or metaphors facilitates capitalist urbanisation through processes of application or persuasion that have little or nothing to do with their original scientific context.

The difficulty in defining the city as a coherent or spatially bounded entity has contributed towards a recent revival of the neo-Lefebvrian distinction between cities and 'urbanisation' as a broader set of processes or operations. At one level it is undoubtedly true that 'the city' cannot be meaningfully restricted to pre-given administrative boundaries or superficial distinctions between urban and 'non-urban'. Yet to deny the ontological significance of the city is also problematic since there are distinctive cultural, political or even bio-physical dimensions to urban space that are not interchangeable or reducible to a generalised theory of the urban. If we take the example of Weimar-era Berlin, there was a set of specific developments spanning fields such art, architecture and sexuality that constituted an experimental kind of cultural and intellectual milieu, which differed from most other German cities. Similarly, aspects of the visual arts scene that emerged in Manhattan in the 1970s, or the Highlife musical efflorescence of post-colonial Lagos in the 1960s, were rooted in the particularities of place as well as international connections and processes. But where do these geographically and historically specific cultural and political manifestations of urban life leave the broader question of what the city is as an object of analysis? If we shift our emphasis from the 'urban process' towards the 'urban experience', it is clear that significant distinctions remain in the material manifestations of urbanisation and the historical development of different forms of urban consciousness.

The interdisciplinary nature of urban research agendas is clear enough, but the term 'interdisciplinary' spans a mix of somewhat contradictory developments.[7] The increasing emphasis on interdisciplinary research, driven in part by the agendas set by funding agencies, poses significant dilemmas for urban research. If interdisciplinary research involves not just working across established disciplines but also enabling connections between the academy and other sources of knowledge production, then this may indirectly alter the criteria by which work is evaluated or even threaten the autonomy of academic work itself. If, for example, university-based research is deployed by the state to advance aspects of public policy, then there are circumstances in which 'evidence-led policy' may become inverted into various forms of 'policy-led evidence' in order to chase diminishing sources of funding or attempt to demonstrate putative forms of influence. Yet the encouragement of interdisciplinary work can also operate in the other direction to challenge institutional barriers to intellectual innovation or to enable critical reflection on the historiography of academic disciplines themselves.

To think of the city as an interdisciplinary terrain holds complex implications for the way in which we approach urban research as well as the context within which our work is produced and received. To expand both the imaginative and methodological scope of urban writing enables everyday observations and experiences to play a potential role in the research process: a few words of overheard conversation, a fleeting view from a moving train or an immersion in an unexpected literary journey. Let's look to both the skyline and the sidewalk.

1 David Harvey, *The Limits to Capital* (Oxford: Blackwell, 1982).
2 T. J. Clark, *The Painting of Modern Life: Paris in the Art of Manet and His Followers* (London: Thames & Hudson, 1985) and Marshall Berman, *All That is Solid Melts into Air: the Experience of Modernity* (New York: Simon and Schuster, 1982).
3 See, for example, Dipesh Chakrabarty, *Provincializing Europe: Postcolonial Thought and Historical Difference* (Princeton, NJ: Princeton University Press, 2000); Rosalyn Deutsche, *Evictions: Art and Spatial Politics* (Cambridge, MA: The MIT Press, 1996); and Gyan Prakash, 'Subaltern Studies as Postcolonial Criticism', *The American Historical Review,* 99 (5) (1994): 1475–90.
4 See, for example, Paul Duvigneaud, 'Étude écologique de l'écosystème urbain bruxellois: 1. L'écosystème "urbs"', *Mémoires de la Société Royale de Botanique de Belgique*, 6 (1974): 5–35 and Herbert Sukopp, *Stadtökologie* (Berlin: Dietrich Reimer, 1990).
5 William Cronon, *Nature's Metropolis: Chicago and the Great West* (New York: Norton, 1991).
6 Mike Davis, *Ecology of Fear: Los Angeles and the Imagination of Disaster* (New York: Metropolitan Books, 1998).
7 Andrew Barry and Georgina Born (eds.), *Interdisciplinarity: Reconfigurations of the Social and Natural Sciences* (London and New York: Routledge, 2013).

II

Site-Specific Collaborations

3

SITE-WRITING

Jane Rendell with Adriana Keramida,
Povilas Marozas and Mrinal Rammohan

In *Site-Writing: The Architecture of Art Criticism*, I experiment with possibilities for writing the situatedness of criticism.[1] This method, which I call 'site-writing', configures what happens when discussions concerning situatedness and site-specificity extend to involve art, architectural and urban criticism, and the spatial qualities of writing become as important in conveying meaning as the content of the criticism. Site-writing seeks to question the separation of critical analysis and creative work in urban research by aiming to 'write sites' rather than to write about sites. My hope is that by operating as a mode of practice in its own right, one which takes into account its own sites and situations, this kind of criticism can raise ethical questions concerning the relation of the critic to the work positioned 'under' critique and propose alternative ways for researchers and writers to 'relate' to their own 'objects' as subjects of study. Drawing on Howard Caygill's notion of strategic critique, which shares with immanent critique the capacity for discovering or inventing the criteria of critical judgement in the course of criticism', I suggest that with their responsibility to address the work and an audience, critics occupy a discrete position as mediators, and that this situatedness plays a part in conditioning the performance of their interpretative role.[2] I am interested in how the often-changing but specifically spatial aspects of the positions we occupy as critics — materially, conceptually, emotionally and ideologically — create conditions that make possible acts of interpretation and constructions of meaning.

The transdisciplinary spirit of my ongoing 'site-writing' project generates spatial and textual processes of criticism out of psychoanalytic modes of operation. Following the feminist figurations of Rosi Braidotti and Donna Haraway, site-writing could be described as a process of figuration, one that is strongly informed by psychoanalytic understandings of subjectivity and representation, where relations between critic and site, as well as between text and reader, are figured, configured and reconfigured through the process of writing and re-writing.[3] Site-writing tries to position words in relation to one another, in a manner akin to Jean-François Lyotard's description of a 'figure' as opposed to a discourse:

> This present book ... still stakes out a position in signification; not being an artist's book, deconstruction here does not operate directly but is signified. No doubt its signification is fragmentary, with omissions and, I hope, rebuses. Nevertheless, this makes it only an uncertain and intermediary object, which I would like to excuse by calling it an interworld (after Klee) or a transitional object (after Winnicott); but it does not really warrant these qualifications, since they pertain only to such figural things as games and paintings. Once again, it is not a question here of letting the figural insinuate itself into words according to its own rules, but rather of insisting on the word's capacity to utter the preeminence of the figure. The ambition is to signify the other of signification.[4]

When Lyotard talks of his book *Discourse, Figure* (1971) operating like 'a transitional object', the assumption is that the work is located somewhere between the more conventional literary modes of discourse and the poetic textual practice of the figure, but Lyotard is aware that this characterisation is limited by the fact that, on the one hand, transitional space is figural and, on the other, that the figure is not simply set in opposition to discourse but by drawing on the unconscious is 'other' to it, challenging the very forms of discursive signification. Following André Green's consideration of the 'analytic object' as the third element in analysis, formed through the analytic association between analyst and analysand, my own practice of 'site-writing' is also located in a transitional space.[5] Green, a French psychoanalyst who uses both Freudian and Winnicottian concepts in his work, considers the analytic object from a spatial perspective, to be 'neither internal (to the analysand or to the analyst), nor external (to either the one or the other)' but situated between the two so corresponding precisely in his view to 'Winnicott's definition of the transitional object and to its location in the intermediate area of potential space'.[6] Working with some of the psychic present in psychoanalytic exchange, those experienced by the analysand, such as free association, as well as those more consciously practised by the analyst, like evenly suspended attentiveness, interpretation and 'construction', my aim, through site-writing, is to configure new positions of relation between critic and site, essay and reader, that respond to psychic attitudes and conditions.

6 → 59 20 → 173 26 → 217 29 → 237 32 → 259

Site-Writing/Site-Reading, Cities Methodologies, Slade Research Centre, London, 2013. View of the exhibit during opening night. Photo: David Roberts.

SITE-WRITING/SITE-READING: Adriana Keramida, Povilas Marozas, Mrinal Rammohan with Jane Rendell

Site-Writing/Site-Reading was a Cities Methodologies exhibit curated by a group of students — Anna Ulrikke Andersen, Polly Gould, Adriana Keramida, Povilas Marozas, Azzurra Muzzonigro, Mrinal Rammohan and Ishita Shah — from the Theorising Practices/Practising Theory: Architecture, Art and Urbanism course run by Jane Rendell as part of the MA in Architectural History at the Bartlett School of Architecture, UCL. In this module, master's and PhD students explore the intersections of transdisciplinary research, focusing on critical analysis of architectural and artistic practices through the process of site-writing.[7]

For the final project of the course, students were asked to select a location and to develop a site-specific methodology by which to interrogate, analyse and interpret their subject, using the theories and criticisms presented over the course of the term. Within the class of 2013 alone, these chosen sites were spread over three continents and ranged in size from the cityscape as a whole, to the layout space in AutoCAD software. As opposed to the normative way of writing about the site, the students were instead asked to write sites as a critique of, reaction to, insertion in or interpretation of the site. Due to the variety of sites and methods employed, these resulted in a variety of forms, from a collage to a book to an in-situ performance piece.

The exhibit *Site-Writing/Site-Reading* provided a 'taster' of nearly twenty different ways of approaching the built environment and therefore presented a number of curatorial challenges. As a situated methodology, and with the wide variety of methods and media, how would site-writing and site-reading translate into a gallery environment? A major requirement of the show was therefore to develop a strategy that could showcase, for example, performative and static pieces on equal terms. Another issue that came up was that participants began to adapt their projects to fit the conventions of a white-walled gallery space. From a curatorial perspective, we sought to actively combat this tendency by designing a framework that would be flexible enough not only to display a range of media but also to conceal and reveal projects durationally in order to provide a sense of balance between the visual and performative. Throughout the exhibition, different projects were highlighted at different times by spotlighting and placing them in more prominent locations. A series of performances took place at specific times during the day.

The idea of using a bookshelf as the central object in the exhibit was part design and part coincidence. A member of our team had come across a 1970s Scandinavian shelving unit. A precursor to the IKEA-style ranges of modular furniture, it could be reconfigured in multiple ways and adapted to fit almost any project, and even hold those projects not on display. The bookshelf also seemed to be an apt metaphor to house what would be the products of a site-writing exercise. The shelving unit, which became the understated focal point of the exhibition, further inspired the third driving concept behind the design of our exhibit: its domestic aesthetic.

Ultimately, the exhibition evolved into a site itself to be read and written by its visitors. While the intentions of the curatorial team were for the exhibit to be as flexible as possible, not all the projects could be accommodated equally well. The resulting friction from these imperfections added a sense of authenticity to the experience. Sites do not always cooperate with the methodologies developed for them, and, similarly, the needs of the exhibition required us to constantly alter our strategy and design, and the outcome encouraged the same flexibility and discovery in the viewer.

For the exhibition, *Site-Writing/Site-Reading*, the sites chosen as research foci varied from the streets of Cairo to a hospital in the south of England, originally constructed for the treatment of tuberculosis. The mode of the responses — composed of words, combined with images, sounds

Site-Writing/Site-Reading, Cities Methodologies, Slade Research Centre, London, 2013. The space was curated to have a domestic aesthetic, encouraging visitors to explore the shelves and sit down to read. Photo: Mrinal Rammohan.

and artefacts — adapted processes used in film, poetry, fine art and fiction to reconsider the relation of form and content in academic urban writing. The transdisciplinary methodologies that developed were presented as films, books and installations. An assemblage of shelves and cupboards contained the various site-writings as artefacts, which, over the three days of the exhibition, surprised us all as they opened out at specific moments into site-readings, where acts of reading and viewing — public and private — transformed the sites referred to as 'over there' into sites also occupied and performed 'right here' in the presence of others in the lived space of the exhibition.

SITE-WRITING
SITE-READING

Site-Writing (Rendell 2005, 2010) experiments with possibilities for writing the situatedness of criticism, with this in mind, the brief for this module questions the separation of critical analysis and creative work in urban research and asks students to 'write sites', rather than write about sites. The responses are textual/written works, which reconsider the relation of form and content in academic writing. An assemblage of shelves and cupboards contains the various site-writings as artefacts, which over the three days of the exhibition open out into site-readings – public presentations, such as poetry readings and film screenings – where relations between sites and writings develop into a performative display through the design and curation of site-readings. Thanks to the Bartlett School of Architecture, UCL, who have funded this exhibition.

Site-Writing/Site-Reading is an exhibit by students from the UCL Bartlett MA Architectural History module: Theorising Practices/Practicing Theory: Art, Architecture and Urbanism, led by course tutor Jane Rendell and including PhD students: Katy Beinart and Polly Gould; affiliate PhD students: Azzurra Muzzonigro and Signe Brink Pedersen; MA Architectural History students: Anna Ulrikke Andersen, Natalie Carter, Can Cevik, Adriana Keramida, Povilas Marozas, Carlo Menon, Mrinal Rammohan, Ishita Shah, Eda Soyal and Magd Zahran; MSc Urban Studies students: Mattie Alston, Andrea Cetrulo, Nayutaka Fukuda and Merav Kaddar; Brunel University Creative Writing student: Chioma Paul. The curatorial team consists of: Anna Ulrikke Andersen, Polly Gould, Adriana Keramida, Povilas Marozas, Azzurra Muzzonigro, Mrinal Rammohan and Ishita Shah.

Tuesday 23.04
Exhibition Launch
18.30-21.00

Wednesday 24.04
Presentations & Critique
10.00-18.00

Thursday 25.04
Individual Presentations
15: 10.00 **19:** 14.00
6: 10.30 **13:** 15.00
9: 11.00 **16:** 16.00
18: 12.00 **17:** 17.00

Friday 26.04
Individual Presentations
10: 10.00 **4:** 14.00
12: 11.00 **8:** 15.30
14: 12.00 **2:** 17.00

1-Mattie Alston
2-Anna Ulrikke Andersen
3-Katy Beinart
4-Natalie Carter
5-Andrea Cetrulo
6-Can Cevik
7-Nayutaka Fukuda
8-Polly Gould
9-Merav Kaddar
10-Adriana Keramida
11-Povilas Marozas
12-Carlo Menon
13-Azzurra Muzzonigro
14-Chioma Paul
15-Signe Brink Pedersen
16-Mrinal Rammohan
17-Ishita Shah
18-Eda Soyal
19-Magd Zahran

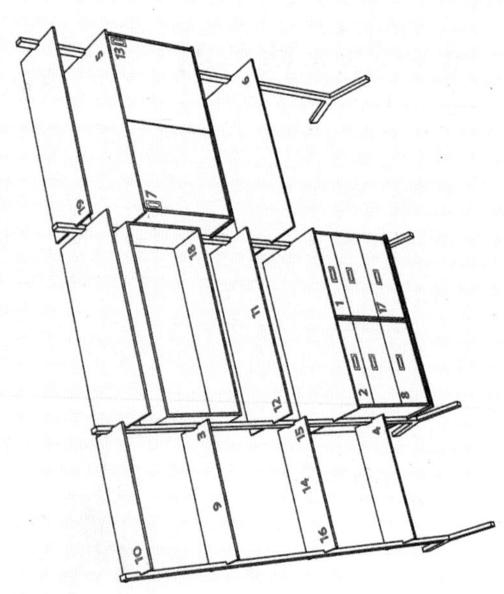

Expand beyond the Shelf

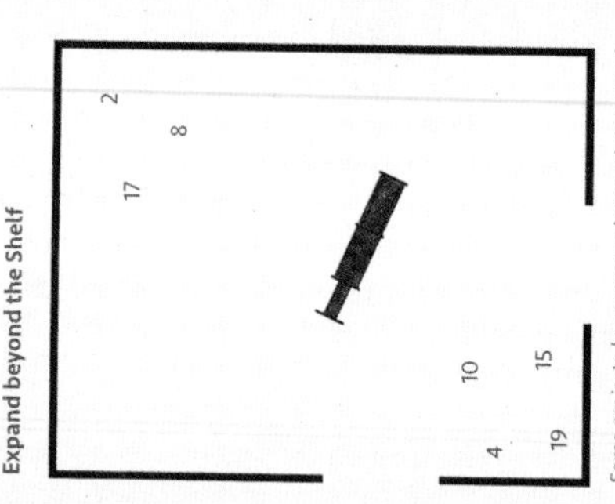

Some projects have a more interactive or visual component--please explore the space to interact with the works marked on the map above

Adriana Keramida, exhibition brochure, 2013. Side A of pamphlet with general course descriptions, performance schedule and 'map' illustrating the location(s) of each piece. Photo: Povilas Marozas.

6 → 59 20 → 173 26 → 217 29 → 237 32 → 259

SITE-WRITING/SITE-READING

PROJECT
ARTIST
DESCRIPTION

1 The Arena - A Play - Written 2013 - Perform 2061

Mattie Alston

The Arena is a play, to be performed in 2061. A reconceptualisation of Arena, a sculpture outside the National Theatre in London, it reimagines and (re)presents the work as a juxtaposition of timeless and zeitgeist, at once the product of modern rationality and ancient ritual, alongside exploring the surrounding context.

2 The Spirit of the [Natural] Place

Anna Ulrikke Andersen

Based on a chapter of Genius Loci, this film questions Norberg-Schulz' categories of landscape by juxtaposing images from the romantic (Norway) and cosmic (Jordan). The Window is 'displaced', creating an ambiguity within a dynamic network of focalizer and focalized.

3 A Game of Dominoes

Katy Beinart

The game is based on a series of recordings made through playing dominoes with an elders group in Brixton, London and through other interviews in and around Brixton Market, which explore memories of arrival, making home, creating identities and how current changes taking place affect residents' sense of belonging.

4 The (Un)wanted History

Natalie Carter

The future of Heatherwood Hospital is being decided. Following a long-neglected history, this archive of materials charts the little evidence of the early history of the hospital. You are invited to select pieces from the archive and place them on the wall, creating an exhibition, combining and juxtaposing history with current debate to produce a new discourse.

5 SE17

Andrea Cetrulo

This project explores how the regeneration plans for the Elephant and Castle area will have an impact on the adjacent Walworth Road, specifically on the site's existing economic, cultural and social relations. An interactive prototype and a piece of writing reproduce certain physical details and oral traditions.

6 A Journey in Between

Can Cevik

Exploring the land of New Zealand, each corner unveils the story behind how it also came to be known as the land of Tolkien's The Lord of the Rings. See how the choices you make reshape your story as you travel in between the stories of fiction, depiction and reality...

7 Scarred Letter

Nayutaka Fukuda

Abstract painting of the alphabet 'T' with 'scars' deliberately etched by the artist, the coarse surface of the canvas shall expose the metaphor conjured up by the materiality of the scarred furniture, which is the main theme of the experimental writing. Furthermore, the scarred letter also implies the deconstructed written text employed in the written work.

8 Horizon

Polly Gould

Horizon is a response to watercolours by Antarctic explorer, Edward Wilson 1872-1912. The site referenced is the polar environment, but mediated through the paintings of landscape now housed in the archive. Glass slides, watercolour swatches, copies of topographical drawing, and narrative derived from the expedition journal and Wilson's annotated sketches, inform the work.

9 Construction Sight

Merav Kaddar

The hoardings of the construction-site outside my window pose the question – where does creativity live? *Construction Sight* summarises a 6 month observation of this site. Shifting from site to sight, the language frames the experience, while the viewer chooses how to engage. The site-sight is always subjective, disclosing while concealing, constructing through interpretation..

10 City on the Shelf

Adriana Keramida

Through a parallel reading of a skyline and a shelf of books, this project offers an alternative impression of one of London's most iconic views; looking East from Waterloo Bridge. Exctracted words from representive texts describe what the area around each building in the skyline is/should be/was/could have been/will be/might become.

11 Back From Where I Am

Povilas Marozas

This work is a speculative attempt to articulate Freudian ideas of uncanny strangeness and memory into an architectural-historical inquiry. It is a visual diary of a brief journey to Visaginas, a Soviet-built satellite town on the north-eastern edge of Lithuania that was once planned as the biggest nuclear power-plant in Soviet Russia.

12 The Sphere and the Labyrinth

Carlo Menon

In 1980, Italian historian Manfredo Tafuri published an enigmatic book on the crisis of architectural language and the artistic avant-gardes. After a huge impact, The Sphere and the Labyrinth is disappearing. Not an elegy nor a call for the dead, this project is more a leaflet pointing at its graveyard.

13 Reading Chester to London: 5 km/h

Azzurra Muzzonigro

Starting in Chester in March and ending in London in April. This project is written on a narrowboat with two-fix crew members -me and my partner - plus occasional visitors and random encounters. Anything that happens will be moving at an average speed of 5 km/h.

14 Working with the Burnett Archive of Working Class Autobiographies

Chioma Paul

Adapting the literary form of two stories from the Burnett Archive of Working Class Autobiographies. The project is a story, written in verse that explores my experiences and those of previous generations of my family against the backdrop of migration.

15 It Happened Here

Signe Brink Pedersen

Ths project examines the concept of temporality in the Olympic fringe of Hackney Wick East London.

It questions what has happened here? And asks what does 'Making It Happen' mean? This is discussed through a curatorial site-specific practice-based project following the temporary attitudes found on the site.

16 Neo-Waste-tery/Set Tone Weary/ Near Testy Woe

Mrinal Rammohan

It's all downhill from here. Is that a good thing? Depends on which way you're looking. Inspired by Walter Benjamin's One Way Street, this project is a search for the blatantly obvious by reading the streets against the grain.

17 Cite. Recite. Incite. Excite.

Ishita Shah

Local street markets are a unique part of every city. But the 'new city' is constantly challenging this timeless system of exchanges. The project is a critique of the act of 'mall-ification' of markets by emphasizing the hybrid nature of these markets, through a play of words, forms and sounds.

18 Object Stories

Eda Soyal

The project arises from my personal experiences with a Turkish migrant family who has been living in London for ten years. Particular objects that are part of their everyday life evoke memories of a time in the family's life and illustrate a relationship with unfamiliar urban-life.

19 Spleen Cairo

Magd Zahran

Remaining a mysterious entity, multiple historical, artistic and political studies take place in order to identify Cairo's character and identity. This project is an attempt to adopt a new urban understanding of Cairo through investigating interdisciplinary poems written by Cairo resident poets as well as through investigating these poets' lives.

Adriana Keramida, exhibition brochure, Cities Methodologies, 2013. Side B of pamphlet describing each contributor's project. Photo: Povilas Marozas.

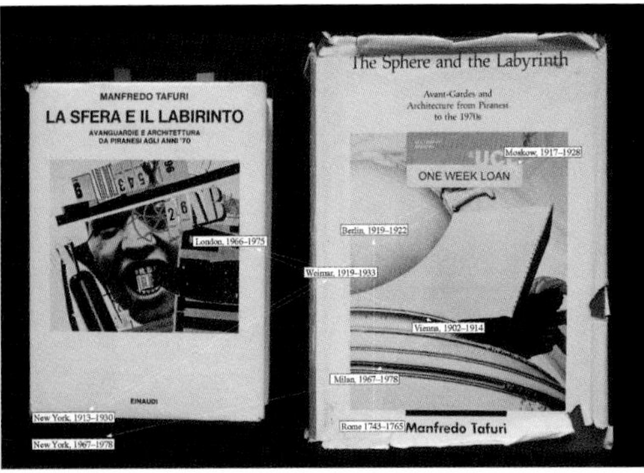

Carlo Menon, *The Sphere and the Labyrinth*, 2013. A temporal and spatial map positioned over the original and English translation provides a matrix of clues pointing toward the disappearance of Tafuri's seminal text.

Anna Ulrikke Andersen, *The Spirit of a [Natural] Place*, 2013. Petra, Jordan. A window design by Norwegian architect Ove Bang, displaced in Petra, Jordan. Still from *The Spirit of a [Natural] Place*.

Povilas Marozas, *Back From Where I Am*, 2013. Visaginas, Lithuania. Excerpt from the visual diary of the artist exploring the efficacy of memory in an architectural historical context.

Adriana Keramida, *City on the Shelf*, Cities Methodologies, 2013. Two elements of *City on the Shelf* on display during the exhibition. Photo: Mrinal Rammohan.

Anna Ulrikke Andersen, *The Spirit of a [Natural] Place*, 2013. Petra and Wadi Rum Desert, Jordan. Andersen shooting the 'cosmic' portion for her film *The Spirit of a [Natural] Place*. Photo: Mikkel Due.

Site-Writing/Site-Reading, Cities Methodologies, 2013. One of the temporal elements of the exhibition, the work displayed on the kitchen table was rotated on a set schedule and could be changed by visitors to the space. Photo: Mrinal Rammohan.

Mrinal Rammohan, Neo-Waste-tery/Set Weary Tone/Near Testy Woe, 2013. Title page from a book of photography produced as an exploration of the obvious in directive signage.

Natalie Carter, *The (Un)wanted History*, Cities Methodologies, 2013. Interactive archives, documenting the history of Heatherwood Hospital, allow visitors to display their own version of events. Photo: Mrinal Rammohan.

6 → 59 20 → 173 26 → 217 29 → 237 32 → 259

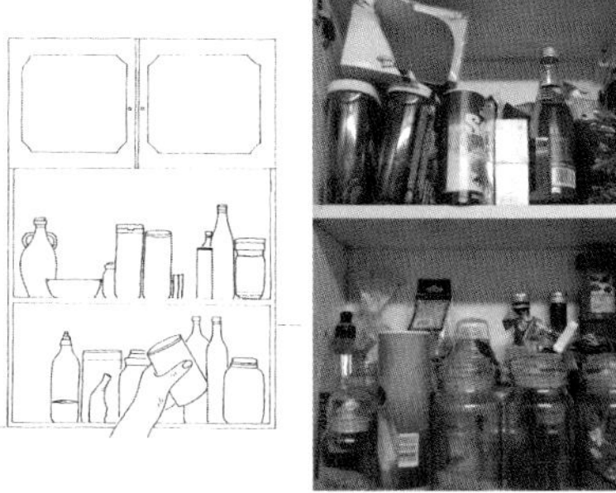

Eda Soyal, *Object Stories*, 2013.

Merav Kaddar, *Construction Sight*, 2013. Image from *Construction Sight*, posing the question that inspired Kaddar to monitor and analyse the construction site opposite her flat for six months.

Site-Writing/Site-Reading, Cities Methodologies, 2013. Detail of central shelf element during the exhibition. Photo: Adriana Keramida.

Site-Writing/Site-Reading, Cities Methodologies, 2013. Contributor Polly Gould presenting her doctoral work 'Horizon' during the final critique. Photo: Azzurra Muzzonigro.

Site-Writing/Site-Reading, Cities Methodologies, 2013. The Site-Reading/Site-Writing class culminated in a final presentation and critique of each project, which was open to the public in the exhibition space. Photo: Azzurra Muzzonigro.

1 My site-writing project was initiated as a mode of spatialising writing first in Jane Rendell, 'Doing it, (Un)Doing it, (Over) Doing it Yourself: Rhetorics of Architectural Abuse', in *Occupying Architecture*, edited by Jonathan Hill (London and New York: Routledge, 1998), 229–46. I then first named it as a form of site-specific practice in Jane Rendell, 'Site-Writing', in *Transmission: Speaking and Listening*, vol. IV, edited by Sharon Kivland, Jaspar Joseph-Lester and Emma Cocker (Sheffield: Sheffield Hallam University and Site Gallery, 2005), 169–76. I then developed it through a series of essays and texts, brought together in Jane Rendell, *Site-Writing: The Architecture of Art Criticism* (London: I.B. Tauris, 2010). I have also worked with 'site-writing' as a pedagogic practice since 2001 at the Bartlett School of Architecture, UCL.

2 Howard Caygill, *Walter Benjamin: The Colour of Experience* (London and New York: Routledge, 1998), 34 and 79. For a discussion of the politics of spectatorship, see, for example, Umberto Eco, 'The Poetics of the Open Work [1962]', in *Participation: Documents of Contemporary Art*, edited by Claire Bishop (London and Cambridge, MA: Whitechapel and MIT Press, 2006), 20–40. See also Claire Bishop, *Installation Art: A Critical History* (London: Tate Publishing, 2005), 13 and 131.

3 For their definitions of feminist figuration, see, for example, Donna Haraway, 'Cyborgs, Coyotes and Dogs: A Kinship of Feminist Figurations and There Are Always More Things Going on Than You Thought! Methodologies as Thinking Technologies: An Interview with Donna Haraway Conducted in Two Parts by Nina Lykke, Randi Markussen, and Finn Olesen', in *The Donna Haraway Reader* (London and New York: Routledge, 2004), 321–42; Rosi Braidotti, *Nomadic Subjects* (New York: Columbia University Press, 1994), 4–5 and 113; Rosi Braidotti, *Transpositions: On Nomadic Ethics* (Cambridge: Polity Press, 2006), 90 and 170.

4 Jean-François Lyotard, 'The Bias of the Figural', in *Discourse, Figure* (Minneapolis, MN: University of Minnesota Press, 2011), 3–19, 13.

5 André Green, 'The Analyst, Symbolization and Absence in the Analytic Setting (On Changes in Analytic Practice and Analytic Experience) – In Memory of D. W. Winnicott', *International Journal of Psycho-Analysis*, 56 (1975): 1–22, 12.

6 André Green, 'Potential Space in Psychoanalysis: The Object in the Setting', in *Between Reality and Fantasy: Transitional Objects and Phenomena*, edited by S. A. Grolnick and L. Barkin (London and New York: Routledge, 1978), 169–89, 180.

7 The exhibit presented work by PhD students Katy Beinart and Polly Gould; affiliate PhD students Azzurra Muzzonigro and Signe Brink Pedersen; MA Architectural History students Anna Ulrikke Andersen, Natalie Carter, Can Cevik, Adriana Keramida, Povilas Marozas, Carlo Menon, Mrinal Rammohan, Ishita Shah, Eda Soyal and Magd Zahran; and MSc Urban Studies students Mattie Alston, Andrea Cetrulo, Nayutaka Fukuda and Merav Kaddar. It was funded by the Bartlett School of Architecture, with thanks to Dr Marcos Cruz and Professor Adrian Forty.

4

TOWARDS AN ARCHITECTURE OF ENGAGEMENT

Researching contested urbanism and informalities

Camillo Boano, Caroline Newton and Giorgio Talocci

Action-orientation Participatory design Relational urban design

In this chapter, we connect a number of seemingly disparate urban research activities, initiated, conducted and developed with students and staff of the UCL Development Planning Unit's MSc Building and Urban Design in Development active collaboration with partners and urban activist groups. All were action-oriented, using a theoretical yet pragmatic approach, attempting to uncover and research the hidden forces that shape material urban worlds and, vice versa, investigating how the material and everyday conditions shape relationships, imaginations and people. They each show how design is essentially about the production of space, not as fixed and abstract reality but as something actively and contingently produced. As such, design is understood as an impure and discrepant practice, as a way to address urban challenges from the perspective of excluded groups in contested urban spaces. Each project shows that the potential of design can no longer remain within the realms of intent, form or representation but needs to tie these to its consequences and effects.

From a collective design process in the complex and multifaceted territory of Dharavi in Mumbai to a stroll in Beirut across the green line and the Solidere's downtown, and an immersion inside a real heterotopia, a squatter-occupied building in Rome and its spatial narratives, these projects are examples of how urban designers are pushed to actively question their practice and to dig deep into the multilayered complexity of material and immaterial realities and processes encountered in a given context. We call for a recalibration of the practice in order to get a better understanding of how to deal with the non-designed and the un-designable, be it power relations, informal organisational structures, collective and individual imaginations and aspirations.[1] Architecture and design in situations of informality and marginality require engagement with a less-than-ideal world and an appreciation of architecture beyond its mainstream. Design methods must proceed from the current state of affairs and existing modes of spatial production. Such a statement is not to claim for revolution; it is, rather, to call for an investigation of political subjectivities along with their material and spatial conditions.

The projects are exemplary of this renewed engagement of urban professionals and of the coming back of advocacy at the forefront of architecture: in Rome we were actively engaging with a community of squatters and constructing an altogether new mythology around the spaces they occupy and creatively shape, against any social stigma or rhetoric of exclusion from the rest of the urban social and built fabric; in Mumbai, after working with the activist group SPARC (Society for the Promotion of Area Resource Centre) in the struggle against the Dharavi Redevelopment Project's imposition of a vocabulary of comprehensive planning aiming to 'fix' slums in a 'world-class city', we conceived design strategies as acts of resistance, envisioning alternative spatial scenarios and imaginations that encompass the existing situated urban human resilience and material and relational resourcefulness;[2] in Beirut, finally, one question hangs permanently above the head of the practitioner who is strolling and traversing the city's post-conflict landscape and its new neo-liberal developments: 'What [design] methodology can be discerned in the middle of this landscape? ... And, perhaps a better question here, under such conditions is, is it possible to design such an environment at all?'[3]

Collage titled *The Vertical Slum: a Contestation of the Dharavi Redevelopment Plan Vision,* which emerged during the work in Mumbai to reflect on conflicting narratives and imaginations. Credit: MSc Building & Urban Design in Development students, 2010.

AN ARCHITECTURE OF ENGAGEMENT

Over 1 billion people now live in 'slums' or 'informal settlements', a number expected to double by 2030, making what can be labelled 'informal urbanism' globally into the dominant expression of urban form. In our view, architects should formulate appropriate answers in the form of a responsive architecture, an architecture of engagement that has the capacity to reconsider and recalibrate design process within this contemporary urban condition, which could be called 'un-designed' or even 'un-designable'. We make a plea for an urban design approach that engages with situated urban realities and practices and is active, relational, collective, embedded, reflexive and transdisciplinary.

'Active' primarily refers to a practice that engages with material conditions and their complex social and political conditions. It vacillates between refraining from taking action and engagement as an ongoing balancing act, as it seeks to cultivate a collective imagination spawning transformative action. In practice, such an approach entails engaging both with activist approaches to research (e.g., building on practices of insurgent planning, creating platforms and visible actions) and with methods for institutional development that seek out negotiation and establish consensus in what is a messy and contingent process of collaboration between government, business and civil-society actors. This was clear, for instance, in Mumbai, where the methodology hinged upon an analysis of the possibilities already in place, the knowledge produced inside Dharavi, and the subsequent transformations and historical layers, spawning a design process that capitalises on these local conditions and resources, on the people that work for progress, the imperfect and aborted actions, the incremental changes and the windows of opportunity that they implied.

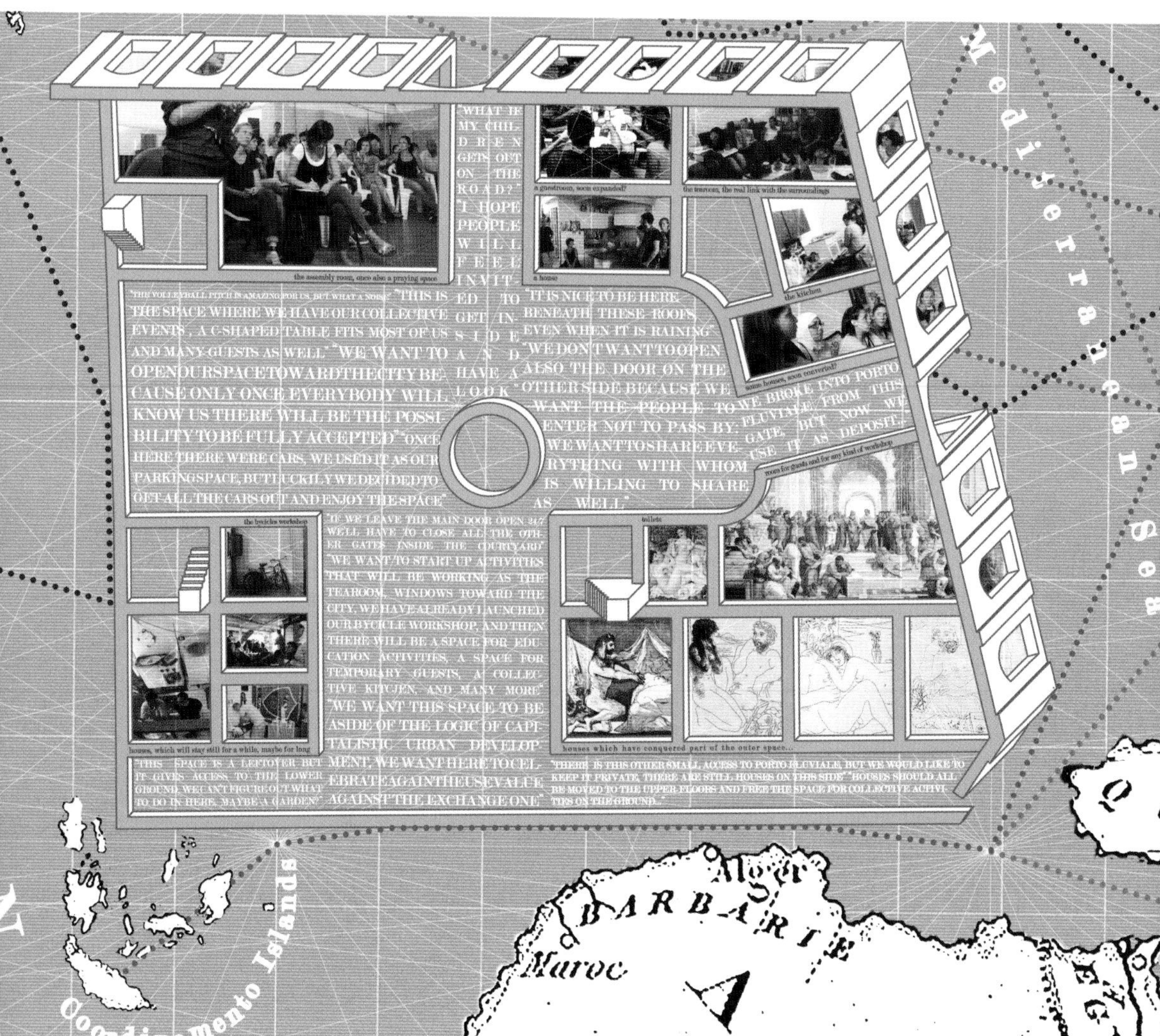

Conflictive narratives and aspirations interweave on the ground floor of Porto Fluviale squat.

15 → 131

Such design practices entail research of the local context, and they are, therefore, also necessarily relational, recognising that knowledge production and learning are defined within relative positions, and in conversation with existing discourses, material processes and local actors with their socially constructed and mediated cognitive resources and cultural meanings through which they make sense of the world. In our work we lay out these configurations, helping us to see the constraints for action as well as the potentials to open up new spaces, new possibilities and new visions. The work in Porto Fluviale — squatter-occupied space in Rome — was exemplary in this sense. Different overlapping layers of narratives — both spatial as well as personal — were interpreted and mapped out. The everyday mediations and negotiations between a multitude of individual aspirations and a supposedly consensual collective will, render evident conflictive views, aspirations and representations. Illustrating an 'archaeology' of Porto Fluviale allows remapping new pathways and new narratives of the inhabited place).

The work is then inevitably collective, whereby knowledge production is understood as a common endeavour pursued by networks of individuals, community organisations, NGOs and public (and private) sector institutions that share the values of both aesthetics and ethics alike. The starting point is to question the role of the expert and the ways in which discourses of expertise are constituted in particular contexts, as this so-called expertise often puts a break on 'out-of-the-box' thinking, thus limiting possible alternatives and outcomes. In the short animated movie, *Dwelling the Threshold*, Muzzonigro and Zacchi called for collective moments and spaces

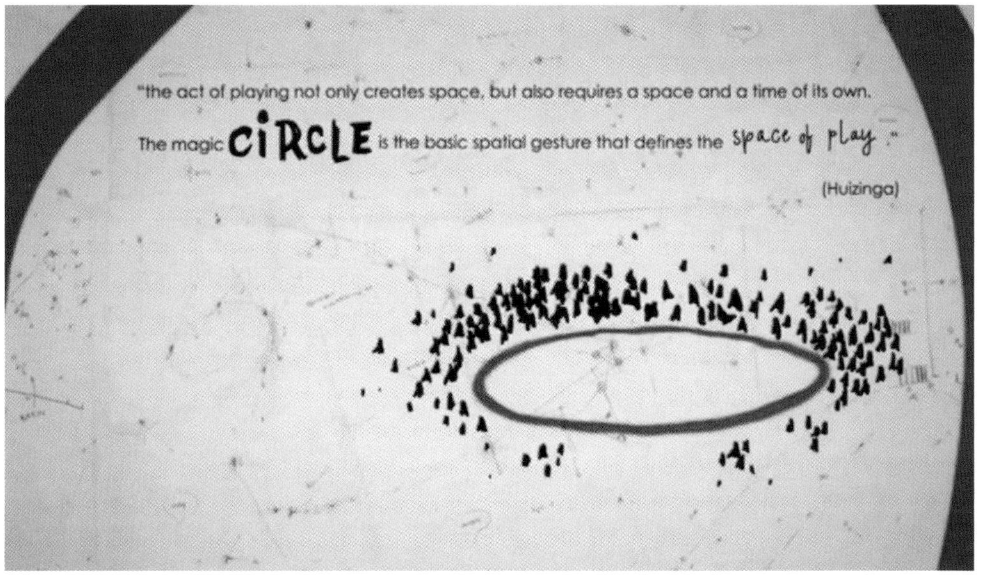

The 'circle' as a space of play and encounter. Frame from Azzurra Muzzonigro and Daniele Zacchi's 'Dwelling the Threshold'.

of encounter in 'circles', 'borders' and 'interstices', searching respectively for performances and events, 'common' limits and 'contiguity' of spaces, 'residual' fragments: all of them necessary elements of a renewed approach to design. Here the authors pragmatically operationalised the Foucauldian notion of heterotopia, able to suggest new territories of investigation beyond the one immediately visible suggesting poetically the possible encounter of both knowledge and space as a common, non-partial and unique endeavour.

Research and design are also embedded: learning and knowledge production are dependent on the practices and lived experiences of people in specific settings and locations. This means recognising development as a collective endeavour that crystallises from the interaction of multiple subjectivities, being sensitive to emotional worlds and ways of engaging with the world. How can this be possible in a landscape as complex as the one in Beirut? In tune with the historical roots of critical theory and critical urban commentary, the research also has to be reflexive, self-consciously and explicitly acknowledging the contexts in which it is produced. More specifically, the approaches question fixed understandings of the world as these are unable to produce alternative and counter-hegemonic outcomes. Again in Beirut, this comes to the fore:

> This was ground zero for a decade, the area adjacent to the green line suffering the greatest physical damage during the war. And it is because of this that the area has undergone the greatest reconstruction in the post-war years. A playground for a conglomerate developer, Solidere has attempted to incorporate both the aesthetic of pre-war Beirut 'charm', and post-modern neoliberal design into the development of the 21st century city.[4]

A counter-hegemonic outcome was impossible here, and it should instead be the role of the designer to grasp how to move towards new inclusive possibilities. Strolling and discussing, while observing Beirut's urban environments and everyday life, impressions were gathered and walking become a 'primary act in the symbolic transformation of the territory, an aesthetic instrument of knowledge and a physical transformation of the "negotiated" space, which is converted into an urban intervention'.[5]

Finally, transdisciplinarity, where complexity is recognised and celebrated in the form of critical engagement with multiple partial perspectives, is fundamental. This is not an attempt to address complexity through a relativist engagement with all possible forms of knowledge. Rather, it is a perspective that prioritises listening, without prejudice, to multiple voices, to the extent that listening can generate and enable fresh perspectives on the world. The project in Beirut brought together four academics with very different backgrounds, initially offering a kind of impossible mix but eventually producing an amusing experiment exchanging knowledge and perspectives. A new situated vocabulary emerged centred on the abandonment of expert knowledge. Complexity was recognised and celebrated through the promotion of a critical engagement with multiple partial perspectives and vocabularies.

Visiting the Solidere office in Beirut, discussing their vision and masterplan for the city, 2013. Photo: Camillo Boano.

NEW SITES OF CRITICAL INTERVENTIONS

The projects presented here are all experiments in the rediscovery of the practices and lived experiences of people in specific settings and locations. They relate to multiple subjectivities, emotions and ways of engaging with the world and they offer different readings of the contemporary city and activating new sites of critical intervention. They contest the contemporary detachment or social and contextual 'drift' of design and architectural practices primarily focused on enhancing and validating the role of 'the architect'. Rather, they call for another type of architect, one who is, as Jeremy Till suggests, 'bound to the earth but with the vision, environmental sense, and ethical imagination to project new (social) spatial futures on behalf of others'.[6]

The projects were an attempt to move beyond the domain of 'expert' knowledge as conventionally understood, expressing care for both the process by which places and spaces are produced and the outcome and design product that emerges out of such collaboration, understood as a kind of wiki-process with open-source contributions. Such collaborative processes require everyone to render their relevant beliefs and knowledge systems, including professional expertise, vulnerable. Design becomes a collective and community-based practice, in which aesthetics is both a means and an end in terms of addressing social and political challenges.

1 Camillo Boano, Melissa Garcia-LaMarca and William Hunter, 'Deconstructing and Recalibrating Urban Design in the Global South', in *Explorations in Urban Design: An Urban Design Research Primer*, edited by Matthew Carmona (London: Ashgate, 2014), 25–34.
2 Camillo Boano, William Hunter and Caroline Newton (eds.), *Contested Urbanism in Dharavi: Writings and Projects for the Resilient City* (London: Development Planning Unit, 2013).
3 Camillo Boano and Dalia Chabarek, 'A Stroll Down Memory Lane: The Battle of the Hotels', *The Journal of Space Syntax*, 4 (1) (2013): 242–5.
4 William Hunter, 'Four men and a methodology (?) in Beirut', *The Journal of Space Syntax*, 4 (2) (2013), 242–5, 245.
5 Francesco Careri, *Walkscapes: Walking as Aesthetic Practice* (Barcelona: Editorial Gustavo Gili SL, 2002), 3.
6 Jeremy Till, *Architecture Depends* (Minneapolis, MN: University of Minnesota Press, 2014), 195.

5

'WORLDING' THE STUDIO

Methodological experiments and the art of being social

Worlding Visual ethnography Iterative design

Suzanne Hall and Juliet Davis

1 ↑ 23

Worlding cities, to paraphrase the anthropologist Aihwa Ong, is the situated, everyday practice of reimagining and remaking alternative social futures, incorporating a variety of ways of shaping the urban by resisting the hierarchical economic logic of globalisation.[1] 'Worlding' essentially denotes the experimental practices that arise through actively engaging with local and worldwide connections. In the context of urban life, such experiments result in a reconfiguration of social and spatial relations, what Ong refers to as 'the art of being global'. Worlding provides a way of engaging with processes of city-making in a global world through acknowledging a wide spectrum of creativity that includes but also extends beyond the confines of professionalised experts. New channels for ideas, association and governance that reflect the inter-relationships between near and far worlds potentially emerge. New practices of worlding cities can be seen in transnational forms of civic resistance, such as Occupy, where opposition is expressed in situated and symbolic urban spaces, but simultaneously resonates across cities, translating, for example, into the 99 per cent campaign. Worlding incorporates everyday political practices, or a 'deep democracy', such as those fine-tuned by slum dwellers who construct a web of local and international collaborations to secure housing for the urban poor.[2]

Here, we stretch the worlding analogy to embrace the activities of teaching and learning in an urban research and design studio. To begin with, our students are increasingly drawn from varied geographic localities, opening up questions not only of what design is, but also how a range of urbanisms and diverse experiences are core to understanding what constitutes the urban and can be productive for understanding and conceptualising the difference between specific urbanisms too. From the platform of a diverse disciplinary and cultural base, part of our studio challenge is to experiment with empirical heterogeneity, engaging with wide-ranging methods from statistical, to visual, to archival and ethnographic ways of seeing. We encourage testing and, if necessary, adapting conventions of interviewing, photographing and drawing, as well as investigating the different forms of information yielded by qualitative and quantitative techniques. But core to the process is having a specific site within easy access to allow for direct, visceral immersion. These methodological explorations are underpinned by the primary working principle of our studio, where embedding students in the spatial and social life of the city is fundamental.

Our second working principle is that conceptual exploration is integral to analytic exploration. An understanding of the 'city' emerges from the iterative process of seeing and assessing what is already there, together with conceiving the possibilities of what might be. Students are encouraged to draw on urban literatures and urban experience, so that a London field site is also understood through the wider worlds of theory and diverse cultural references. The studio findings therefore emerge out of several related explorations: an understanding of the forces, activities and spaces that shape a site; a provocation as to the key issues at stake; and detailed understandings of strategic focus within the particular economic and political milieu.

Our third principle relates to a particular orientation towards design. Students are encouraged to see design as an integral part of the research process and not as the point of creative departure from diverse forms of research and contextual analysis. Design is therefore considered as an exploratory process throughout the studio — as a research method that can bring together and express different ways of seeing places and also as a way of seeing in itself. Treating design in this way

Centring and dispersing: relocations of former business occupants of the Olympic site across London and beyond, 2007.

— as much as a process of observation as of intervention — has important implications for how design is able to engage with the existing qualities and experience of urban places and yet also be propositional and transformative. All too often, design is interpreted as fundamentally change-oriented, creating blueprints devised to prescribe and even fix future action. Emphasising the exploratory aspects of design through the life-worlds of people, places and processes encourages an alternative view of its outcomes.

Urban design which is conceptualised as a way of intervening in unfolding processes rather than as the delivery of finished 'products' provides a means to link the past, present and future of places. Exploratory design through interdisciplinary urban research facilitates a questioning process, which goes to the heart of the ethics of city-making. From here, it is crucial to emphasise the importance of being critical through design, using the insights of exploration to take a position. Design involves the construction of arguments about what we are seeing or witnessing and where we stand and with whom. The aim of critical design should be, as suggested by Jane

Rendell, to 'question dominant processes that seek to control intellectual and creative production' and, indeed, that create many of the disparities of wealth and opportunity that characterise global cities today.[3]

These principles are reflected in a studio project undertaken in 2009–10 that focused on the challenges faced by locales around the perimeter of the London 2012 Olympic site.[4] Students aimed to valorise existing local resources in the face of the tendency of regeneration to undervalue the qualities and complexities of places deemed to be run-down, in this case surviving at the margins of London's 'post-industrial' economy. The students' reflections began not long after the enclosure of the Olympic site for redevelopment had resulted in the dispersal of former business, residential and cultural users across London and its surrounding counties. Students looked at what the new 'centre' being forged inside the enclosure meant for the construction of new urban peripheries; they also looked at local experiences of being positioned at the cusp of change. Research identified rich intersections of urban forms explored through spatial mapping at macro, meso and micro scales. Activities and voices were captured through in-situ observations and interviews, while longevities and attachments were traced through combining oral histories with archival research. Plans and oppositions to authorised interventions were pursued through policy documents and face-to-face meetings with bureaucrats, designers and activists, all in their distinctive ways seeking to make a new set of possibilities in an urban fringe. These varieties of methods provided different forms and modes of conceptualising the precariousness of the fringe in the context of large-scale regeneration and the varied agendas and perspectives at play. The projects arose simultaneously in the design studio, drawing on knowledge and references from farther afield, much as the specifics of sites themselves are assembled from cultural materials from far and wide. In the context of large-scale development projects, the socio-spatial approach revealed not only the profound political and economic complexity of the regeneration impetus but also the absolute significance of sustained and new forms of human presence in the regeneration area. The student projects highlighted the extent to which the creative capacities of individuals and groups in the area had been largely overshadowed by global interests in Olympic-scale urban redevelopment and then went further to propose how on-the-ground capacities could explicitly engage in the long-term remaking of East London.

'Worlding' the studio therefore provides an experimental orientation to learning about design, one invested in the prospects of reimagining alternative social futures and attuned to the diversity of everyday life that shapes a variegated city.

1 Aihwa Ong, 'Worlding Cities; or, The Art of Being Global', in *Worlding Cities: Asian Experiments and the Art of Being Global* (Oxford: Blackwell Publishing, 2011), 1–26.

2 Arjun Appadurai, 'Deep Democracy: Urban Governmentality and the Horizon of Politics', *Environment and Urbanization*, 13 (2) (2001): 23–43.

3 Jane Rendell, 'Critical Architecture: Between Criticism and Design', in *Critical Architecture*, edited by Jane Rendell, Jonathan Hill and Mark Dorrian (London and New York: Routledge, 2007), 1–2.

4 Juliet Davis and Suzanne Hall (eds.), *Olympic Fringe* (London: The Cities Programme, London School of Economics and Political Science, 2010).

III

Performance and Participation

6

FROM 'HEROIN' TO HEROINES

Collaborative workshops Participatory film-making Re-enactment

David Roberts with Anne Louise Buckley, Briony Campbell, Chantel Forrester, Elam Forrester, Jahcheyse Forrester, Lorna Forrester, Rosie Fowler, Taina Galis, Steve Hart, Therese Henningsen, Lasse Johansson, Gillian McIver, Lewis Osbourne, Eric Phillip, Adam Rosenthal, Georgia Sangster, Ruth-Marie Tunkara, Smart Urhiofe, Julie Vandemark, Julia Vandemark, Cathy Ward and Andrea Luka Zimmerman

I am part of the collaborative art platform Fugitive Images, established by Andrea Luka Zimmerman and Lasse Johansson, two long-term residents of the Haggerston West Estate in Hackney, East London. The housing estate was built by the London County Council from 1935 to 1938 as part of a ten-year 'crusade to eliminate the slums'.[1] Following three decades of shelved refurbishment plans under the ownership of a local authority unable and unwilling to perform adequate maintenance, it was demolished in autumn 2014 to make way for mixed-tenure apartments as part of an urban-regeneration scheme.

In the long moment of suspended transformation, the informed and organised tenants of Haggerston's last-standing block secured a right of return to the new housing development and compensation for delayed works. Rather than lament the loss of their estate, they remade its anonymous and bare courtyard into a joyful celebration of defiance against urban policy that threatens to separate and stratify.[2] It became filled with table-tennis and picnic tables, delicately painted murals and a communal programme of events that cultivated creativity and sociability. As Bertolt Brecht urged of us all, they were interested in building from the bad new days, not pining for the good old ones.[3]

The trilogy of works presented here sought to draw on residents' creativity and to amplify their critical voices, developing playful methods to trace the passing of their estate and the promises of public housing. They were made with an ever-growing group of residents and local artists united by a desire to share their experiences and who generously collaborated year on year in the process and content to different degrees: tailoring historical costumes, operating cameras, exchanging stories and skills, while crammed in stairwells and balconies, kitchens and bathrooms.

I acknowledge these two dozen contributors in this chapter, but I have not written it collaboratively with them. Language itself can separate, as bell hooks reminds us; it is also a place of struggle.[4] The works convey the necessity and excitement of confronting original political, archival and academic texts without filtering terminology or flattening complexity.

This short piece is in my words only, but I have invited all the contributors to write around and between and over my text to see the projects from their eyes: how they understood it, where they stand now, what is to be done. Their writings from the margin are available online.[5]

Backbench Business

Social Housing in London

Work 1

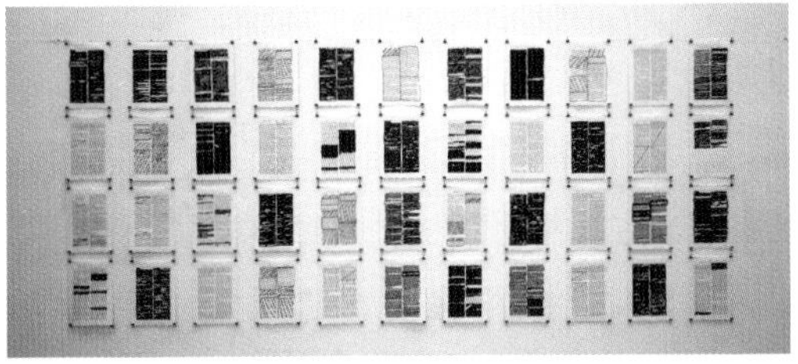

Exhibition view of forty-five photocopies, 297 × 420 mm, 2011. Photo: Fugitive Images.

Hansard is the edited verbatim transcript of proceedings of the UK Parliament's House of Commons, and on 5 May 2011 it featured a backbench debate dedicated to social housing in London. Members of Parliament discussed legislative changes which independent analyses estimated would make 60 per cent of the city that pioneered the modern ideal of social housing unaffordable by 2030, with up to a quarter of a million people facing eviction or forced relocation.[6]

As the public housing stock and spaces in the city are increasingly privatised, so is access to information about it — hidden behind paywalls, tangled within government literature and buried under corporate financial confidentiality. Public scrutiny of these documents is vital to collapse the distance between those defining policy and those affected by it.[7]

I gave residents a black marker pen and asked each to read several pages of *Hansard*, to leave in words they believed represented their opinions and experience and to black out everything else, opening up political text as a site for intervention. I returned after a week to collect the pages. Each resident had adopted a different style to interpret and reclaim the words used to define their futures, from delicate diagonal strokes to dense and disorderly effacing. I gave copies of the full, redacted transcript back to each resident and posted them anonymously to the twenty MPs who spoke in the debate. They will have seen their own words transformed by every shroud, strike-through and slash of text.

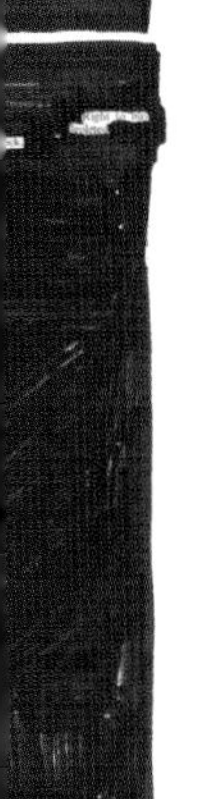

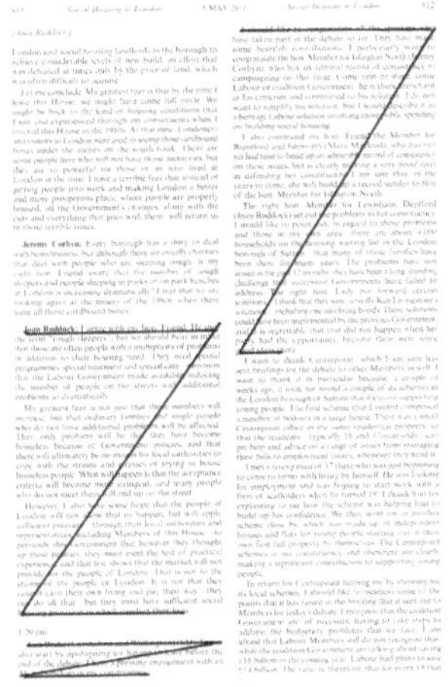

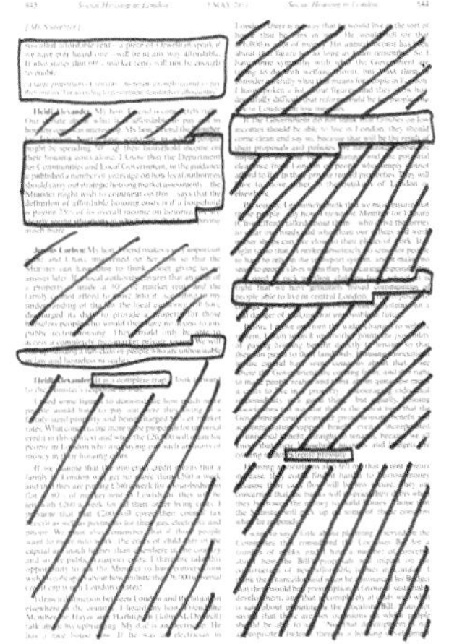

Photocopies of *Hansard* verbatim transcripts of proceedings of the House of Commons, 5 May 2011, redacted by residents of the Haggerston Estate.

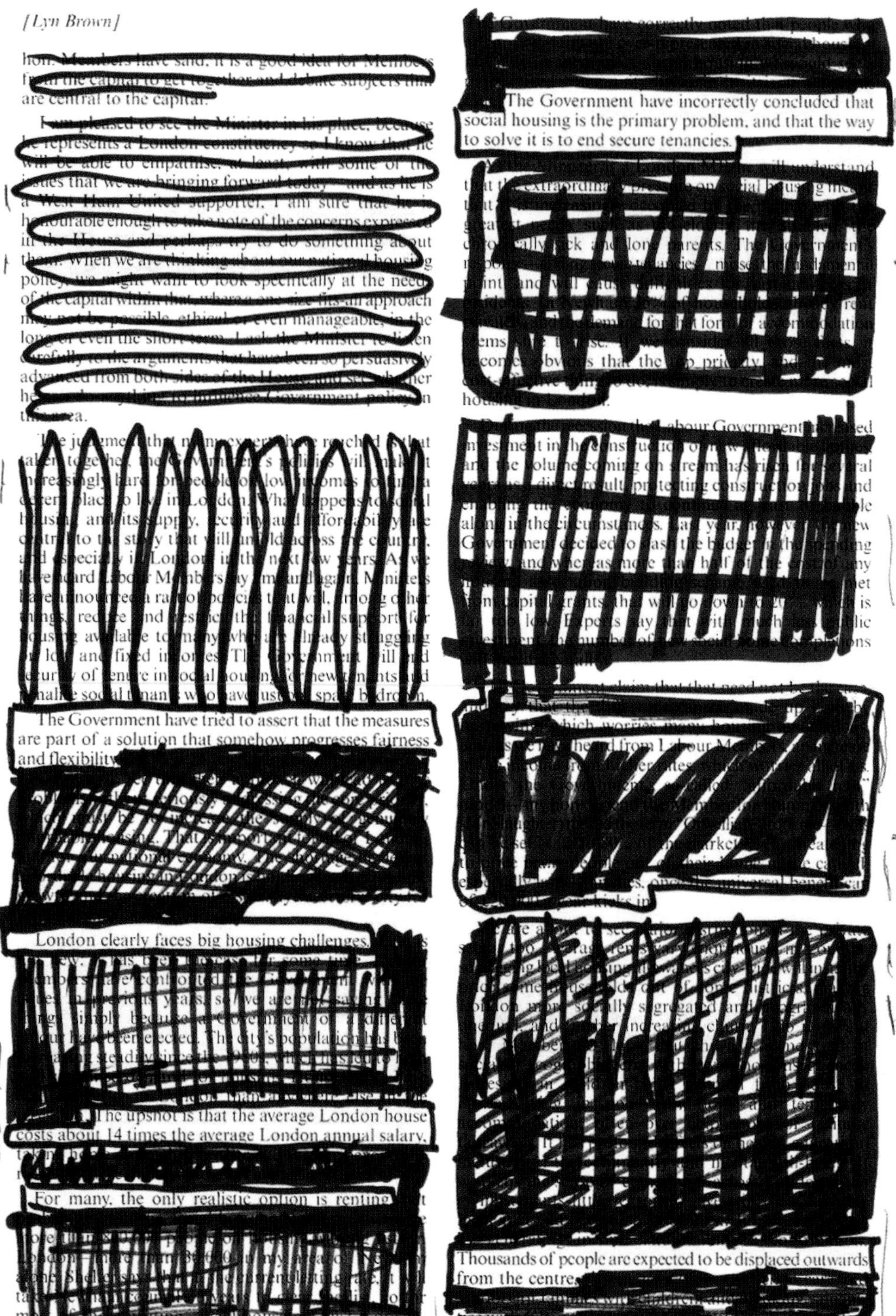

867 *Social Housing in London* 5 MAY 2011 *Social Housing in London* 868

[Lyn Brown]

The Government have tried to assert that the measures are part of a solution that somehow progresses fairness and flexibility

London clearly faces big housing challenges.

The upshot is that the average London house costs about 14 times the average London annual salary.

For many, the only realistic option is renting

The Government have incorrectly concluded that social housing is the primary problem, and that the way to solve it is to end secure tenancies.

Thousands of people are expected to be displaced outwards from the centre

principle could be set

he rules are unfair

people left on waiting lists.

he Localism Bill
will give landlords
lexible tenancies and greater control
over homes

foolishly considered

the Minister mentions
Government
the Government
ocus on greater social mobility
making
people
hange, to change where they live.
Government
make decisions to
stop people becoming

individuals.
my
important
contributions; to
the Minister's response.

1.8 million people on the housing waiting list.

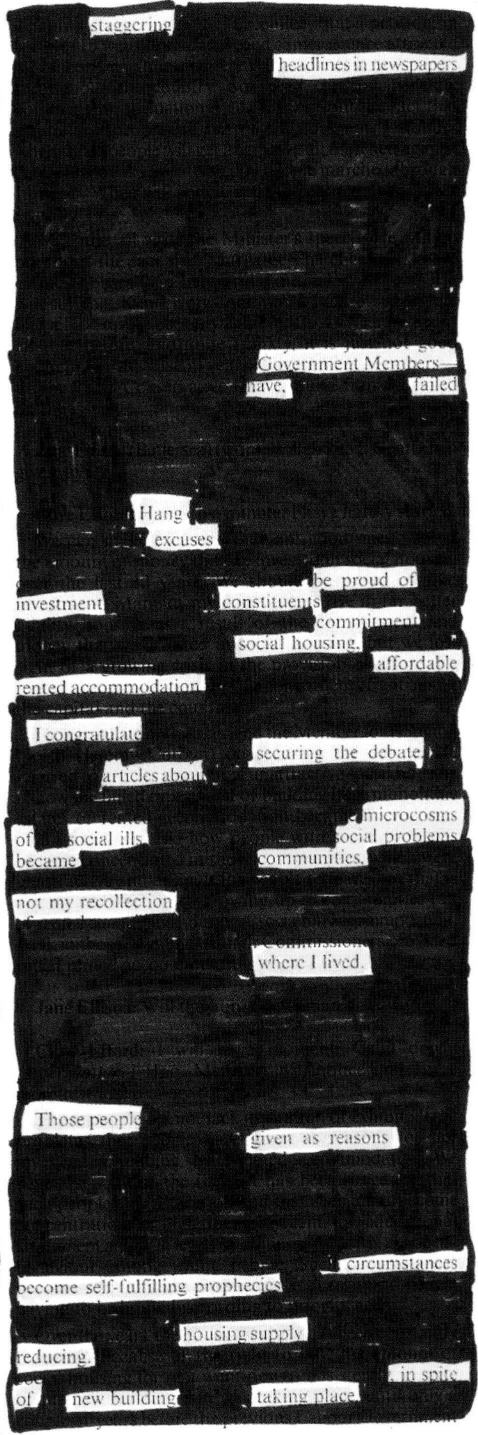

staggering
headlines in newspapers

Government Members—
have, failed

Hang
excuses
be proud of
investment constituents
commitment
social housing.
affordable
rented accommodation

I congratulate
securing the debate
articles abou
microcosms
of social ills social problems
became communities.

not my recollection

where I lived.

Those people
given as reasons

circumstances
become self-fulfilling prophecies
housing supply
reducing.
in spite
of new building taking place.

3 ↑ 35

Over the course of six weeks in summer 2012, Fugitive Images ran a sequence of workshops, filmed as part of the film *Estate* by artist Andrea Luka Zimmerman, using performance as a medium for residents to gather, embody and enact Haggerston's history, invoking original ideals and offering them for collective analysis against lived experience and critical texts.[8]

As original plans and documents of the estate were unavailable, our workshops were inspired by the only fragments of the designers' intent that remained: the names of the different blocks that comprised the estate — Lovelace, Pamela, Lowther, Harlowe, and Samuel, characters taken from the novels of eighteenth-century author Samuel Richardson.[9] Richardson was a devout Christian dismayed at the immorality of Georgian London. He wrote tales of virtuous heroines to reform readers socially and spiritually, in which each chapter takes the form of a letter to give the illusion of reality to fictitious characters and events. The decision by the London County Council to borrow these names implies a belief, like Richardson's, in moral improvement, where the instrument of reform was not ink but brick.

We dressed in eighteenth-century costume to embody Richardson's protagonists. Inspired by his epistolary novels, each workshop began with a letter addressed to participants in the voice of different people who had

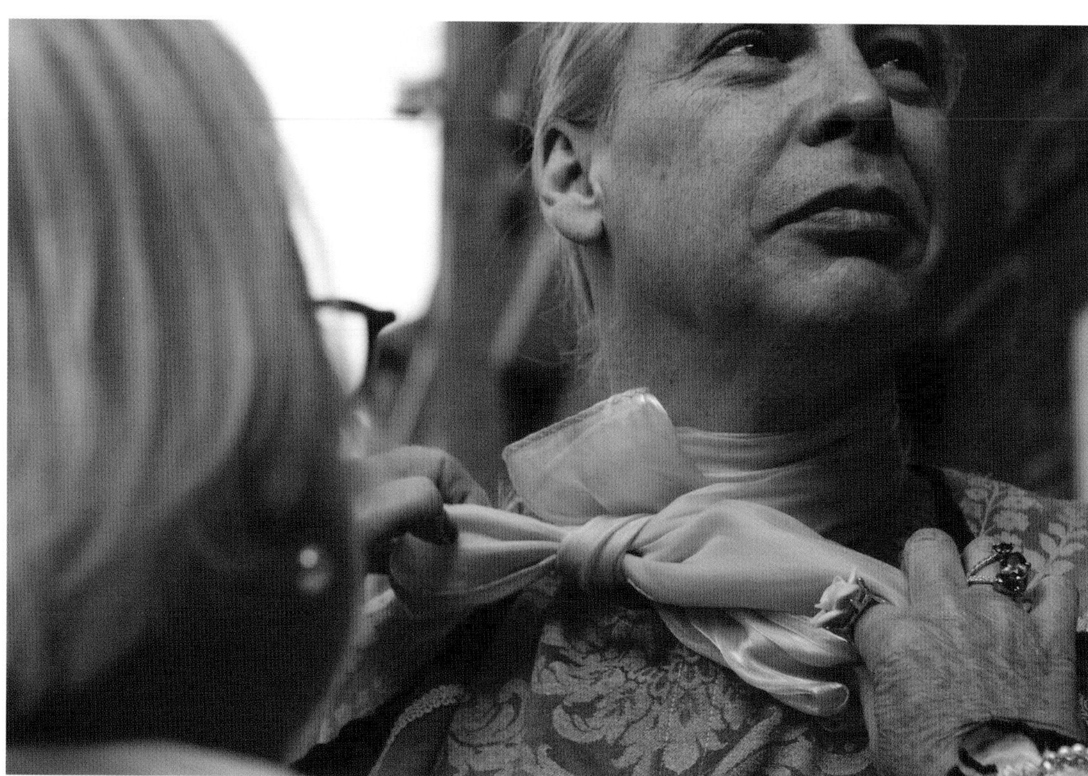

Costume fitting before third workshop re-enacting the history of the Haggerston Estate. Photo: Fugitive Images.

Second workshop in the estate courtyard. Photo: Fugitive Images.

influenced the nature and perception of the estate — the author, architect, journalist and politician — using methods of dramaturgy, devising and site-writing.[10] The letters were accompanied by contextual literature and read aloud before opening to wider discussions, questioning the vision and virtue of Haggerston's designers and Richardson's heroines and sharing opinions and expertise that cast aside stereotypes of this estate once unjustly labelled the 'heroin capital of Europe'.[11]

Still from scene of *Estate* depicting a duel between Richardson's two heroines, Pamela and Clarissa, on the skeleton of City Mills rising alongside the Haggerston Estate, 2012. Photo: Briony Campbell.

3 ↑ 35

The final series of filmed workshops took place in spring 2013 in which a wider group of current and former residents tackled the history of public housing in London. Instead of letters, each workshop began with a short lecture charting this history through key legislative Housing Acts.[12] They were staged in different spaces of the estates, using archival and architectural materials to choreograph an encounter between building and texts.

Critical questions came to life as we debated how each room, flat and block was made and is managed in response to a set of ideas about how society works, who does what and who goes where. Oscar Newman's highly influential defensible-space theory was disputed while participants were standing beside security railings on an access gallery.[13] Marion Roberts' historical analysis of how housing design is inflected by gender was considered while they crowded around the stove.[14] This negotiation of alternative histories informed by everyday experience challenged that most common biography of housing estates propagated by the media: an abrupt descent from utopian golden age to dystopian reality, which presents a narrative that appears closed and finite, a premature announcement of the death of public housing.[15]

Ninth workshop on the balcony of Samuel House performing the history of public housing in London. Photo: Fugitive Images.

10 → 87

Work 3

Seventh workshop in a kitchen of Samuel House. Photo: Fugitive Images.

These collaborative methods conceptually and physically bring ideas and people together on site. When we exhibit the work and screen the film, we reveal the socio-economic effects of spatial changes, we celebrate the richness of residents' knowledge, we share experiences and resources with other communities of interest, and we show those who claim to build 'lively', 'diverse' and 'vibrant' communities through regeneration schemes that these communities are already here.

Tenth workshop in the stairwell bay of Samuel House. Photo: Fugitive Images.

1 National Government, 1933. Quoted in Alison Ravetz, *Council Housing and Culture: The History of a Social Experiment* (London and New York: Routledge, 2001), 89.
2 The accelerated retreat of social welfare under austerity measures has paved the way for a dismantling of public housing in ideal and form. See Andrea Phillips and Fulya Erdemci (eds.), *Social Housing: Housing the Social – Art, Property and Spatial Justice* (Amsterdam: SKOR, 2012). See also Loretta Lees, Just Space, The London Tenant's Federation and Southwark Notes Archives Group, 'The Social Cleansing of Council Estates in London', in *Urban Pamphleteer #2: Regeneration Realities*, edited by Ben Campkin, David Roberts and Rebecca Ross (Northampton: Belmont Press, 2013), 6–10.
3 Bertolt Brecht, 'Against Georg Lukács', *New Left Review*, 84 (March–April 1974): 36–8. See also Hal Foster, 'Towards a Grammar of Emergency', in *Establishing a Critical Corpus*, edited by Thomas Hirschhorn (Zurich: JRP/Ringier, 2011), 162–81.
4 bell hooks, 'Choosing the Margin as a Space of Radical Openness', in *Yearnings: Race, Gender and Cultural Politics* (London: Turnaround Press, 1989), 145–53.
5 Fugitive Images, 'Collaborating from the Margins'. http://www.davidjamesroberts.com/files/citiesmethodologies.pdf (accessed 8 September 2014).
6 Alex Fenton, *Housing Benefit Reform and the Spatial Segregation of Low-Income Households in London* (Cambridge: Cambridge Centre for Housing and Planning Research, 2011), 21.
7 Commentators have long described a crisis of representation in British politics; see Owen Jones, *Chavs: The Demonization of the Working Classes* (London: Verso, 2011).
8 *Estate: A Reverie*. Directed by Andrea Luka Zimmerman. (London: LUX, 2015). See also http://www.estatefilm.co.uk (accessed 8 September 2014).
9 See Gillian McIver, 'i am here', in *Critical Cities: Volume 2*, edited by Deepa Naik and Trenton Oldfield (London: Myrdle Court Press, 2010), 146–55.
10 See Jane Rendell, *Site-Writing: The Architecture of Art Criticism* (London: I.B.Tauris, 2010).
11 Fugitive Images, *Estate* (London: Myrdle Court Press, 2010). For a critical examination of discourses of public-housing tenants, see Paul Watt, '"Underclass" and "Ordinary People" Discourses: Representing/Re-presenting Council Tenants in a Housing Campaign', *Critical Discourse Studies*, 5 (4) (2008): 345–57.
12 Housing of the Working Classes Act, 1890; Housing and Town Planning Act, 1919; Housing Act, 1949; Housing Act, 1980; and Localism Act, 2011.
13 Oscar Newman, *Defensible Space: Crime Prevention through Urban Design* (London: MacMillan, 1972).
14 Marion Roberts, *Living in a Man-Made World: Gender Assumptions in Modern Housing Design* (London and New York: Routledge, 1991).
15 Stuart Moss, 'The Death of a Housing Ideal', *The Guardian*, 4 March 2011.

7

FOUR PALIMPSESTS ON THE ERASURE OF THE HEYGATE ESTATE

Visual palimpsest Experimental photography In situ modelling

Felipe Lanuza Rilling

INTRODUCTION

The original name of my contribution to the Cities Methodologies exhibition in April 2013 was 'Materialising Absence: The Present of the Heygate Estate'. It consisted of four palimpsests intended to recreate the sense of absence that emanated from the site during its interim condition of disuse, prior to demolition. As I write now, the erasure of 1,260 housing units and public green areas is actually taking place and will presumably be completed before this book's publication. It is unlikely that there will be any physical presence of the Heygate left, as the project for the forthcoming regeneration regards the site as a blank page. The absence my work referred to then, therefore, has now acquired a different meaning, pointing to the total absence of the estate.

TWO ERASURES

The Heygate Estate was located in the Elephant and Castle area of Southwark, in South London. Designed in the late 1960s by a council team headed by architect Tim Tinker, it was built between 1970 and 1974. During its first days it provided a high-standard environment for its inhabitants, who developed a strong sense of community as a result of this.[1] From the 1980s onwards, however, the Heygate progressively declined, as did many other council estates built by the welfare state. There have been fierce debates about whether this resulted from neglect, housing policies or the architecture itself.[2] Yet an appraisal study commissioned by Southwark Council in 1998 found no structural damage in the Heygate's buildings and instead pointed to the need for refurbishment and appropriate maintenance.[3]

There were also more than 450 mature trees in the site, which were planted in the early 1970s as part of the original project. They formed a dense urban forest. The qualities of these green areas, together with the well-ventilated and bright spacious flats, represented the main assets of an estate that in 1998 was in sound material condition, with the majority of its residents preferring to stay.[4]

However, Southwark Council deemed the decline to be irreversible. A year later, they confirmed the complete demolition of the estate in order to clear the way for an ambitious regeneration project to be developed within what they called the Elephant and Castle 'opportunity area'.[5] This was a repeat of the erasure and total urban renewal that took place in the postwar period, when a series of old tenement blocks and terraced houses where knocked down to make way for the Heygate itself.

Although sharing similar features, the historical contexts and the reasons behind these major urban operations are quite different. Whereas in the first case the renovation was a centralised authority effort aimed

9 → 83 17 → 147

to provide homes for people of middle and lower classes, the second is basically a market-driven plan where investors intend to take the maximum advantage of a large plot in one of London's property prime spots. The amount of social housing in the new scheme is indeed dramatically diminished in favour of more expensive flats.[6]

The last remaining occupants, together with a network of neighbours and supporters, strongly resisted the regeneration plans that involved the demolition of the Heygate Estate, critiquing the process as gentrification accompanied by the privatisation of public space.[7] The unfair decanting of residents forced to leave without a just compensation, the environmental damage caused by felling mature trees, and the approach of demolishing only to build again from scratch rather than repairing or refurbishing, were all issues raised in opposition to this comprehensive redevelopment, part of the now ongoing urban renovation of the Elephant and Castle area.[8] In this sense, to characterise the Heygate as a dysfunctional and dilapidated estate was instrumental in justifying the whole operation of demolition and replacement.[9]

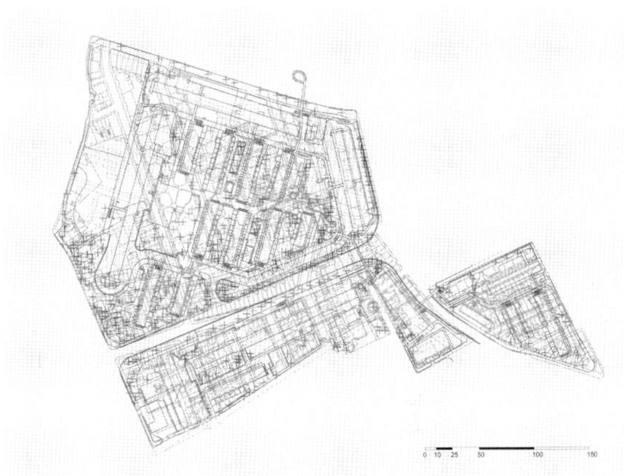

Overlay of three plans for the Heygate Estate site, 1950, 1990 and the redevelopment plan for 2025.

FOUR PALIMPSESTS

The metaphor of the palimpsest has been used in urban history to describe the continuous process of 'over-writing' of urban landscapes, accumulating traces and elements of past uses and physical configurations: different stages of history are 'inscribed' in the materiality of the city. The superimposition of urban plans from different periods is a way of representing this kind of situation. In the case of the Heygate Estate site, however, the palimpsest consists of three totally different physical configurations imposed on the same site during a period of fifty years. The first palimpsest presented here is a representation evidencing the discontinuity of different times fictionally collapsed in a complex and disparate matrix. It reproduces the footprints of what has been and is being erased, and also of what is yet to be built.

Overlay of sixteen photographs taken in the north-eastern part of the Heygate Estate (formerly Pollock Road).

At the moment, the site of the Heygate Estate is not accessible, but before demolition started, when almost all residents had been decanted, it was like a quiet garden, surrounded by modernist slabs standing like impenetrable ruins. Divorced from the regular flows of the city, the Heygate simultaneously evoked its original purpose, the life it had hosted and its impending disappearance after demolition.

In my design-led research, I reworked the sense of absence that emanated from the evocative qualities of the site as a projection of different presences that do not overwrite each other. I did this by digitally overlaying photographs taken from different points of view within the site and allowing a degree of transparency so that they can be observed simultaneously. The photographs in this second kind of palimpsest seem to merge into each other, as vanishing memories of a place about to be effaced.

Photography literally means 'writing with light' or 'writing of light', and a photograph itself is a projection of the light of a past moment, so these images can be seen as palimpsests of light that recreate the environmental qualities of the Heygate, closer to a blurred and fragmentary memory than to a fixed image of it.

For the third piece I printed copies of architectural drawings of the original project of 1969 as well as images of the current redevelopment project and stored them together with soil and rubbish I picked up from the actual site. A process of deterioration occurred as the collected material

9 → 83 17 → 147

soiled and decomposed the drawings. Displayed altogether they constituted a palimpsest made by found objects, soil and representations of expected futures of the site, providing a complementary tactile and olfactory dimension to the layered photographs.

Print of an original drawing of the 1969 Heygate Estate project decomposed by soil and waste collected from the site in April 2013.

Print image of the redevelopment project of the Heygate Estate site for 2025, decomposed by soil and waste collected from the site in April 2013.

The point here was to trigger a reflection on the discourses of urban decline and renovation that converge on the Heygate Estate, observing how its idealised representations are altered by the vestiges of a site as an actual leftover. The areas from which I collected soil and waste materials, as well as the photographs I took in the site, were defined by sixteen old photographs of the Victorian constructions that stood there before the Heygate.

Still of a video taken in the north-eastern part of the Heygate Estate in April 2013, overlaid with a photograph of Pollock Road in 1967, courtesy of Southwark Local History Library and Archive, both taken from the same position and framing the same view.

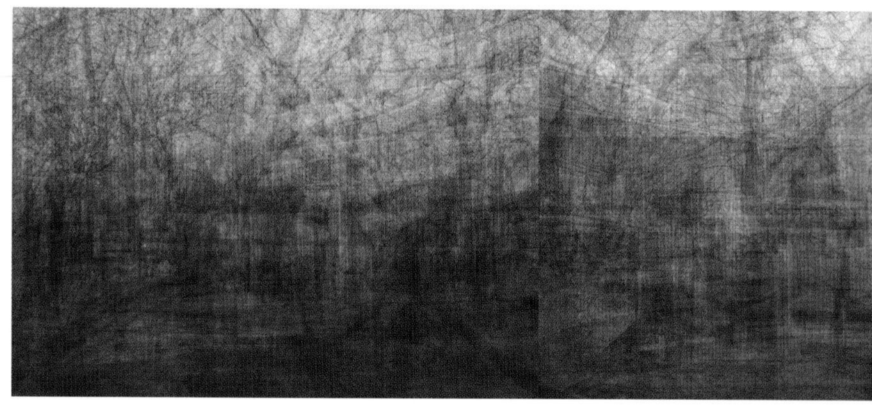

Series of overlaid photographs presented alongside the soil and objects found on the site in April 2013, resembling the original display in the corresponding Cities Methodologies exhibition.

9 → 83 17 → 147

I selected eight of them to determine the videos that I took on site, matching the standpoints and framing the same views of the old photos.[10] The videos were superimposed over the photos and then superimposed over each other, constituting a fourth palimpsest encompassing the slight sounds and movements of the disused place in order to generate an impression of its quiet and transient time.

WHY THE PALIMPSEST AS A METHOD TO REPRESENT ABSENCE?

Absence means to be away, it is a distant kind of presence. Urban leftovers, as the Heygate was in its last several years, are openings for memory, retrospective and prospective imaginations, forms of social resistance and possible alternatives to be formulated against the imposing market-driven regeneration dynamics. The palimpsests featured here intend to recreate that sense of openness and fullness that appeared in and through the Heygate Estate while it stood absent from its busy surroundings, reflecting both the memory of what it was and the dream of what it could have been.[11]

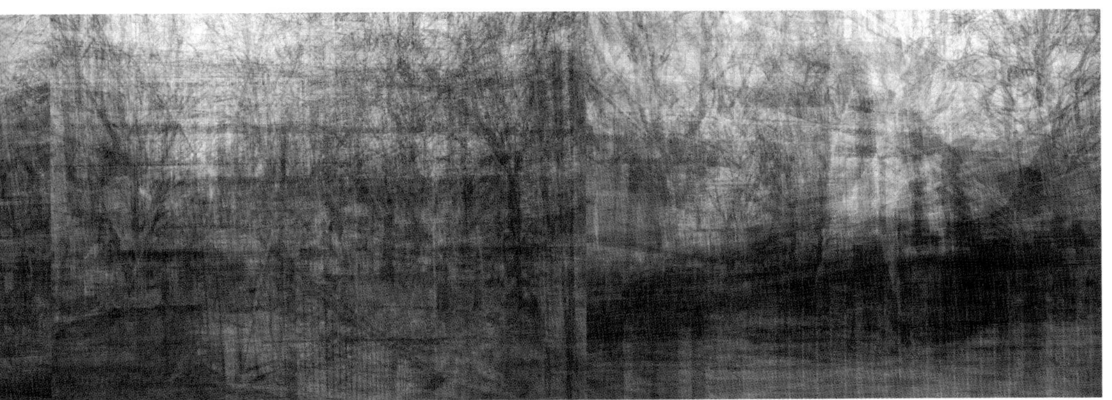

1 *Heygate Was Home.* http://heygate.github.io (accessed 9 September 2014). See also Daniel Clarke, *Debris of the Heygate Estate* (London: Issuu, 2011). http://www.daniel-clarke.com/debris-of-the-heygate (accessed 9 September 2014).
2 Specifically referring to Margaret Thatcher's Conservative government's housing policies promoting private ownership and limiting public investment in council estates.
3 Allot & Lomax Consulting Engineers. Heygate Estate, Option Appraisal Studies. 4.8.2 Description of Existing Structures, 1998. Available in 'Better Elephant', The Surprisingly True Cost of Keeping the Heygate. http://halag.files.wordpress.com/2012/01/allot_max_survey_heygate_1998.pdf (accessed 9 September 2014).
4 Allot & Lomax Consulting Engineers. Heygate Estate, Option Appraisal Studies. Appendix F, Social Background, 1998. Available in 'Better Elephant', The Surprisingly True Cost of Keeping the Heygate. http://halag.files.wordpress.com/2012/01/appendices.pdf (accessed 9 September 2014).
5 Southwark Council. 'Regeneration News.' http://www.southwark.gov.uk/news/200079/regeneration (accessed 24 July 2014).
6 Greater London Authority. Planning report PDU/2149/02. Heygate Estate, Elephant and Castle. 27 February 2013. Southwark Council, Planning Applications. http://planningonline.southwark.gov.uk/DocsOnline/Documents/281820_1.pdf (accessed 9 September 2014). See also details of the S106 agreements on Heygate Estate redevelopment. http://35percent.org/blog/2013/05/26/peters-denial/ (accessed 9 September 2014).
7 Elephant Amenity Network. http://elephantamenity.wordpress.com/about/ (accessed 24 July 2014).
8 Loretta Lees, Just Space, The London Tenants' Federation and Southwark Notes Archives Group, 'The Social Cleansing of Council Estates in London', *Urban Pamphleteer*, 2 (2013), Ben Campkin, David Roberts and Rebecca Ross (eds.), 6–10; Better Elephant, 'Sustainable Development?' http://betterelephant.org/Environmental/ (accessed 9 September 2014); Southwark Council, 'Elephant and Castle.' http://www.southwark.gov.uk/info/200183/elephant_and_castle (accessed 24 July 2014).
9 Francesco Sebregondi, 'Notes on the Potential of Void', *City: Analysis of Urban Trends, Culture, Theory, Policy, Action,* 16 (3) (2012): 337–44; see page 341 for a broader analysis of the production of the void of the Heygate as a matter of market speculation.
10 The positions of the old photographs were marked on the Heygate Estate plan in order to locate them in the actual site. In this way, they determined the areas where photos and videos were shot, and soil and objects were collected in April 2013.
11 This work forms part of the author's PhD by Architectural Design thesis, being developed at the Bartlett School of Architecture, UCL, under the supervision of Ben Campkin and Jonathan Hill. This PhD is funded by CONICYT (Becas Chile programme).

The series of images presented here are compositions based on: historical plans, photographs and drawings courtesy of Southwark Local History Library and Archive; plans and images of the Heygate Estate site future renovation available on Southwark Council's website (accessed on March 2013); photographs, videos and objects collected on site by the author.

8

HACKING LONDON'S DEMOLITION DECISIONS

A new collaboration to scrutinise the technical justifications for retrofit, refurbishment and demolition

Kate Crawford with Sarah Bell, Felicity Davies, Charlotte Johnson, Sunyoung Joo, Sharon Hayward and Richard Lee

2 ↑ 29

Demolition of social housing is a highly contentious issue in urban regeneration. Residents and communities are often excluded from decisions about demolition or refurbishment of housing, which are justified in complex economic and technical terms, using language, data and arguments that are hard to access without professional training and expertise.

Our work focused on London, but the slippery definition of obsolescence in the built environment and the difficulties the public face finding data on demolition, particularly data that has been disaggregated by the people and places that are displaced or otherwise lose out, are urgent issues in many parts of the world and after disasters and conflicts. This work, in the new 'hacking' tradition of citizens taking apart and remaking ubiquitous technologies, data sets and commonly held beliefs, looks at what underpins the published literature and represents it in a variety of formats, tested with their intended audiences.

The Just Space network and London Tenants Federation (LTF), working with the London Action Research on Regeneration Group, identified a need for communities to have better access to the evidence used in decision making about demolition and refurbishment of social housing. It was felt that improved access would support communities in their engagement with regeneration and policy processes. The two organisations commissioned a review of the evidence for demolition of refurbishment of social housing, which was used to support community input into the London Assembly's Housing Committee investigation into the demolition of social housing. This was the subject of the committee's meetings in June and July 2014.[1]

Clapham Park Estate refurbishment works.

WHO WAS INVOLVED AND HOW DID IT WORK?

An important part of this research was to use the process to reflect on the surprises, challenges and emerging findings from this exchange between community and tenants' groups and engineers. This was a non-traditional approach for engineering academics whose main research sponsors are from industry or government. LTF participated in the exchange, bringing expertise, experiences and research questions from across the boroughs, that is, from organisations of tenants of social-housing providers that are coordinated through LTF as an umbrella organisation. Just Space participated in the exchange to share expertise setting up a London-wide network of voluntary and community groups working together to influence planning policy at the regional, borough and neighbourhood levels. The academic team brought together two doctoral students, two post-doctoral researchers and a senior lecturer convening the group, liaising with Just Space and LTF clients and managing the project. We came to the exchange from different backgrounds — anthropology, architecture, civil engineering, energy and sustainability — to share expertise in doing research on buildings and infrastructure systems.

WHAT DID WE LEARN AND PRODUCE?

LTF and Just Space were aiming to address the two questions posed by the London Assembly's Housing Committee: How are decisions made to either refurbish existing buildings or to demolish and rebuild housing estates? What impacts do these programmes have on communities, households and individuals?

A starting point was the way in which evidence was presented in the London Assembly's investigation scoping paper. These are some extracts:

> If media coverage is to be believed, a significant proportion of tenants on London's largest, most dilapidated estates continue to be very unhappy with the regeneration programmes underway.
>
> Other advantages of demolition over refurbishment for the most dilapidated estates include the availability of capital grant for new homes and the reduced cost of ongoing maintenance as well as improved energy efficiency of new build, though conflicting evidence exists on the environmental benefits of each method.[2]

The voices of tenants in the first extract are just alleged and indirectly reported by 'the media'. In the second extract, the environmental advantages of demolition are asserted, but any possibility that the evidence might point to different conclusions is put down to unhelpful disagreements. Thinking

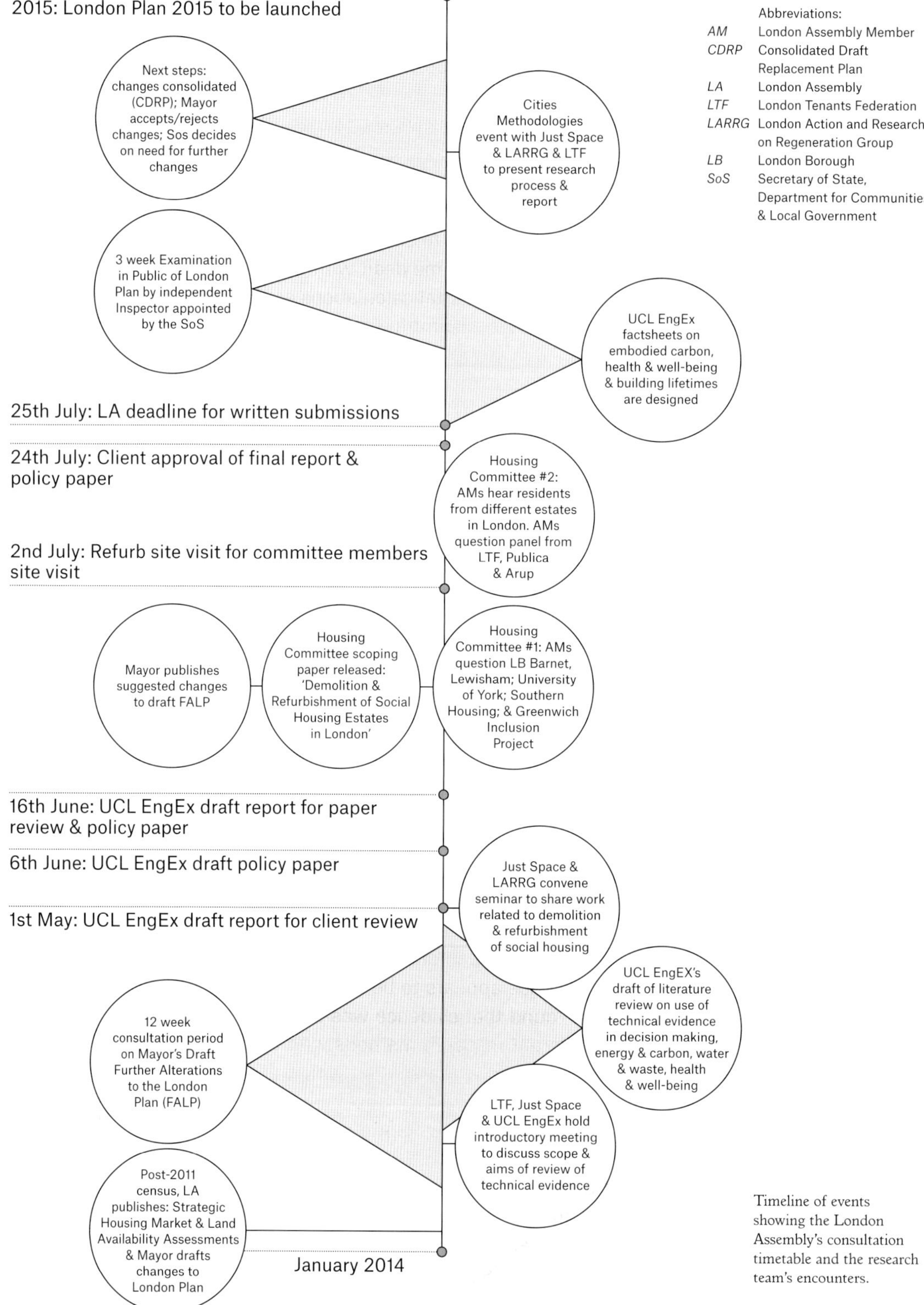

Timeline of events showing the London Assembly's consultation timetable and the research team's encounters.

30 ↑ 249

about this as a group helped us to understand which fields of evidence might be important to engage early with the way that evidence is taken up and represented in this politicised decision-making process.

The review of the technical evidence focused on three themes raised by this investigation. The first of these was the health and well-being of people living with regeneration projects. These data help to understand the experiences of and impacts on social-housing tenants of such projects. The second was building performance, understood in terms of energy, water and waste, because this helps to see whether environmental evidence is really conflicting. The final theme dealt with the assumptions underpinning the economic and environmental calculations applied to refurbishment and demolition because these assumptions may be conflicting.

The review work was conducted alongside a number of events in the university, as well as in community and local government settings.

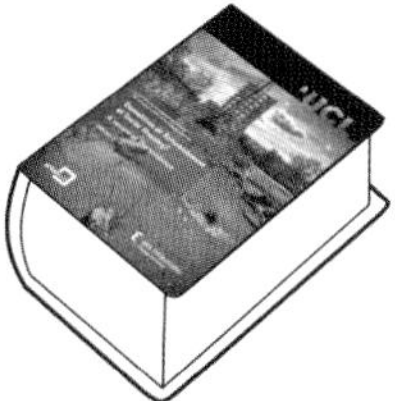

Peer-reviewed academic articles and edited industry reports were examined in order to synthesise evidence from different fields into a conventional report for client review by LTF and Just Space and academic review by leading writers on the subject (eighty pages). An important part of this process was to then present this work again, using feedback from LTF and Just Space, in formats that were easier and faster for all of us to cross-reference and challenge, including balance sheets (four pages each), that referenced and mapped out the positive, negative, vague and absent evidence on each topic and a policy briefing note that summed up the state of the evidence (four pages). To complete this exercise in exchanging and challenging the research, compact fact sheets were developed for 'community review' by members of the networks coordinated by LTF and Just Space (two-sided pamphlets presenting key ideas and case studies).

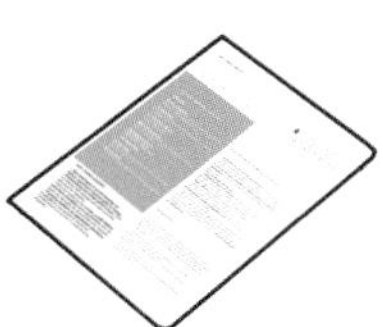

The formats compiled for different audiences.

During this process, we found that rather than contradictory or 'conflicting evidence', most studies were highly context-specific and patchy in their coverage of different places, groups of people and the impacts that had been assessed. It also become clear that although academic literature is potentially available to communities, developers and local authorities, it is not always free to download from academic journals or fast to review. Lastly, other relevant documents and analyses are not always in the public domain, and emerging evidence appears to be or is categorised as anecdotal.

This review found that evidence was sometimes represented in ways that conflated different research methods with different findings, suggesting unreliable data rather than reliable but incompatible data. There also seemed to be a tendency to publish and republish simple, convenient numbers as universal rules of thumb when the original source research was out of date or based on a very few or specific cases that were hard to disentangle or generalise about. For example, embodied energy is rarely accounted for but is critical in reducing overall emissions. While there is now some consistency in the estimates for the embodied energy of different building materials in the UK supply chain, this cannot be extrapolated directly to the embodied

2 → 29

energy of different buildings. Embodied energy is regularly reported as a percentage of the energy used over the lifetime of a building. If this appears to be a low percentage, the significance of embodied energy in decision-making can be dismissed. However, using these percentages to make general claims about the performance of buildings is spurious: the data vary so widely and depend so much on building types, lifetimes and supply chains that they can rarely be compared and should be examined on a case-by-case basis.

In addition, while there is agreement on the principle of a waste hierarchy, much of what was published about construction waste concerned successes in reusing waste materials rather than the prior consideration: to reuse buildings themselves. In terms of water, measures to manage drinking water inside buildings and surface water around neighbourhoods were not just relevant to new buildings but could be retrofitted. Finally, the review showed that modelling any impacts was highly dependent on assumptions about: how long buildings are expected to last; future energy prices; good agreement between the models and real building performance; and the behaviour of people living in buildings.

WHAT WILL HAPPEN NEXT?

The report, policy briefing and fact sheets provide a resource for members of Just Space and the LTF to draw on in their engagement with decision-making about demolition or refurbishment of social housing. The policy briefing note will be distributed and accessible to a range of actors engaged in regeneration decision making, including local and central government.

The project has shown the value of stronger engagement between university researchers and community groups. Just Space and LTF were able to draw on the grounded experience of their members to articulate research needs, as well as to provide experience and expertise in marshalling people and evidence to make an effective impact. The relationship has provided opportunities for increasing the impact of publicly funded university-based research in communities and policy making. The 'client-consultant' nature of the relationship provided a helpful structure for agreeing the scope of the project, steering and reviewing the work and ensuring delivery of useful outputs. The project was useful in identifying how to manage and improve relationships between engineering researchers and community-based organisations in ways that lead to mutually beneficial outcomes.

1 The review was undertaken by the UCL Engineering Exchange (EngEx) to address such needs by facilitating community engagement with engineering research.

2 London Assembly, 'Demolition and Refurbishment of Social Housing Estates in London'. http://www.london.gov.uk/mayor-assembly/london-assembly/investigations/demolition-and-refurbishment-of-social-housing-estates-in-london (accessed 22 July 2016).

9

AUTHORING THE NEIGHBOURHOOD IN WIKIPEDIA

In situ editing Hacking knowledge Crowd production

Rebecca Ross and Chi Nguyen

In June 2014, we convened a community event targeted at those who live and work in the King's Cross area of London with the objective of analysing and expanding upon the existing entry in Wikipedia (the crowd-sourced encyclopedia) for 'King's Cross Central'.[1] The focal point was an eight metre-long print-out of the existing online article, which was used as a basis to discuss what is included in the article and what is missing, and, in both cases, why. The project sought to identify whether and how the Wikipedia article for King's Cross should be updated and to frame a discussion about interactions between text-based and in-depth personal knowledge of a contested urban regeneration site. By focusing on the intersection of Wikipedia and King's Cross, an area with complicated divisions between public and private space and ownership, the event raised questions about power and situatedness. It asked how knowledge about the built environment is generated and shared and how this relates to urban change.

The event emerged out of a 'Digital Urbanism' workshop held at Central Saint Martins in which we reviewed Wikipedia articles for familiar places in London and felt dissatisfied with their content.[2] This was particularly the case for our immediate neighbourhood, King's Cross, to which the college had re-located in 2011. Central Saint Martins was one of the first organisations to take up residence in a large regeneration project situated in the railway lands north of King's Cross station, now under the control of the property developer Argent. Central Saint Martins itself has an intrinsic role within Argent's place-making project. It has been a big chess piece in the ambition to concentrate cultural capital in the area but is also a diverse institution made up of individual students, designers, artists and academics, who are in King's Cross every day, who have many legitimate questions about what has happened and a variety of potential contributions to make to what might happen next. We felt that the existing Wikipedia article for the regeneration area,

This article **needs additional citations for verification**. Please help improve this article by adding citati
sources. Unsourced material may be challenged and removed. *(June 2007)*

KXC) is a multi-billion pound mixe **mixed-use *place* in central** ntral
he site is owned and controlled b ...ays (LCR) and Exel, which
ge to be the developer for King's Cross Central, after an extensive selection process. The site
65 acres (26 ha) of former railway lands, mostly to the north of King's Cross and St Pancras
The site is largely determined by three boundaries: the existing East Coast Main Line
g's Cross; York Way, a road marking the division between Camden and Islington; and the
ed 1 (HS1), formerly known as the Channel Tunnel Rail Link, which curves around the site

ct, known as the "Triangle Site", falls within the boundaries of Islington. Camden Council
rmission for the main part of the site in ~~early~~ MARCH 2006. This has now been approved by the
e Mayor of London, ~~although~~ separate planning permission for the Triangle Site is ~~still~~
ncil. It went ahead following a public inquiry April/May 2007 [MARIAN LARRAGY]

ing's Cross Central was used for HS1 construction purposes from July 2001 until autumn 2007. Foll
ing permission, GLA (Greater London Authority) and GOL approval, the developer Argent Group PL

The Wikipedia entry for King's Cross Central being 'live-edited' by the community with the term 'property development' updated to 'place' (2014).

newly rebranded King's Cross Central, did not seem to tell a complete enough story, given the Wikimedia Foundation's mission to 'to empower and engage people'.[3]

In evaluating the content of the existing Wikipedia article, we were struck by the extent to which it reproduced the narrow description of the area and its history typically favoured by the developer.[4] We also noted that it did not seem to be prepared by anyone with any kind of traceable connection to King's Cross (though this is difficult to confirm). Details of King's Cross's late-nineteenth and early twentieth-century industrial past were described in some depth, where the latter part of the twentieth century was framed only generally as a period of decline, disrepute and abandonment. Wikipedia guidelines state that articles 'must be written neutrally and without bias'.[5] To this end, the Wikipedia community typically deploys standards of 'verifiability', achieved through citations, and, at the same time, has a rule disallowing 'original research'.[6] Wikipedia is a free and open crowd-sourced encyclopedia deriving its credibility from its stewardship by a wide community. However, in the case of an article on a specific contested location, we wondered whether the requirement of references to previously published material and rejection of primary descriptions by those actually present in the area in fact results in a more neutral and less biased general-purpose article.

Around King's Cross, there are two conflicting kinds of texts that are not equally represented on Wikipedia: those initiated by the developer and those of the local community. In addition to the buildings, tenants, street furniture and security, outside of Wikipedia, Argent maintains to a large extent control over the communicative dimensions of King's Cross, in terms of the information, graphics and screens in public areas around the site as well as how King's Cross is portrayed within the media, via well-staffed publicity and marketing teams who maintain Twitter feeds, prepare press releases and underwrite documentaries. Advertisements printed on the hoarding along King's Boulevard to attract new business to the area paint a particularly editorial perspective about King's Cross past:

> The tapper, tallyman and legged are long gone, and there's small chance of catching a rick master and his nipper about their business. You're quite likely to hear a banker's whistle but the tune would have been very different in King's Cross past. Back then a banker's whistle meant the steam-powered shriek of a shunting engine at work. Now it heralds the jaunty approach of someone in high finance, and the steam comes from a hot cappuccino on a cold day.

It is of concern that the embellishments of these kinds of texts are more likely to provide the kind of verifiability sought by Wikipedia's article content guidelines than those being produced by members of the King's Cross community who have less well financed but equally important stories to tell. For instance, the poem below, written by local resident Daniel Zylbersztajn and posted to a community blog, does not qualify as verifiable:

The mayor's promises of years
to calm those roads,
a laughing stock against their speed
and the new high-rise builds.
We who live here,
showing tourists the way on maps.
For you we are peripheral,
best we don't exist at all!
So you raise the rents and price us out,
here's a Waitrose to an Iceland,
a three Pounds coffee shop,
to a local pub.
Improvement, better, gentrified![7]

7 ↑ 69

Zylbersztajn's poem does not meet Wikipedia's criteria of 'verifiability' because it does not put forward a 'neutral point of view' and is published on a community blog. Wikipedia discourages the use of blogs as sources and specifies that where they are used they must be staffed by professionals: 'Anyone can create a personal web page or publish their own book, and also claim to be an expert in a certain field. For that reason, self-published media, such as books, patents, newsletters, personal websites, open wikis, personal or group blogs (as distinguished from newsblogs, above), internet forum postings, and tweets, are largely not acceptable as sources.'[8] Texts such as Zylbersztajn's are also discouraged because they are explicit about the fact that they express an impassioned 'non-neutral' perspective whereas the kind of historical narrative that sustains the predominant narratives underlying the development project is presented as unopinionated fact.

We decided to become involved with the Wikipedia article for King's Cross, in particular, because we saw the need to put these two kinds of texts or media in critical dialogue with one another on a more even playing field. Though Wikipedia and crowd-sourced content does not always live up to its utopian ideals, it is the most prominent and well-used default or first reference information set that, by its own definition, should not actually remain under the control of a single author or interest. This is in the same sense that the long-term development of King's Cross Central will be best served through the participation of a diverse range of people who live, study and work there every day rather than determined exclusively by a single profit-driven entity. One of the edits made during the June 2014 community event was to the first line of the article, from 'King's Cross Central (KXC) is a multi-billion pound property development in central London' to 'King's Cross Central (KXC) is a multi-billion pound mixed-use place in central London': this shift from 'property development' to 'place' exemplifies how a community-based approach to community is distinct from a property developer's approach to community building.[9]

Through our approach to experimenting with the Wikipedia article for King's Cross Central, we are arguing that, in describing conditions in the built environment, contributions made in situ by members of a community should have more credibility than singular contributions made from elsewhere. We also seek to raise questions about how the diversity of a community is intertwined with the diversity of voices contributing to its associated media and critique the instruments by which the principles of 'neutrality' and 'verifiability' are applied by Wikipedia's editors in the specific case of location-based content. As we continue to iterate the design of our approach to facilitating edits to the Wikipedia article for King's Cross Central, we hope to demonstrate the feasibility of alternative methods for crowd production of media and knowledge related to the built environment in a way that could be deployed by communities in other contested spaces around the world.

1 King's Cross Central is a name given to the regeneration area by its developers. See http://www.kingscross.co.uk/whos-developing-kings-cross (accessed 14 October 2015).
2 The workshop was conducted with MA Communication Design students.
3 See http://wikimediafoundation.org/wiki/Mission_statement (accessed 14 October 2015). Wikimedia is the parent organisation of Wikipedia.
4 https://en.wikipedia.org/w/index.php?title=King%27s_Cross_Central&action=history (accessed 14 October 2015) and the user pages for 'Rsrikanth05', 'The Anome', 'Feudonym' and 'Trident 13'.
5 https://en.wikipedia.org/wiki/Wikipedia:List_of_policies#Content (accessed 14 October 2015).
6 https://en.wikipedia.org/wiki/Wikipedia:List_of_policies#Content (accessed 24 July 2014).
7 Excerpt from Daniel Zylbersztajn, 'Mapping Us'. http://kingscrossenvironment.com/2014/06/18/mapping-us (accessed 14 October 2015).
8 http://en.wikipedia.org/wiki/Wikipedia:Verifiability (accessed 14 October 2015).
9 See https://en.wikipedia.org/wiki/King%27s_Cross_Central (accessed 14 October 2015) and its revision history.

10

THE SECRET SECURITY GUARD

Being a G4S employee during the London Olympic Games 2012

Henrietta Williams

6 ↑ 59

G4S training centre, Pitchford Street, 2012.

G4S interview, Pitchford Street, 2012.

G4S interview test, Pitchford Street, 2012.

Fireworks exploded noisily over the stadium at Stratford, bringing the London 2012 Olympic Games to a close. I stood and watched with the other workers at the edges of the Olympic Park. We had spent the past month working as security guards for the company G4S at the Games, and this was the final surreal moment. Unlike my colleagues, I'd been working undercover on a project to document the entire process. As the last firework exploded, I slipped quietly out of the gate, jumped on a train at Stratford and returned to my real life.

The past four weeks had been an extraordinary time. London transformed into a zone of hyper-security, with the fear of a possible terrorist attack used to justify every conceivable counter-measure. The army patrolled the streets, missiles were placed on residential rooftops, battleships were moored on the Thames, surveillance blimps monitored us from the sky above, protests were banned, and a vast number

25 → 211

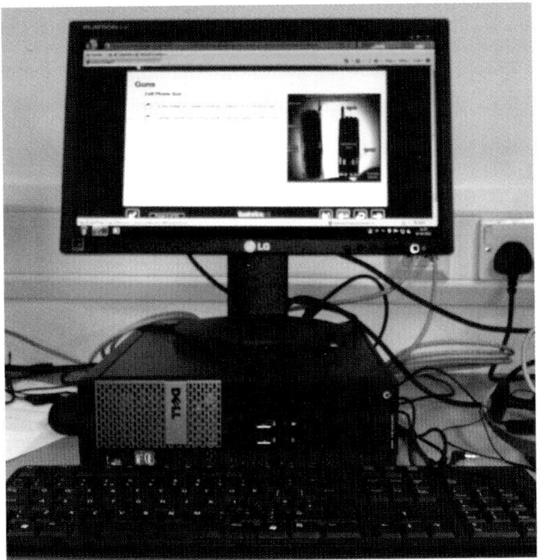

G4S interview test, Pitchford Street. Gun concealed in mobile phone, 2012.

G4S training classroom, Romford Road, 2012.

Restraint training, Romford Road, 2012.

of new CCTV cameras were installed.[1]

Within this state-controlled environment, companies specialising in security and defence reported a massive increase in profits, none more so than G4S, the largest private-security company in the world, employing 657,000 people in 125 countries.[2] G4S were awarded the £284 million contract to deliver security for London 2012, with chaotic consequences.

As an urbanist with a particular focus on security, I had been interested in G4S for some time in advance of the London 2012 Olympic Games. G4S is one of the world's largest private-sector employers but has been connected with reports of human-rights abuses both internationally and in the UK.[3] In October 2010, Jimmy Mubenga tragically died at Heathrow after being restrained by three G4S custody officers on board a plane bound for Angola. The officers have now been charged with manslaughter and will face trial at the end of 2014.[4]

6 ↑ 59

Bag search training, Pitchford Street, 2012.

X-Ray screening training, Pitchford Street, 2012.

Guarding a back entrance, Olympic Park, 2012.

I wanted to research G4S from the inside: to understand its training process, to experience working as a security guard and to document the whole process. So I applied for a job as a security guard at the Olympics. A simple Google search of my full name would have revealed my previous projects on the topic of security, but G4S were so desperate for staff that it seems that anyone would do.[5] I applied in January 2012, and by March I had passed a series of tests, including testing my ability to quickly pick out an improvised explosive device in an X-ray image, and I was on route to becoming an X-ray operator. My training was under way.

In a class with thirty-five others, mainly men, I learned the basics of being a security guard at the Olympics, which, according to my instructors, were: customer service, using force and how to spot a terrorist. The training was at best random, at worst illegal. Our instructor had been in the British Army

25 → 211

Walking to work behind the army, Stratford, 2012.

Guarding a staircase, Olympic Park, 2012.

Workers canteen, Olympic Park, 2012.

and then worked as a bouncer for twenty years. His advice suggested an endemic acceptance of violence within the private-security industry as he taught us how to hit people without leaving a mark: 'You can hit them first', he told us. 'This is known as a pre-emptive strike. If you were to strike someone, use an open hand. This has the same power as a punch but it doesn't leave a mark.'

Beyond the basic illegality of the training described above, the entire process was inadequate and chaotic. I had been given the role of X-ray operator and would be operating the machines at the gates to the main Olympic Park in Stratford. My job was to scan up to 200 bags an hour and to check for bomb components and other weapons. Yet it was only in the final ten days before the Opening Ceremony that I was brought in to start this complex training. I spent twenty minutes on a Rapiscan X-ray machine in advance of full deployment.

Guarding a locked gate, Olympic Park, 2012.

Internal fence, Olympic Park, 2012.

Perimeter fence, Olympic Park, 2012.

The chaos and mismanagement at G4S for training security guards for the Olympics quickly became an international news story. Awarded with a £284 million contract to provide 13,700 guards, it became clear that G4S were going to fail to deliver. As the media waited at the gates to interview us, inside the training centre G4S management became increasingly paranoid.

To guarantee myself some level of legal protection and to try and maximise the reach of the project, I decided to approach the *Guardian* newspaper. They engaged me on a short-term contract to write about my experiences as a G4S security guard. My project had now morphed from personally directed research into becoming an undercover reporter working under the name 'The Secret Security Guard.'[6] I contributed to a number of news stories for the *Guardian*, one of which made the front page, and wrote a series of diary pieces that were published in the paper and online. The protection

25 → 211

River defences, Olympic Park, 2012.

Walking to work, Olympic Park, 2012.

Waiting for work, Olympic Park, 2012.

offered by working for the *Guardian* allowed me to continue to document my experience despite the internal lockdown on offering information to the press. I continued to write careful contemporaneous notes and take photographs covertly on my iPhone.

My work as a G4S security guard was in turns mundane, tiring and sometimes pointless. One day, before being deployed to the X-ray machine, I spent twelve hours guarding a staircase that wasn't in use. The next day, despite the well-publicised scandal over a lack of staff, I waited with other colleagues for six hours to be deployed, but we never received any instructions, and, eventually, most of us went home. The night shifts were particularly bleak as there was little to do except in brief bursts over a twelve-hour shift. But there were good parts to the job as well. Running the X-ray machines was busy and fun for the whole team, as well as genuinely important, and my fellow workers were lovely, interesting

6 → 59

X-Ray screening area, Olympic Park, 2012.

Working as an X-ray screener, Olympic Park, 2012.

Working the night shift, Olympic Park, 2012.

people from all over the world.[7]

As a research project, delving into the world of private security, I felt the time I spent with G4S was hugely informative, not just in terms of the project itself but also in terms of exploring research methodologies. Working as an undercover journalist for the *Guardian* was as much a part of my project as working for G4S. Playing the role of undercover journalist felt much like playing the role of G4S security guard. It felt important at the end of the project to reclaim my research and present it in another fashion, less journalistic and with more depth.

Initially, I had ethical concerns about carrying out a project with undercover elements. I had been particularly concerned about the possibilities of exploiting the trust of my fellow workers. I dealt with this in a number of ways: trying to avoid personal relationships by constantly moving location within the park and being as truthful as

25 → 211

Working the night shift, Olympic Park, 2012.

Working the night shift, Olympic Park, 2012.

Fireworks at the Olympic Closing Ceremony, Olympic Park, 2012.

possible on a personal level in my daily engagements. Ultimately, in the columns I wrote for the *Guardian*, I explained how the fault lay with G4S management rather than with the people I was working with on the ground.

Any concerns I may have had were balanced by the fact that once I'd experienced at first hand the violent undercurrent to our training, it felt vital to complete the research. Ultimately, it felt appropriate to exhibit the project under my own name, to reveal my identity to my former colleagues and to G4S. I decided to do this through a theatrical installation, creating a stage-set illusion from the artefacts of my project: an Olympic-style tent, my training manual and pass, and my lime-green uniform flung over the same model of chair on which we sat as guards. My presentation, as an installation, aimed to describe my experience of being part of the security systems that locked down

6 ↑ 59

Installation shot of the exhibition, *The Secret Security Guard,* 2013.

Installation shot of the exhibition, *The Secret Security Guard,* 2013.

London during the Games.

Perhaps what had struck me most about the experience of working for G4S at the Olympics was how so much of the security in place was about conveying an impression of safety. It began with media photo calls of dramatic security tests before the Games began, army snipers photographed hanging out of planes, prison-grade fences bristling with CCTV cameras. The G4S workers drafted up quickly for the London 2012 Olympic Games were simply dressed as security guards, actors upon a stage, with very little actual training. As 200 handbags and rucksacks whizzed past me on the X-ray belt every hour, I knew that I wouldn't have spotted a makeshift bomb, but I looked the part.

1 Stephen Graham, 'Olympics 2012 Security: Welcome to Lockdown London', *The Guardian.* http://www.theguardian.com/sport/2012/mar/12/london-olympics-security-lockdown-london (accessed 14 October 2015).
2 Described as a 'bonanza' by Graham, 'Olympics 2012 Security'.
3 Clare Sambrook, 'Open Democracy: G4s and Their Human Rights Problem', 6 June 2013. https://www.opendemocracy.net/ourkingdom/clare-sambrook/g4s-and-their-human-rights-problem (accessed 3 November 2015).
4 Crown Prosecution Service, 'Death of Jimmy Mubenga: Charging Following Inquest', 20 March 2014. http://blog.cps.gov.uk/2014/03/death-of-jimmy-mubenga-charging-decisions-following-inquest.html (accessed 22 November 2015)
5 See http://www.henriettawilliams.com (accessed 14 October 2015).
6 The 'Secret Security Guard' was used as a key source in a number of news stories as well as authoring a series of diary pieces in *The Guardian* from 23 July to 13 August 2012. Henrietta Williams, 'The Secret Security Guard', *The Guardian.* http://www.theguardian.com/uk/series/secret-security-guard (accessed 14 October 2015).
7 After I decided to exhibit the project and reveal my identity, I contacted the people I had swapped contacts with. They were highly amused, and we remain in touch through Facebook.

11

HIDE AND SEEK

The dubious nature of plant life in high-security spaces

Max Colson

Hide and Seek is a documentary photography project created by the photojournalist Adam Walker-Smith. Instigated by his discovery of the landscape design programme 'Crime Prevention Through Environmental Design', Walker-Smith realised that privatised public spaces in London, which present themselves as being free and open, actually covertly guide behaviour through landscape design and monitor human activities through extensive surveillance infrastructure. The reason these things are not often observed is because they are carefully hidden and softened by the strategic deployment of foliage. This illuminating finding led to what could only be described as Walker-Smith's intense paranoia as to the 'innocence' of all plant life in these spaces. His photographs dramatically expose the plants of privatised urban areas that he sees as being 'suspect' (these plants are so-called for posing as 'innocent' decoration while actually being hidden parts of the security apparatus).[1]

This project develops, in particular, from the contrasting perspectives of two giants of urban and architectural thought, Oscar Newman and Jane Jacobs. Jacobs and Newman disagreed about the effect that the securitisation of the built environment — or the perception of security — had on people's feelings of safety or alienation. Today, the integration of security design within the UK's built environment is still contentious and, through the work of prominent journalists such as Anna Minton, has been gaining notice in public discussion.[2] The product of a post-9/11 climate and a society polarised by unequal income distribution, modern urban design often betrays fear and social divisions. Security priorities often rule, leading to a design of environments that are increasingly 'paranoid' and defensive, for example the excessive use of metal fencing or crash barricades around private residences and public buildings.[3]

Left Adam Walker-Smith, *Street Level Entrance*, 2013.

Right Adam Walker-Smith, *Natural Surveillance*, 2013.

Recent scholarship has critiqued so-called 'regeneration' projects for favouring the better-off while perpetuating social divisions.[4] In the UK, new commercially oriented and privately run public areas, commonly known as 'Business Improvement Districts' (BIDs) are some of the major examples of urban developments that purport to be directed towards social inclusion, being characterised by exclusionary defensive architecture, surveillance and estate-management regimes. Widely applied policies and design paradigms such as 'Secured by Design' and 'Crime Prevention Through Environmental Design', which encourage designers and planners to anticipate and de-incentivise criminal acts or 'criminal persons', are now the typical but largely unremarked-upon part of many new developments within the built environment.

For *Hide and Seek*, Adam Walker-Smith photographed the plants of securitised urban areas in situ at a number of BIDs in London using high-impact lighting to animate and emphasise their suspicious nature. Yet,

32 → 259

Left Adam Walker-Smith, *Low Lying Bush*, 2013.

Right Adam Walker-Smith, *Ornamentation on Steel Structure*, 2013.

while the narrative and his photographs raise awareness of the way in which security design covertly operates in the urban environment, the bizarre nature of the photographs also invites us, its audience, to consider the politics of the field and whether we are being offered credible interpretations of a city that is arguably becoming increasingly more paranoid, segregated and controlled. As the photographer of the project suggests, because of today's subtle security-design approaches, one can excessively obsess over the notion that forces of control are potentially hidden everywhere.

IMAGES OF ENJOYMENT AND SPECTACLE

This series was produced as part of Max Colson's ten-month residency at the UCL Urban Laboratory. It is featured in his resulting solo exhibition at the Royal Institute of British Architects.[5] It is a sequence of appropriated 'photorealistic' advertising images originally used to market privatised public spaces and luxury housing developments in Britain. Responding to the

Max Colson, *Images of Enjoyment and Spectacle*, 2015.

way in which these urban areas are often promoted as utopian and socially inclusive environments, it recontextualises some of the constituent parts of these marketing images. At first, the buildings and landscape architecture are removed; the people and the skies that remain are then placed onto a computer-generated colour gradient, which is selected from the colours of the original digital image. The title of the project references a slogan that accompanies imagery used to promote one of the most restrictive privatised public spaces in London.

32 → 259

1 Adam Walker-Smith is the alter ego of Max Colson, an artist who uses photography to speculatively explore security design, surveillance and paranoia in the built environment. See http://www.maxcolson.com (accessed 14 October 2015).
2 Anna Minton, *Ground Control: Fear and Happiness in the Twenty-First Century City* (London: Penguin Group, 2012).
3 Lorraine Gamman and Adam Thorpe, *Profit from Paranoia: Design Against 'Paranoid' Products* (London: Design Against Crime Research Centre, 2012). http://www.designagainstcrime.com/output/profit-from-paranoia-design-against-paranoid-products-2/ (accessed 9 September 2014).
4 Minton, *Ground Control.* Ben Campkin, *Remaking London: Decline and Regeneration in Urban Culture* (London: I.B.Tauris, 2013).
5 Max Colson, *Virtual Control: Security and the Urban Imagination,* Royal Institute of British Architects, 9 July–27 September 2015.

IV

Situating Images and Imaginaries

12

THE UPS AND DOWNS OF VISUALISING CONTEMPORARY MUMBAI

Experimental documentation Visual ethnography Infrastructure narratives

Andrew Harris

1 ↑ 23

Since 2009, I have been investigating the construction of elevated roads (flyovers) and walkways (skywalks) in Mumbai. These have proliferated across the Mumbai Metropolitan Region since the mid-1990s, with over fifty flyovers built since 1998 and over thirty skywalks since 2008. My research uses these structures to explore new social and political relations in the city, ones that increasingly are framed and experienced through the vertical dimension.[1] Despite their functionality and lack of obvious aesthetic appeal,

flyovers and skywalks reveal important socio-spatial dimensions to recent elite efforts at remaking Mumbai as a 'world-class' Indian city. They are indicative of a new, selectively accessible, vertical layer across Mumbai over and above an increasingly crowded and congested metropolis.

In order to assess the way in which these large pieces of Mumbai's transport infrastructure operate and perform, I have sought documentation around their conception and reception, including planning reports, technical

31 → 255 32 → 259

Double-decker flyover at Kurla Terminus.

1 ↑ 23

diagrams, newspapers articles and websites. I have also spoken to a range of key actors involved in the promotion, construction and maintenance of flyovers and skywalks: from engineers and planners to politicians, transport consultants and security guards. These archival and interview techniques have been supplemented and extended through visual methods and analysis. Although rarely matching the built reality of these schemes, tenders and promotional materials for flyover and skywalk projects show a city enjoying regulated traffic flows, slum-free residences and pristine engineering, where globally recognisable advertising images and logos are often prominent. I regularly came across these images as I encountered company websites, promotional videos, Powerpoint slides, scale models in foyers, screensavers and office walls. The construction of flyovers and skywalks accordingly need to be understood as part of a new visual regime shaping understandings of Mumbai's urban futures.

Scale model of flyover project.

31 → 255 32 → 259

I have also been keen to explore the visual life of flyovers and skywalks beyond these top-down, official visions. As I travelled around the city, I tried to develop a way of photographing different structures in a consistent fashion. This would involve shots of the 'sweep' of the flyover or skywalk along the road, photographs from centrally underneath, shots of columns or piers, signs and advertising, as well as activities beneath. This approach might be understood as a form of infrastructural *flânerie* that uses photography to reveal a 'different nature' to that of the naked eye.[2] Using keywords in Adobe Lightroom to emphasise recurring categories across over 3,000 digital photos, I began to identify common features to what people did underneath (sleeping, selling, storing, playing) and how this everyday life underneath was regulated and controlled (fences, landscaping, signboards).[3] In this way, I took advantage of how digital photography allows not only for large quantities of photographs to be taken but also for new ways of retrieving and cataloguing visual material. As William J. Mitchell presciently argued in 1992, the digital image 'electronically accelerates the mechanisms of the visual record, enables the weaving of complex networks of interconnection between images to establish multiple and perhaps incommensurable layers of meaning'.[4]

FILMING JJ HOSPITAL FLYOVER

Flip camera, Senapati Bapat Marg, Tulsi Pipe Road.

Although this style of photographic hyper-empiricism provided important insights into Mumbai's infrastructural underworld, the digital camera's fixed gaze did not sufficiently capture the important rhythms and flows that comprise these spaces. As well as still photos, I experimented with video cameras to record flyover and skywalk scenes from a range of vantage points. These included the chaotic bustle (and occasionally surprising stillness) of the roads underneath or the steady processions of people or vehicles above, and I tried to find spots where I could record flows simultaneously above and below. Not only did my use of video indicate some of the variety of flyover and skywalk settings and experiences across Mumbai, it emphasised how these structures create and constitute a two-tiered city. Whereas traffic on flyovers would stream smoothly and regularly along these elevated routes, the streets below were filled with an unpredictable and stop-start array of pedestrians, hawkers, trucks, carts and buses negotiating their way ahead, frequently disrupted and frustrated by policemen, animals, traffic lights and pot-holes. As cars forced their way through this erratic choreography, the main rationale behind constructing skywalks (rechannelling non-vehicular traffic upwards) became clear. These vertical differences were something I sought to exploit in the arrangement of digital photos (single shots and sequences) and videos (complete with soundtrack) of the JJ Hospital flyover for my Cities Methodologies installation in 2010. Taking advantage of the high walls of the Slade Research Centre at UCL, these were organised systematically so that ground-level images were presented by the floor whereas a photograph looking down on the flyover was towards the ceiling (and less accessible to the viewer).

Filming above and below the JJ Hospital Flyover.

Although my photography and video footage importantly revealed some three-dimensional relations of power carved through contemporary Mumbai by flyovers and skywalks, I was aware that this remained an interpretation framed through my own assumptions, as well as the decisions I had made of what to shoot and where to shoot it (and how to display it). I was struck by how people who saw me with my camera in Mumbai would often assume I would prefer to film from raised positions, such as the roof of a building in Kurla looking across at India's first double-decker flyover under construction. Working with colleagues to film underneath the long JJ Hospital flyover that runs down Mohammed Ali Road in central Mumbai, we managed to negotiate to shoot from an elevated post used by the police.[5] This process emphasised how the ability and opportunity to visually capture these spaces inevitably was bound up with a position of power, especially in a predominately Muslim neighbourhood such as this with colonial and post-colonial histories of surveillance.

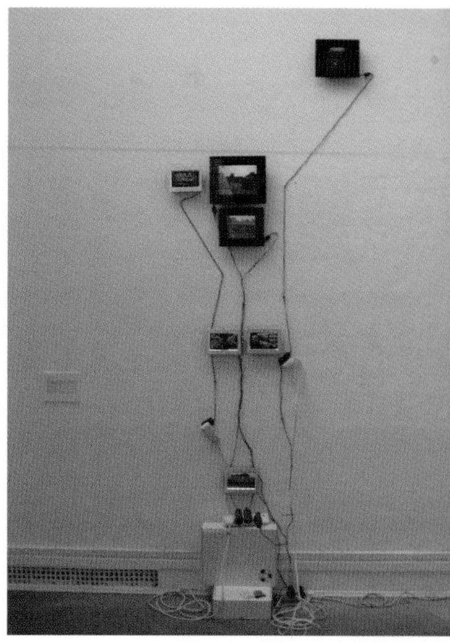

Vertical Urbanism exhibit, Cities Methodologies, 2010.

In order to disrupt straightforward assumptions being drawn and unreflexive positions being taken in a visual 'audit', this project emphasised the need to combine visual methods with the ethnographic focus of my research. As Mumbai's global profile has grown over the past decade, there has been a tendency to rely on a shorthand set of key visual images to represent and understand the city.[6] A good example is the large water pipes that pass through a large 'informal' settlement called Dharavi, which have featured in an iconic photo by Sebastião Salgado and director Danny Boyle's film, *Slumdog Millionaire*.[7] Although the use of this image importantly captures a scene displaying modern

Filming from police platform, Mohammed Ali Road.

infrastructural provision yet limited accessibility for those people featured, there is rarely much more detail around the thoughts and experiences of those shown. In my flyover and skywalk research, I wanted to ensure I had some idea of what the people who lived and worked underneath actually made of these structures. Informal conversations revealed that many people, even those without access to flyovers as they did not own a private vehicle, actually quite liked the way these large structures provided shade from the sun and shelter during the monsoons and often saw them as vindications of Mumbai's modern progress. Future work might try not only to talk to those underneath but to collaborate with them to photograph or film (and discuss) how they understand and experience these spaces.

Another aspect to unsettling the analytical scope of visual methods

1 ↑ 23

in this research was to find ways of acknowledging the opaque qualities of everyday life in Mumbai. In many respects, the city thrives on its unknowability, and, indeed, I struggled to find certain planning reports despite persistent attempts at locating them. Thus, in presenting material visually, I tried to develop outputs that were deliberately fragmentary and could be understood as strategically incomplete. The project website presents photographs, film clips, sound recordings and newspaper and interview quotes without clear statements about what they necessarily represent.[8] The website was also deliberately created before I subsequently wrote up material in academic papers so that it became part of the process of the research rather than simply a final outcome. Although the material is categorised in both English and Hindi (from Lightroom tags and transcript coding) and located on a map, there is limited guiding narrative and explanation of categories. Visitors to the site have to reach their own judgements (in a manner similar to myself) as they navigate the material, and there is a facility to submit their own opinions and thoughts. Investigating an array of visual components to contemporary Mumbai may be an essential feature of understanding the social and political dynamics of this city, but it is also crucial to question how this visual material is interpreted and re-presented.

1 See Andrew Harris, 'Vertical Urbanism: Flyovers and Skywalks in Mumbai', in *Urban Constellations*, edited by Matthew Gandy (Berlin: Jovis, 2011), 118–23; Andrew Harris, 'Concrete Geographies: Assembling Global Mumbai through Transport Infrastructure', *City*, 17 (3) (2013): 343–60. This project was funded by the ESRC (Award RES-000-22-3127).
2 As Walter Benjamin argues, a camera enhances the practice of *flânerie* 'by focusing on hidden details of familiar objects' such that 'a different nature opens itself to the camera than opens to the naked eye'. Walter Benjamin, *Illuminations* (London: Pimlico, 1999), 229–30.
3 See my photo-essay, 'Mumbai's Underworld: Life Beneath Transport Infrastructure', *Moving Worlds*, 13 (2) (2013): 151–60.
4 William J. Mitchell, *The Reconfigured Eye: Visual Truth in the Post-Photographic Era* (Cambridge, MA: MIT Press, 1992), 85.
5 My thanks to Savitri Medhatul and Rahul Dandekar.
6 Andrew Harris, 'The Metonymic Urbanism of Twenty-First-Century Mumbai', *Urban Studies*, 49 (13) (2012): 2955–73.
7 See also the discussion on page 2 of Stephen Graham and Simon Marvin's *Splintering Urbanism: Networked Infrastructures, Technological Mobilities and the Urban Condition* (London: Routledge, 2001).
8 http://www.verticalurbanism.com (created with the assistance of Sanjay Bhangar from CAMP).

13

CREATING SYSTEMATIC RECORDS THROUGH TIME

The destruction and reconstruction of heritage areas affected by earthquakes in Chile

Bernadette Devilat

Systematic photography 3D laser scanning Survey

In Chile, built heritage is at risk of disappearing. Historic buildings are particularly vulnerable not only to disasters such as earthquakes and fires but also to the emergency and reconstruction approaches applied in the aftermath. Other causes that contribute to the poor conservation of heritage buildings are their cultural undervaluation, their lack of maintenance, their accumulated damage over the years and the weak regulations to protect them. These aspects have a higher impact in the constructions after an earthquake than in a regular situation, intensifying conservation issues. But Chile has earthquakes regularly; thus, this process of change has often affected heritage buildings several times in their history. In this context, the record of historic buildings and settlements designated as heritage is relevant, especially before and after a disaster, and before and after their reconstruction.

In this essay, I explore the compilation and creation of systematic records (photographic and 3D laser scan) as a methodology to study the heritage area of San Lorenzo de Tarapacá, which has experienced constant changes in recent years since a large earthquake of 7.9 in Moment Magnitude scale (Mw) affected it in 2005 and a reconstruction process followed after that. That process was mainly done by the government by adapting social-housing subsidies and was finished in 2013. The method used in this essay is the juxtaposition of records taken in this case during different periods of time, in order to reveal imperceptible variations and to question that reconstruction process. The aim is to bring out aspects of the destruction and reconstruction that can inform future approaches, which will be needed in forthcoming earthquakes for this and other Chilean heritage areas.[1]

The images on the right are a series of photographs based on five archive photographs taken before the seismic event and from the same standpoint in 2005, 2006, 2007 and 2013.[2] The production of a longitudinal systematic record has been possible because of my involvement in the study of San Lorenzo de Tarapacá since the 2005 earthquake, when I was an architecture student and volunteered to record the post-earthquake situation with other students. Back then I used only photography as a way to quickly assess the destruction produced by that earthquake when compared to previous photographs from two years before the seismic event. This exercise was extremely helpful for us, as we never had been there before; so old photographs, drawings, records, imagination and experience of what was left by the earthquake were a way to figure out how the historic area of San Lorenzo de Tarapacá used to be. The full record that we created aimed at communicating the devastation to others and providing a basis for the reconstruction, for which we started an initiative called Tarapacá Project.[3] Because of that initiative, I continued working in that village during consequent years, in addition to taking my master's in architecture research, which was based on the same case study. I continued the series when the reconstruction was finished in 2013, as a way of seeing the extent and the

2003 2005 2006 2007 2013 2013 3D Scan

View of Los Libertadores Street from the same standpoint starting with the 2003 photograph onwards, until 2013.

View of 'Casona de las seis aguas' from the same standpoint starting with the 2003 photograph onwards, until 2013.

View of Ramírez Street from the same standpoint starting with the 2003 photograph onwards, until 2013.

View of North Façade over the main square from the same standpoint starting with the 2003 photograph onwards, until 2013.

View of Chintuya Street from the same standpoint starting with the 2003 photograph onwards, until 2013.

changes generated by it. This latest record is part of my doctoral research, where I use the case again to study the now completed reconstruction process and to compare it to two other cases — Zúñiga and Lolol — undergoing reconstruction after being affected by an earthquake in 2010.[4]

The use of photography as a recording method is not new and has been used (and continues to be used) widely because it is fast, easy and

portable, especially today with the use of digital and satellite photographs. Documenting disasters using this recording method has been used historically since the middle of the nineteenth century, when the long exposures needed to photograph at that time were unable to record people in movement or actions; thus, buildings became the main focus in the representation of a disaster or a conflict by using a 'before and after' sequence of images.[5]

However, photography is only two-dimensional and fixed to the specific standpoint and view defined by the author, in this case, by the photographer of the archival photographs from before the earthquake, used as a basis for the whole sequence. Because of that, several aspects of the destruction

19 → 163

Photographic elevations of Los Libertadores Street in San Lorenzo de Tarapacá.
Above: just after the 2005 earthquake. Centre: after the reconstruction in 2013.
Below: 3D scanned elevation from 2013, used to scale the photographic records above.

and reconstruction cannot be seen. This is why I also began another record in 2005: the photographic elevations of the whole heritage area as a more comprehensive visual survey. Being only visual is another weak point of photography as a recording method for architecture, as no measurements can be obtained with it, unless complemented with dimensions taken on site, plans or drawings. In this case, the photographic elevations were taken using a 1-metre stick that allowed scaling the snapshots in a posterior process of mapping, in order to obtain dimensions closer to the reality. I re-shot the photographic elevations in 2013 as a way to compare with the record obtained just after the 2005 earthquake.

Over the years, new technologies for recording the built environment have become available, which can remedy some of photography's weaknesses. One of them is 3D laser scanning, a quick technology that provides a measurable 3D digital model of the buildings, coloured and with precision to a matter of millimetres. Images, technical drawings and even physical models can be generated from this method in a short period of time. I used this technology to scan the heritage area of San Lorenzo de Tarapacá in 2013, when the reconstruction was over. With 3D scanning, the record is much more comprehensive, with a multiplicity of viewpoints and editing possibilities that can be defined according to need. The 3D aspect of this type of record allows for flexibility in the decision of viewpoints, which can be defined after the work on site. One example of this is the last image of the series of photographs on page 119, rendered in 2014 using the 3D scanned data obtained in 2013, taken from the same standpoint as the rest of the photographic sequence.

In addition, as 3D scan data are measurable, the old photographic elevations were scaled to fit into the real dimensions obtained with the laser, making a much more accurate version of the 2005 photographic record possible. The idea behind putting all these records together is to closely observe and better understand what has happened during the reconstruction, considering the state of San Lorenzo de Tarapacá immediately after the 2005 earthquake and after the reconstruction process in 2013.

This comprehensive, spatially and temporally precise 'before and after' visual recording generates a virtual database for archiving the built environment in its different stages, with the potential to influence decisions about demolition, intervention and replication in reconstruction projects. Because of the measuring component given by the 3D scan data, the possibility to impact reconstruction approaches is higher than by using only visual records. This is relevant because in earthquake zones, scattered records and photographs are possible to find, especially of monuments, but they do not provide a systematic record of the same place over a number of years.

The idea of repeatedly taking images from the same standpoint is an interesting method to expose the changes, and the consistencies, to housing. Some houses may be still damaged, while the owners have built other houses or dwellings instead, and some dwellings have been part of the official reconstruction carried out by the state. In this last case, the heritage value of this historic area was only addressed superficially, since the new houses were designed to replicate the shape of 'traditional' houses, lacking understanding of the sustainable building techniques that characterised their original construction, and demonstrating little attention to architectonic elements of the majority of existent dwellings. In addition, the reconstructed houses used non-local materials and external contractors instead of local materials and labour. In the photographic elevations from 2005 and 2013, the lack of an integral approach for reconstruction is evident, where only newly built housing units were considered based on two designs that were

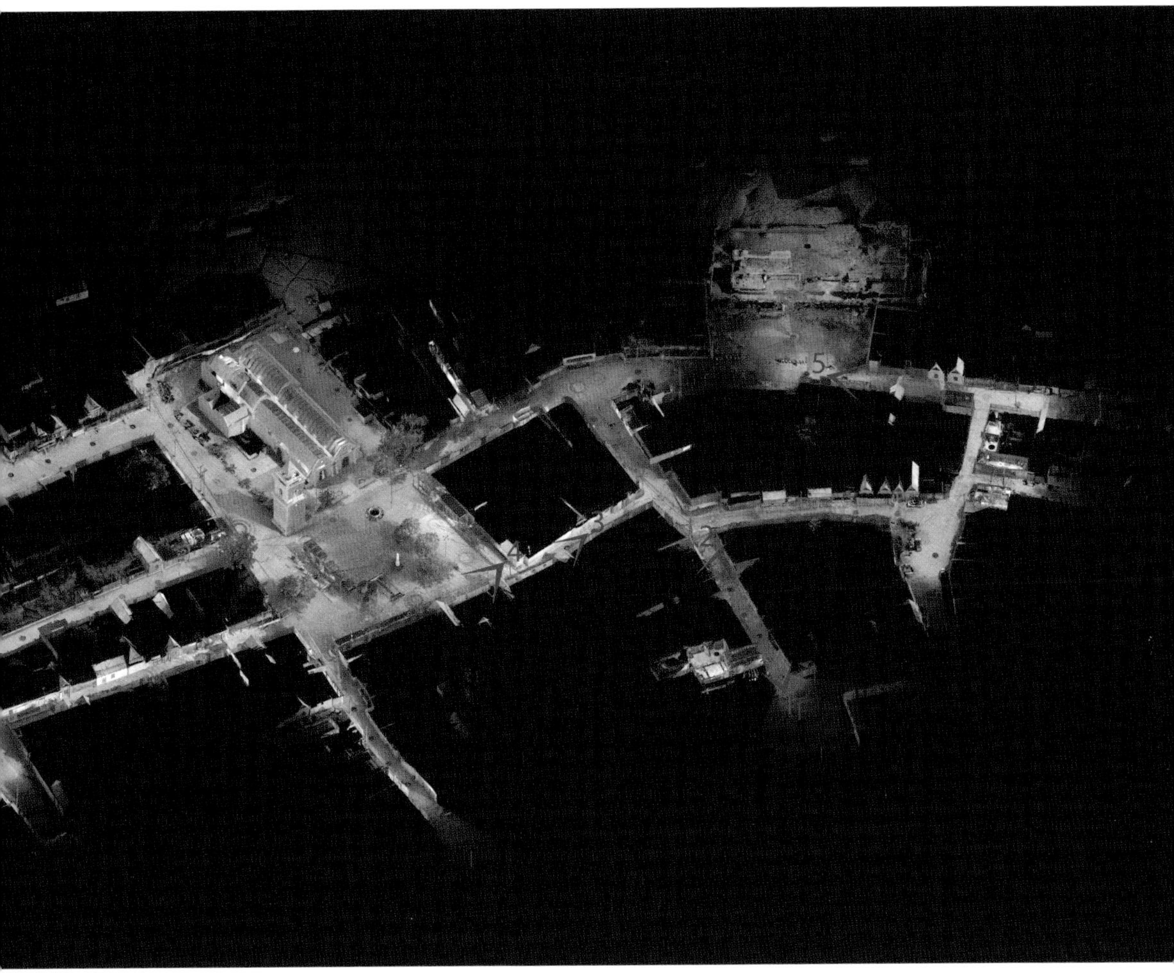

Top view of the village of San Lorenzo de Tarapacá, based on the 3D scanning record of 2013, indicating the standpoint of the sequences of photographs on page 119.

developed with the aforementioned criteria. This left damaged dwellings, also affected by the earthquake but potentially recoverable, without proper reinforcement or retrofit, and they can be seen still in ruins. This represents a risk for inhabitants as these dwellings may collapse in a future seismic event. There is also a bigger question of authenticity of the newly built houses that have erased layers of history to make them look 'as before' even when that previous state is not yet clear because of the non-existence of systematic records before the earthquake. Thus, to what extent methodically created records can influence the design of reconstruction projects in historic areas and define what is and should be considered heritage?

Surveys of this nature become relevant not only as visual and spatial records that enable us to recognise things that would otherwise be imperceptible but also as statements about reconstruction issues. It might also become a point of reference for other photographers in the future, allowing sequences to be continued. If we have a methodical record through time, reconstruction design can move on from formal replica to more creative, sustainable and site-responsive approaches, in this case, more like the heritage dwellings that were damaged.

1 This essay is part of my PhD research titled 'Re-construction and Record: Alternatives for Heritage Areas after Earthquakes in Chile', currently in progress under the supervision of Stephen Gage and Camillo Boano at the Bartlett School of Architecture, UCL, funded by a CONICYT scholarship (Becas Chile Programme 72100578). The thesis explores further the role of systematic and accurate recording techniques for creating intervention approaches in earthquake affected heritage areas of Chile.
2 The photographs from before the earthquake (2003) were given to the Tarapacá Project by the Heritage Department of the Ministry of Housing and Urban Development of the I Region of Chile. Each one of them had a plan indicating where the photo was taken, which I used to find the exact location for the sequence of the years following the 2005 earthquake.
3 The Tarapacá Project is an initiative for the reconstruction of architectural heritage that proposes new guidelines, both theoretical and technological, to address reconstruction issues in heritage villages affected by natural catastrophes, such as earthquakes. This project started as an answer to the 2005 earthquake that occurred in the north of Chile, and was led by architects from the Catholic University of Chile.
4 The 2010 earthquake occurred in the central and southern areas of Chile, where Zúñiga and Lolol are located, and had a magnitude of 8.8 on the Moment Magnitude scale (Mw). Zúñiga and Lolol were affected by that earthquake and have been under repair and reconstruction ever since. Like San Lorenzo de Tarapacá, these two villages have been given the denomination of 'Typical Zone' by the Council of National Monuments of Chile, in order to protect and preserve their built heritage.
5 Eyal Weizman and Ines Weizman, *Before and After: Documenting the Architecture of Disaster* (London: Strelka Press, 2013).

14

PAINT. BUFF. SHOOT. REPEAT

Re-photographing graffiti in London

Repeat photography Documenting inscriptions Surface analysis

Sabina Andron

Paint. Buff. Shoot. Repeat is a photographic project that zooms in on the location and lifespan of street art and graffiti in the urban environment. It is a response to online image banks that often capture street art and graffiti with a focus on the image rather than its setting and arrange photo archives by artist, style or production medium. In opposition, this project uses the method of repeat photography to capture the transformative processes street art and graffiti go through and argues for the capacity of this method to reveal changes on city surfaces.[1]

This project presents a systematic observation of three locations prolific in street art in the Shoreditch area of London and the changes that took place on their surfaces over a period of one year. The use of repeat photography makes apparent certain aspects about the inscriptions' lifespans, their competition for visibility and the influence of specific kinds of surface materiality on their production. It also provides evidence through which we can observe management strategies applied distinctively to street art and graffiti, pointing towards various degrees of perceived entitlement about their presence on city walls. While type-based graffiti interventions such as tags or throw-ups (which are basic forms of signature graffiti) seem to be removed or pushed into the background more often, figurative street-art works are approached with increased tolerance and seem to be allowed longer, more privileged occupations of surface territories.

Photography is the main tool that has acknowledged and popularised the existence of street art and graffiti, long before the internet, and is still being used to archive and collect images of the often impermanent marks on urban surfaces. Repeat photography captures not only the individual images

Surface battles for visibility: murals versus throw-ups.

17 ↑ 147

but also the ways in which inscriptions evolve or change and reveals the dynamics between fixed material elements and the changing graphic marks. The procedure clarifies the relations not only between places and graffiti but also between graffiti production and the policies and processes through which it is regulated.

The image sequence shows a large-scale street art work on Chance Street in London, produced by prolific Belgian artist ROA in April 2012. The first photo is dated February 2014, and it shows the painted hedgehog with a bubble-letter inscription painted on top of it, an additional layer that behaves like a visual parasite, occupying a highly visible and popular wall destination.

Since the mural went up in 2012, many such inscriptions have been painted over it, highlighting the right to occupy the same wall surface irrespective of permission or painting skill. While the mural had been executed with permission, the bubble-letter graffiti throw-up is claiming access to the same territory from outside the authorisation system. The reaction can be seen in the second image, where the throw-up was promptly sent back into the background of the frame, in order to restore the prominence of the hedgehog mural, within just two weeks. In fact, if one takes a closer look at the initial image, one can see that this was not the first time the hedgehog piece had been retouched, and a separation had been repeatedly enforced between more fleeting graffiti tags and the enduring piece of street art.

This visual battle cannot be won, as is apparent from the new tag that appears in the image to the right. Although the act of vandalising a street art work seems ironic at first, this is an increasingly common practice as

the gap between the management of invited murals and that of independent tags widens. Permissioned street art is treated increasingly like sanctioned public art in a cycle of restoration, conservation and durability, while uninvited inscriptions are often the easier targets of graffiti removals, mural restorations and natural degradation.

The image sequence below shows the activity happening under the nose of ROA's hedgehog, focusing on the apparently less visible, or less significant, marks occupying that wall. These are more likely to fall under the radar of authorities and street-art fans alike as they are smaller, more layered and have less individual potential of attracting attention. This sequence is representative of often-overlooked graphic activity on city walls, taking place in the shadow of bigger, more privileged murals. Although these inscriptions might not be as visually arresting as sanctioned or invited murals, repeat photography can help bring them in the spotlight by revealing the more everyday life of urban walls. The photographs of these inscriptions also illustrate the roles different surface materials play as context.

The sequence shows how the metal doorway tends to support paper marks such as paste-ups and posters while the brick wall next to it is mostly occupied by aerosol inscriptions. These are tendencies that only become apparent through a repeated observation of the same surfaces, revealing the influence of surface materials in accommodating inscriptions of various natures.

A final sequence suggests a narrative provocation whose story only becomes apparent through consecutive photos. This particular inscription was conceived by artist Mobstr, who is part of a well-established London graffiti crew, Burning Candy, where he goes by the alias 'HUH?' or simply '?' His work as street artist Mobstr is based on messages stencilled in capital letters, while his graffiti activity consists mostly of painting his '?' tag by using a roller instead of aerosol paint, for a deliberately less polished look.

Material affordances of city walls.

17 ↑ 147

Manipulating the buff.

Mobstr's provocation on this wall started by repeatedly stencilling the word 'BUFF' (that is, erase graffiti) high up on a brick wall at different intervals, inviting local authorities to come and paint over the unwanted marks. In London, this process is handled either by council employees or by appointed graffiti-removal contractors who respond to specific complaints from the public or monitor different areas, removing inscriptions at regular intervals. As the graffiti-removal contractors took the bait and painted over the words, they ended up forming the contours of a new image with their own paint: Mobstr's characteristic '?', seemingly painted in his own rough style but executed by the local authority-appointed contractors. While the two photos are valuable in understanding the sequential production of this mark, they do not provide hard evidence as to whether it was graffiti-removal contractors who actually painted over the words or if it was Mobstr who did

Manipulating the buff.

it himself. Whichever the case, the use of the repeat photography method proves insightful for the visual development of the wall.

When performed systematically over a set period, repeat photography can be a useful method for understanding street art and graffiti, the way they occupy city surfaces and responses to them. It can show how there are different degrees of value attributed to inscriptions and how this impacts on the way they are allowed to take over surfaces. Repeat photography also reveals the predilection of certain surfaces as a frame and support for particular types of inscriptions and can bring to life the energies involved in graffiti writing as a repetitive practice.[2]

Repeat photography can be an insightful method when used to capture urban phenomena as they happen and not just as a way of reconstituting historical scenery in order to observe changes that have already taken place. It allows for observations of localised material phenomena of the city such as street art and graffiti and clarifies their symbiotic relation with the urban environment. If performed over wider time spans, repeat photography of street art and graffiti can produce knowledge not just about inscriptions and their development but also about changes in availability, management and popularity of different surface locations.

1 Repeat photography (or re-photography) is a method used by disciplines such as natural and social sciences, in land management or landscape research, in order to chart visual change over a set period of time by duplicating existing archival photography. More frequently than not, this is employed in relation to natural landscapes, as exemplified by Cliff White, *Lens of Time: A Repeat Photography of Landscape Change in the Canadian Rockies* (Calgary: University of Calgary Press, 2007); Trudi Smith, 'Repeat Photography as a Method in Visual Anthropology', *Visual Anthropology*, 20 (2) (2007): 179–200; Robert H. Webb, Diane E. Boyer and R. M. Turner, *Repeat Photography: Methods and Applications in the Natural Sciences* (London and Washington, DC: Island Press, 2010). The two articles on repeat photography in *The Sage Handbook of Visual Analysis* (2011) focus on the relations between time and image and on the use of historical photographic material. There seem to be very few mentions of the relevance of repeat photography in an urban environment, or when performed in a contemporary setting to obtain information about ongoing, rather than past, phenomena. See John Rieger, 'Rephotography for Documenting Social Change' in *The Sage Handbook of Visual Research Methods*, edited by Eric Margolis and Luc Pauwels (London and Thousand Oaks, CA: Sage, 2011), 132–50; and Mark Klett, 'Repeat Photography in Landscape Research', in *The Sage Handbook of Visual Research Methods*, edited by Eric Margolis and Luc Pauwels (London and Thousand Oaks, CA: Sage, 2011), 114–32.

2 The website Graffarc (short for Graffiti Archaeology) does this by accumulating a number of photographs of the same walls into a single database, which can be browsed by location and year. Cassidy Curtis, who is responsible for the project, collects images from different photographers to create what he calls a 'grassroots assemblage', 'chronomontage' or 'timelapse collage' of graffiti: http://grafarc.org/about.html (accessed 14 October 2015). See also http://sabinaandron.com/leake-street (accessed 14 October 2015).

15

CRITICAL URBAN LEARNING THROUGH PARTICIPATORY PHOTOGRAPHY

Participatory photography Workshops Visual lobbying

Alexandre Apsan Frediani and Laura Hirst

4 ← 45 9 ← 83

In 2014, in collaboration with international NGO Practical Action and the Kisumu Informal Settlement Network (a grass-roots network involving representatives from informal traders' collectives and neighbourhood planning associations), we and our students from the MSc in Social Development Practice of the Bartlett Development Planning Unit, UCL were tasked with researching neighbourhood planning and urban governance in the city of Kisumu, Kenya.[1] The aim was to document learning around ongoing processes of participatory governance within informal settlements as supported by a Practical Action initiative, 'People's Plans into Practice' (2008—12), which aimed to improve the well-being, productivity and living conditions of poor people in informal settlements in Kenya and the East African region. The research also endeavoured to generate recommendations for strengthening the capacity of neighbourhood associations and enhancing participatory planning processes in a context of increasingly private development and regeneration. Based on these activities, a report was produced for local, national and international partners in advocacy work, with a view to formulating key principles regarding participatory urban governance. A combination of research methods was used to thoroughly examine prevailing and alternative discourses, experiences and realities within the city. Participatory photography was adopted as one of the methods to sustain the module's concern with 'critical urban learning', which, as defined by McFarlane, involves 'questioning and antagonising existing urban knowledges and formulations, learning alternatives in participatory collective and proposing alternative formulations'.[2]

While more broadly 'participation' in visual research has a long history, participatory photography or 'photo voice' is a method initially developed as a participatory-action research method by Caroline Wang and her colleagues working on public-health programmes with women in China. It involves providing (marginalised categories of) people with cameras to record their realities and perspectives. The process of taking photographs and subsequent group discussion (which can take the form of storytelling, coding, explaining choices in image-making) provides new spaces for critical dialogue and knowledge production about personal and community issues, productively feeding processes of social transformation.[3] In many cases, the resulting photographs are themselves used as a powerful advocacy tool, attempting to inspire change by bringing stories and experiences to the attention of decision makers and the wider public. As well as having roots in Freire's notion of 'conscientisation', where a critical awareness of one's social reality is developed through reflection and action, the method also draws from feminist theory defining research participants as actors rather than objects of study and identifying the empowering potential of knowledge production for participants.[4]

In the field, researchers and students used participatory photography with small groups of residents to explore institutional relationships and networks, issues of diversity and processes of representation in informal

Left and top Participatory photography workshop with Gonda self-help disability group, Manyatta ward, Kisumu, May 2014.

Right Workshop participants practising camera techniques.

settlements. Participants were identified through local partners and facilitators and were either part of existing self-help groups or self-selecting individuals. The visiting students and researchers organised introductory workshops to instruct participants on basic camera use with a number of themes in mind: spaces and conditions of participatory practices; participation of people with disabilities; housing rights; and the right to water. The resulting photographs were used in focus group discussions and one-to-one interviews, in order to elicit stories and experiences. Conversation aimed to move beyond assumptions about the surface content of images and to explore the processes, practices and relationships behind them, communicating different individual and shared perspectives on living in the city.

The fieldwork timeframe limited the potential for any training in photography beyond a very basic introduction to equipment, yet each

4 ↑ 45 9 ↑ 83

Opportunities for people with disabilities to earn a living in Manyatta ward, Kisumu, May 2014. Photo: George Otieno, workshop participant.

participant brought back a selection of photographs that could be used as a basis for discussion. The participatory analysis through photo elicitation yielded rich information on everyday urban practices and gave visibility to challenges that might not otherwise have been revealed using more conventional methods of interrogation such as straightforward interviews or focus-group discussions. The visual immediacy of a photograph as a talking point often sparked discussion revealing nuanced emotions, values, opinions and practices without a need for overly intrusive questioning from the researchers. Some researchers worked with groups to code photographs into themes, whereby participants took part in physically moving and grouping prints, which lent a particular dynamism to discussions as photographs were arranged and rearranged. This also allowed participants to look at and discuss both their and others' photographs, expressing unique interpretations as well as sharing similar views, experiences and practices.

Accessibility challenges for children with disabilities living in Manyatta ward, Kisumu, May 2014. Photo: Jane Ouma, workshop participant.

Other researchers worked on individual photo-interviews to talk about issues and stories that would have been sensitive to talk about in a group setting.

The process of taking photographs and telling stories changed the dynamic between researcher and participant, facilitating communication and allowing participants to relax and open up. For example, the workshops with people with disabilities and carers revealed sensitive issues around the everyday realities of living with stigma as well as a perceived lack of representation within neighbourhood planning associations despite formal inclusion. Reflections around urban practices emerged organically in some cases; on the topic of water collection, images taken inspired discussion on the gendered nature of everyday collection practices and highlighted gaps in service provision more generally. In exploring spaces of participation in local neighbourhoods, different types of spaces were revealed through the photographs themselves while group discussion and elicitation of people's

4 ↑ 45 9 ↑ 83

Gathering water for everyday use in Manyatta ward, Kisumu, May 2014.
Photo: Elizabeth Ochieng, workshop participant.

Informal spaces of participation in Nyalenda B Ward, Kisumu, May 2014.
Photo: Joseph Otieno Odhiambo, workshop participant.

Workshop participants discussing concepts of home and housing in Nyalenda A ward, Kisumu, May 2014.

motivations related to communal use of these urban spaces showed them often to be linked to economic marginalisation and strategies of resource mobilisation and income generation. Researchers exploring housing rights and neighbourhood planning were able to prompt more personal discussions around housing experiences and narratives around the meaning of 'home' related to people's needs and aspirations. Researchers found that exploring issues in a facilitated session often also led to a more propositional discussion related to potential spaces where urban institutional relationships and networks could be utilised and strengthened.

Operating within a short timeframe of just over two weeks inevitably required trade-offs between the different levels of potential social transformation and empowerment that are often promised by participatory research methods.[5] The photography workshops provided space and opportunities for participants to articulate their knowledge and experiences

4 ↑ 45 9 ↑ 83

and to discuss aspirations. Yet the discrete timeframe limited their opportunities to control the direction of the research or to turn reflection into action themselves. A longer term engagement using participatory photography with a more explicit advocacy focus could go some way to address this shortcoming. Future iterations of the research therefore aim to work more closely with participants to devise collaborative digital storytelling campaigns combining photographs and audio that can be used to bring stories to the attention of local authorities.

The transformative potential of the method was perhaps more visible at the level of the research process, whereby new narratives, local knowledge and ways of seeing urban marginalisation were revealed, allowing for a process of reflection by the visiting students, representatives of the Kisumu Informal Settlement Network (KISN) and those organisations working locally and nationally on participatory urban governance in informal settlements. The overall findings, shared in a public meeting that was attended by over 100 people, fed into Practical Action's activities in Kisumu as well as into wider debates on diversity planning within the Development Planning Unit. Meanwhile, the Social Development Practice programme's long-term engagement in Kisumu means that the year's findings will be taken forward in future iterations of action-learning and research aiming to support the ongoing work of KISN in challenging exclusionary urban development trends in Kisumu currently espoused by city policy makers and developers.

1 The Bartlett Development Planning Unit has a research and teaching agenda that builds on a long-standing commitment to just development and transformative change in cities in the Global South. A critical engagement with existing knowledge, participation and learning drives its work in tracing and exploring new directions in the field of development planning. This is reflected by its ongoing efforts to embed innovative methodologies of research and knowledge production into its teaching. The MSc Social Development Practice explores processes of social change, mobilisation and development that can generate greater equity and well-being for people with diverse identities living in cities of the Global South. Concerned with the relationship between active citizenship and development, its teaching is based on the recognition that diverse identities and aspirations are critical components of social change.

2 Colin McFarlane, *Learning the City: Knowledge and Translocal Assemblage* (Oxford: Wiley-Blackwell, 2011).

3 Caroline Wang, 'Photovoice: A Participatory Action Research Strategy Applied to Women's Health', *Journal of Women's Health*, 8 (2) (1999): 185–92.

4 Paolo Freire, *Pedagogy of the Oppressed* (Harmondsworth: Penguin, 1970).

5 Thea Shahrokh and Joanna Wheeler, *Knowledge from the Margins: An Anthology from a Global Network on Participatory Practice and Policy Influence* (Brighton: Institute of Development Studies, 2014).

16

ASSISTED SELF-PORTRAITS AND GUESTURES

Excerpts from a discussion on photography and participation

Documentary Collaborative photography Assisted self-portraiture

Margareta Kern and Anthony Luvera

15 ↑ 131

The following text is an updated excerpt from a longer, published, conversational piece.[1] In the practice of both Anthony Luvera and Margareta Kern, participation and collaboration play an important role in the production of lens-based imagery. In the following conversation they reflect on the challenges as well as advantages of such an approach, looking at aspects of control and authorship and the ethical concerns that surround it. Employing participatory strategies in making and displaying their work, Kern and Luvera share an interest in how documentary representations are constructed by artists, audiences and subjects alike. Both artists work mainly in urban contexts. Based in Berlin, Belfast, Brighton and London, the projects they discuss here deal respectively with migrant guest workers and people who have experienced homelessness.

Workbook for Assisted Self-Portraits, featuring works in progress with and of Ruben Torosyan, 2004–2005. Photo: Ruben Torosyan and Anthony Luvera.

ASSISTED SELF-PORTRAITS: CREATING PHOTOGRAPHS TOGETHER

AL I often begin by asking participants: 'How would you like to be represented?' 'What do you think about being described in this way?' I've always been interested in seeing how I might involve subjects in processes of creating representations of themselves, their experiences and their points of view. Through this I am keen to hear about their experiences of photography and to learn about how they feel about being described or represented as homeless.

To make an *Assisted Self-Portrait*, I meet with each individual in locations they choose, over repeated sessions, to teach them how to use a 5×4 field camera with Polaroid and Quickload film stock or a digital medium format camera equipment tethered to a laptop, with a tripod, handheld flashgun and a cable shutter release. The final *Assisted Self-Portrait* is then edited with the participant.

23 ↑ 199

MK In the *Assisted Self-Portraits*, we can see the subjects operating the cable release. This seems a key component to your work: the fact that the camera is triggered by the person in the photograph. Homelessness is associated with a lot of uncertainty and vulnerability, and seeing them using the cable release becomes an incredibly potent symbol of their own agency over their lives and over the production of the image.

Assisted Self-Portrait of Maggie Irvine. Photo: Maggie Irvine and Anthony Luvera, from *Residency*, 2006–8.

GUESTURES: ARCHIVES AND WORKSTATIONS

AL I am curious about the relationship photography has to processes of acquiring and representing knowledge, especially in archives, where photographs can be put to uses that may be unexpected, different or contrary to the creator's original intentions. In a sense, it is in archives that photographs are able to function in their purest state as free-floating bundles of information poised to be anchored by context, yet this can have all kinds of implications in terms of representation. The slip and slide of a photograph, in and out of contexts, triggered by different archive-users is potent.

One of the things I find fascinating in your work is how the construction and manufacture of other people's memories or experiences takes place through the active participation of the audience. I like how you create a kind of workstation in which the

15 ↑ 131

audience is invited to construct his or her own route through the material and how there is not just one line of narrative the viewer is invited or prompted to follow but rather a number of different storylines to pursue and assemble. I've found it interesting to watch you develop this body of work over a number of years, unfolding different presentation strategies for the same collection of visual and written material.

MK My project started during a two-month residency in Berlin, and I was expected to complete a piece of work for an exhibition within that period. I had only just made connections with the migrant women who came to Berlin in the late 1960s as part of an organised labour migration from the socialist Yugoslavia (the official term used was 'guest workers'). I was initially focused on hearing about the women's personal experiences of migration as well as their experiences of working predominantly in telecommunications factories, as I found that these stories were largely missing from the official histories and national archives. I was looking at ways to record their stories and at the same time be sensitive to their privacy. I questioned the relationship of portrait photography and personal testimonies and was seeking ways to work with the complex historical, political and gendered context of their migration. All this meant that my engagement with the work went beyond the scope of the residency and became a long-term project.

Installation view, Margareta Kern, *GUESTures*, Cities Methodologies, Bucharest, October–November 2010.

23 → 199

The project developed in several stages, being exhibited in London in 2009 and Bucharest in 2010, when I used different strategies of display in order to work through the research process and to understand different types of materials and vantage points. I'm glad that this key idea of manufacturing or constructing multiple narratives comes across as I felt this was important to convey. I wanted to bring into the piece that experience of working through the material and to give the viewer an active position as a creator of meanings and narratives. I wanted to make the process of creating stories by the viewer more conscious, which is why the work is set up as a cross between a research space, an archive and a workstation. The project then culminated in the making of a double-screen video titled *GUESTures*, in which I worked with an actress using a verbatim theatre technique of re-enacting the voices and words of those interviewed. I juxtaposed the re-enactment of an actress with my own remaking of interviewee's domestic interiors and with an archival footage from the factories in which the migrant women worked. I enjoyed that process very much as it not only enabled me to bring their narratives into the space of the moving image, and to be more experimental, but it also enabled me to contest the desires and needs of the documentary process with its attachments to 'truth' and 'authenticity'.

Installation view, Margareta Kern, *GUESTures*, SC Gallery, Zagreb, 2011.

15 ↑ 131

THE MECHANISMS AND LAYERS OF CONSTRUCTION

MK When I started working on *GUESTures*, I became fascinated with how academics negotiate the research process, producing some tangible outcomes and taking a degree of 'fictionality' that the process brings with it for granted. I think every text is a construction.

AL Yes, in my work I'm interested in how those processes of transcription, editing, quotation or selection might alter the original documents, the original terms of the invitation issued to the participant or the interviewee's intentions for agreeing to take part in the work. When it comes to editing and transcribing, the conversations will be transformed and be manufactured into something else.

MK In a way, the editing process already happens before transcription. We know for instance that we are being recorded and in a way we become more aware of editing ourselves before we speak.

AL It seems to me that there will always be a level of interference, manipulation or construction involved. In *Prologue to Isha*, I used the video camera with the intention of making something for public display about a woman living with mental-health issues. I wanted to record the whole of my encounter with Isha — the process of preparing for the interview as well as the actual interview — so I switched the camera on pretty much as soon as I stepped through the door. When editing

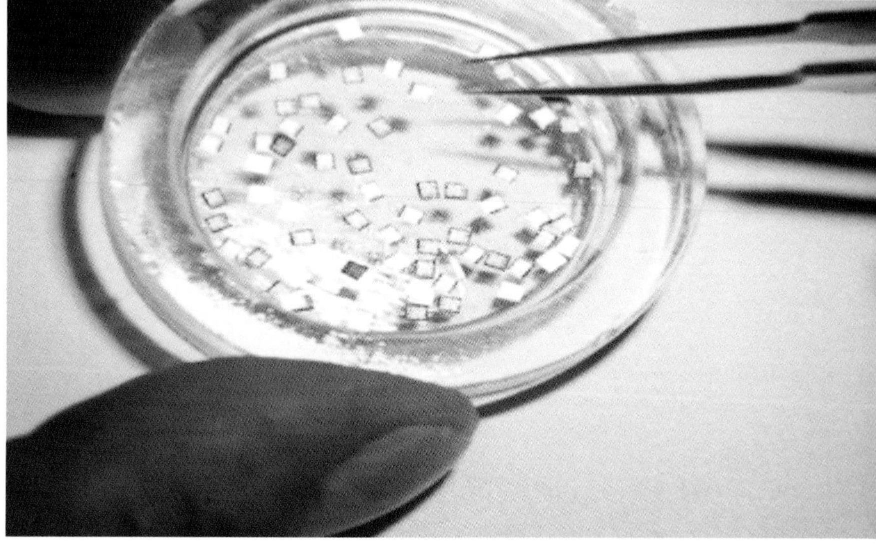

Installation view, Anthony Luvera. Prologue to Isha and Residency, Cities Methodologies, Bucharest, October–November 2010. Photo: Simona Dumitriu.

Margareta Kern, *GUESTures*, Double-channel HD Video, 33 minutes, 2011.

15 ↑ 131

the footage, this process of setting up seemed most pertinent to me: the push and pull between myself as the photographer, and Isha as the subject and the recording equipment as a conduit between us. It seemed right to dispense with the documentary interview itself, which framed Isha in a very particular way, and just retain the prologue to the interview, which seemed closer to my experience of knowing her.

MK You turned the camera on to the mechanism and layers of construction rather than the constructed story. What both our practices are trying to engage in, I believe, are the social realities of others and the critical issues around their representation. There is a tension between different modes of construction, or different realities, and their representation.

AL Indeed, attempting to seek out possibilities for the creation and understanding of the subjectivities presented in my work, and to represent the process of doing this is what drives me. More recently, I've taken my work with people who have experienced homelessness to Brighton to create a body of work called *Assembly*. Along with inviting participants to make photographs of their experiences and the things they're interested in, I've been asking participants to create and share sound recordings with me and to record conversations about photography, homelessness and representation. The role of dialogue in the work I make is pivotal, and I'm increasingly interested in interrogating this further. The idea of a pure depiction of reality is flawed, of course, and while I don't think any of these depictions created by participants or me are any more authentic or closer to the truth, I hope they may take us a little closer to understanding the questions that might be asked of representation.

1 Margareta Kern and Anthony Luvera, 'A Rocky Boat: Reflections on Research, Process, and Representation', in *Cities Methodologies Bucharest*, edited by Ger Duijzings, Simona Dumitriu and Aurora Király (Bucharest: Editura UNARTE, 2011), 36–41.

17

PICTURING PLACE

The agency of images in urban change

Image interview   Visual interaction   Public conversation

Ben Campkin, Mariana Mogilevich
and Rebecca Ross

1 ↑ 23 7 ↑ 69 11 ↑ 97 14 ↑ 125

How do images shape cities? The answer might seem obvious: from impressionist paintings of Paris, to contemporary photographs of China's boom cities, images produced in different media and genres depict and interpret urban change. But beyond the decorative or documentary, they also have profound impacts on the ground. Maps, plans, photographs, renders, CGIs, street art and signage drive physical changes and are central to perceptions of place and claims to territory. They are used as evidence in a wide range of ways: to credit, discredit, authorise, inform, imagine, project, propose, question, prove, disprove, enlighten, deceive, inspire, seduce, anger, create, destroy, preserve. To make things visible typically means to make them public and subject to debate. Urban images not only offer insights to help analyse and understand cities but also point to ways of radically altering their futures.

Picturing Place is a research project that proposes a method to critically explore the agency of images in urban change.[1] It investigates how images work in contemporary urbanisation as media through which different political imaginaries are articulated, operating as discursive sites, with direct and increasingly powerful impacts on the built environment. One of our main concerns in this project is that the increased proliferation and circulation of images in urban change, and the sophistication and availability of new image-making technologies, have not, as one might have hoped, led to greater transparency or meaningful participation in urban life and the production of the built environment. Providing a framework and method for more critical engagement, Picturing Place seeks to reposition images in the production of better cities.

The visual culture theorist W. J. T. Mitchell asks, 'as a kind of thought experiment', 'What do pictures want?' Although Mitchell acknowledges reifying, animating or fetishising images as autonomous agents may be problematic, he nevertheless positions images as 'desiring objects' in order to elicit new ways of considering their significance.[2] To frame an analysis of how images operate as a question of 'their desires' rather than as an assertion of independent agency shifts the burden of answer onto the way in which an image becomes significant through and in relation to broader conditions and institutions:

> What pictures want is not the same as the message they communicate or the effect they produce; it's not even the same as what they say they want. Like people, pictures may not know what they want; they have to be helped to recollect it through a dialogue with others.[3]

We build from this thought experiment, adding the question, 'what do we want from urban images?' Our project sets up frameworks to consider images in and of cities across different media, historical period and geographical location. This has involved writing a generalised questionnaire designed to survey urban images in terms of their production, meaning, reception and circulation; using the questionnaire as a basis to curate a digital catalogue of images; convening panel discussions (again using the questionnaire) to bring together diverse image-makers and to ask them to narrate one image in order to start a common conversation about the roles of images in the production of specific cities; and a set of online articles about ten images, using an international news media platform and social media to generate a public conversation about the agency of images in urban change. Through each of these mechanisms, the project initiated a debate about images and the kinds of knowledge they generate, bringing to light image-making processes and expertise and highlighting unexpected relationships between different types of image in order to consider how visual languages influence struggles over urban space.

In order to demonstrate how this works, we have selected three examples of the kinds of images that we have been considering: a signage system, a digital render and a hand-drawn map. These are accompanied by brief texts that demonstrate how the methodology operates to elucidate the agency of images in relation to a range of contemporary urban situations. They demonstrate how images service different interests and are deployed to bring about change in varied ways. The first example focuses on the signage system that supports Mexico City's public transportation system, facilitating circulation and serving the public welfare. The second is a digital render of a projected development in Shanghai, illustrating the ambiguous qualities of contemporary images and the ways in which they help leverage and mediate power for developers, in this case the state, and for visual and built-environment practitioners. The final case, a community map from Brooklyn, New York, shows how images can work to bring about change and to increase grass-roots participation, reclaiming the city. These three cases of imaging demonstrate how images connect to 'change' in a variety of ways.

THE SYMBOLIC SIMPLICITY OF MEXICO CITY'S METRO SIGNS

When work began in 1967, Mexico City's metro system enacted a dramatic modernisation of the cityscape. Making room for the metro meant clearing away familiar aspects of the urban landscape as well as introducing residents to the strange new spaces of the network's underground tunnels and stations. To integrate this new layer of urban infrastructure with the existing city's pre-Columbian, colonial and contemporary layers, the authors of the subway relied on a pictographic system. Lance Wyman, a New York-based graphic designer, designed icons to identify each metro station.

Instead of carrying just a name, the stations, as new geographic entities, were visually connected to an existing historical or geographical

1 ↑ 23 7 ↑ 69 11 ↑ 97 14 ↑ 125

feature. Thus, the sign for Balderas station, where Line 1 met Line 3 in the historic centre, referenced a cannon on display in a library above ground, while nearby Pino Suárez station was identified by the Aztec ruin that was uncovered (and destroyed) during excavations for the station.

Wyman's pictorial system connected the surface to the subterranean. He created a visible match between the familiar spaces of the city, which were now connected to the new stations via street signs and the far more abstract underground space of the metro system. In the dark tunnel, each pictograph would help travellers to connect their locations to familiar references above ground. With Mexico City's modernisation still a work in progress, the pictorial system also negotiated the fact that many of the system's new passengers could not read.

Signage for Metro system designed by Lance Wyman, Mexico City, 1968–9.
Photos: Lance Wyman.

Other way-finding projects similarly use graphic elements to bring order and legibility to a chaotic system. Harry Beck's 1931 London Underground map turned the Tube system into a diagram to make navigation easier irrespective of actual station locations. More abstract than Mexico's system but equally iconic, this map and others like it create a total image of the city that affords both a sense of pleasure and collectivity. Underground aside, street graphics have a much broader role in demarcating the functions of different urban spaces. We need only think of the stripes of white paint that turn a road into a crosswalk, bicycle lane or parking space.[4]

The specific problem of aiding travellers who may not be able to read the relevant language in an unfamiliar (or familiar) city is a context to which pictographic symbols are especially well suited. On the surface, it might

18 → 155

seem that the mundane practicality or everydayness of transportation stands in sharp contrast with some of the larger political aims associated with the mid-twentieth-century isotype movement, which employed graphic symbols in pursuit of broad socio-political change.[5] However, both Wyman's system for Mexico City and Beck's map for the London Underground have had political and functional implications that continue to play a role in the future of both cities.

THIS 'HERO SHOT' OF SHANGHAI'S
FUTURE SKYLINE PROJECTS CHINA'S SUCCESS

Pudong, Lujiazui, overview, 2008. Image: Gensler.

One of the most prolific forms of image in shaping contemporary cities is the 'render'. The term has come to describe digital visualisations that have the authority, the apparent 'realism', of digital photographs and are often viewed and interpreted as such but are actually hybrid images comprised of layers of data from different sources.

The image above is a render of Pudong, Shanghai that was produced for the Chinese government, the client of the commercial architectural

1 ↑ 23 7 ↑ 69 11 ↑ 97 14 ↑ 125

practice Gensler's Shanghai Tower. The spiralling building is seen in a state of perfect completion on the right hand of the skyline, the tallest of a planned trio, but the image was made in 2008, before construction had started. In an age of intense competition between the world's cities, governments and city authorities have become increasingly focused on presenting an image for global consumption, and this dramatic skyline is the exemplar par excellence, capturing the heady power of capital and the spirit of the city and the nation's modernisation.

The render plays an important role within this process of city imaging and branding, produced to communicate what the towers would look and feel like in context. In this case, the government did not provide a brief for the production of this specific image, but Gensler, who market themselves as globally networked facilitators, 'leveraging the power of design to create a better world', were attuned to their client's desire to produce what they call a 'hero shot', not only aiding visualisation of the tower as a powerful icon within an urban landscape but also projecting the future success of China.[6] The image is not entirely futuristic, however. It shows tourists consuming the spectacle of the nascent skyline of Lujiazui, the city's new financial district, but from a viewing platform on the Bund, the old city, on the point of a bend in the Huangpu river.

The authorship of such renders is as ambiguous as their status as visual artefacts. In this case, Gensler outsourced its production to a specialist and well-known international visualisation firm, Crystal CG, which works across sectors such as entertainment, the car industry and real estate as well as architecture. Gensler provided them with drawings made in Vectorworks architectural software and a digital photograph to show the viewpoint, the former being superimposed onto the latter. Those working in visualisation companies and their less high-profile equivalents (rendering shops and factories) might be trained or part-trained as architects, or in computer game design.

Renders such as this blur the lines between planned and existing built environments.[7] They circulate widely within development processes, taking the place of photographs and drawings as the main means for architects and their clients to disseminate projected (and completed) buildings via the web, corporate brochures, architectural publications and exhibitions. They reassure clients about what it is they are investing in, and are used to garner allies to help sell and realise large and small-scale projects.

It is not clear, however, whether the prevalence of what are understood as 'realistic' simulations in contemporary negotiations about the future or the built environment opens up dialogue in a way that is productive for the public. Does the circulation of a high-resolution and high-production-value image leave room for debate about the future of the built environment or might it actually shut down the potential for a genuinely open discussion?

18 → 155

'THERE'S LAND IF YOU WANT IT': HOW A HAND-DRAWN MAP IS TRANSFORMING VACANT LOTS IN BROOKLYN

How does a map become a garden? In 2011, open-space activists in New York City compiled a list of all the publicly owned vacant land in Brooklyn. It amounted to 596 acres, almost the same size as Brooklyn's Prospect Park. This spreadsheet was an abstraction until it was translated by a graphic artist into a hand-drawn map and printed. In a design meant to communicate abundance, the footprint of all the borough's vacant lots was coloured green. Trapped behind chain-link fence (barbed wire in the poster's more rhetorical depiction), these potential farms, gardens or other community gathering spaces were filled with possibility. Mounted outside the lots themselves and accompanied by a hand-written note encouraging readers to reclaim the publicly owned property, the posters were the beginning of imagining what the space could be.

There's Land if you Want It, poster illustration by Julia Samuels, Brooklyn, New York City, 2012. Photo: 596 Acres.

They were coupled with an online map, which has now expanded to cover more of New York City. Subsequent versions of the posters provide illustrated step-by-step instructions for potential lot-recoverers, as well as pointing passers-by to the website, which, in addition to the map, helps neighbours to organise to request access to the space from the city.

Many experiments had been tried before that entailed community participation in digital maps. There is an entire sub-field of Geographic Information Systems (GIS) referred to as Public Participation GIS (PPGIS).[8] An important element of *596 Acres*, however, is that it moves fluidly

1 → 23 7 → 69 11 → 97 14 → 125

between signage, paper and screen. It has the accessibility of signage and benefits from the potential for happenstance encounters by pedestrians. At the same time, it leverages the communicative and political benefits of a digitalised network-based collaboration via its online presence.

To date, the combined poster-map tool has made it possible for groups in the city to gain access to almost forty lots and convert them to protected parkland, and the technique is being applied in other cities: Berlin, Philadelphia, Pittsburgh, Los Angeles, New Orleans, Montreal, Melbourne, Sydney and Toronto have also begun to map and mark vacant lots.

No mere posters, *596 Acres*' signs make visible an opportunity to reclaim space. Not only might someone pass by an eyesore and be pointed to see it fresh as a common good, but they are also connected with information on how to realise that potential — an especially valuable tool in the neighbourhoods where such lots are concentrated, not coincidentally underserved by municipal and commercial infrastructure. Map-making and signposting are not only the means by which cities order and explain space; they can also be a tool for citizens to make claims on it.

1 In pilot form, the method was exhibited with the installation of a digital catalogue and questionnaire in the 2010 edition of Cities Methodologies, and it also informed the production of *Real-Time London*, Cities Methodologies (2012), a piece exploring the streams of vernacular images in and of cities being uploaded to the internet every minute.

2 W. J. T. Mitchell, *What Do Pictures Want? The Lives and Loves of Images* (Chicago, IL: University of Chicago Press, 2005).

3 Mitchell, *What Do Pictures Want?*, 46.

4 Luis Castañeda, 'Choreographing the Metropolis: Networks of Circulation and Power in Olympic Mexico', *Journal of Design History*, 25 (3) (2012): 285–303.

5 For example, see Eve Blau, 'Isotype and Architecture in Red Vienna: The Modern Projects of Otto Neurath and Josef Frank', *Austrian Studies*, 14 (2006): 227–59.

6 Interview with Monica Schaffer, Gensler, 23 September 2014.

7 For a close ethnographic study of the production of architectural renders, see Sophie Houdart, 'Copying, Cutting and Pasting Social Spheres: Computer Designers' Participation in Architectural Projects', *Science Studies*, 21 (1) (2008): 47–63. For detailed discussion of the ways in which digital visualisations circulate within the context of one development in Doha, Qatar, see Clare Melhuish, Monica Degen and Gillian Rose, 'Architectural Atmospheres: Affect and Agency of Mobile Digital Images in the Material Transformation of the Urban Landscape in Doha', *Tasmeem*, 4 (2014): 1–14; Gillian Rose, Monica Degen and Clare Melhuish, 'Networks, Interfaces, and Computer-Generated Images: Learning from Digital Visualisations of Urban Redevelopment Projects', *Environment and Planning D: Society and Space*, 32 (3) (2014): 386–403; and 'Heritage and Renewal in Doha', *Urban Pamphleteer #4*, 2014, edited by Clare Melhuish, Ben Campkin and Rebecca Ross.

8 William J. Craig, Trevor M. Harris and Daniel Weiner (eds.), *Community Participation and Geographical Information Systems* (London and New York: Taylor & Francis: 2002).

18

SEEING IS BELIEVING

The social life of urban decay and rebirth

Photo biography Visual analysis Archival interpretation

Wes Aelbrecht

17 ↑ 147

What can an in-depth analysis of a photograph reveal of the complexity of urban renewal? Furthermore, what methods can we use to unravel such a history through the study of photographs? Used for research, educational and promotional purposes, photographs offer a window into the visual discourse of urban renewal. In other words, following Gillian Rose's definition of discourse analysis, they offer us insight into 'the discursive production of some kind of authoritative account … [and] the social practices in which that production is embedded and which it itself produces'.[1] Because photography is a medium for mass communication, easily reproduced, disseminated and affective in multiple contexts, it lends itself well to examine the discourse on urban reform. Photographs, I argue, help explain how a discourse of urban renewal was constructed and how the idea of renewal took hold in the minds of a whole population, shaping as such the citizens' urban imaginary. Contrary to certain modes of art history where the focus is placed on what lies behind and beyond the image surface, the method proposed here emphasises instead the visual and material exchange(s) produced in the sites of production, consumption and audiencing.[2] The discussion centres on the politics of representing the city as well as the visual evocation of the city.[3] Only one photograph is discussed (one which uses visual contrast to make an argument), allowing for an in-depth empirical analysis on its 'life' and on visual exchanges between the city and its citizens.

On 26 September 1951, one the most well-known female urban-renewal photographers of Chicago, Mildred Mead, pointed her camera at the demolition and construction site of the new Illinois Institute of Technology (IIT) campus on the South Side of Chicago. Little did she know that the resulting photograph *Urban Decay and Rebirth* would become one of the most successful depictions of Chicago's urban renewal story (1940s—60s).[4] Whether the photograph was enlarged and hung in ballrooms, performed and projected in dark school refectories or community rooms, exhibited in housing exhibitions or published in reports and schoolbooks, from the mid-1950s it came to represent and influence Chicago's urban-redevelopment programmes in multiple ways. When the historian Arnold Hirsch picked up the image for publication in his path-breaking work *Making the Second Ghetto* in 1983, he emphasised the instability of the signifiers of 'old' and 'new' in Mead's photograph. Instead of a pathway to civilisation he reversed the 1950s narrative of progress and stated, 'A new Illinois Institute of Technology dormitory looms behind the lone survivor on a nearby block.'[5]

In the face of the photograph's constant reappearances and the different meaning-making processes, albeit in different contexts and formats, the question we have to ask is, 'What was the role of this image (and other visual images and methods) in the promotion and execution of one of the largest programmes to transform the urban landscape in the twentieth century in the United States?' By placing photographs of renewal and decline at the centre of postwar renewal culture, I approach them as primary research material and debunk the idea that whole collections of photographs produced and disseminated by citywide organisations and the City of Chicago merely illustrate, rather than help to produce, a historical moment in the urban development of Chicago. Most studies of this turbulent period focus on the legal frameworks and planning policies, or racial and social segregation, neglecting how photography was intertwined with and shaped the culture of renewal and demolition from the 1940s to the 1960s. If, as the Women's Council for City Renewal (one of the organisations Mead volunteered for) argues, 'seeing is believing', we must investigate and try to know what citizens needed to believe in front of these images and subsequently the city.[6]

As reproducible and malleable mediators of meaning, photographs are suitable carriers of utopian and dystopian messages of redevelopment. In that sense, you could say that photography is one of the key contributors to the construction of 'the imaginary', in other words, to the formation of a culture or shared mental life, which in this case we could refer to as an 'urban imaginary' or 'place imaginary'.[7] Like the 'social imaginary', this offers a 'widely shared sense of legitimacy' and can thus be a useful tool in any redevelopment project.[8] Faced with boxes of photographs in dusty and local archives in Chicago, what I did is what the visual anthropologist Elizabeth Edwards calls 'a social biography of the photograph'.[9] In it, the photograph is seen as an object 'in a continuing process of meaning, production, exchange and usage'.[10] Investigating how the image was produced, who displayed and disseminated it and in which contexts can reveal further exchanges between the image, the city and the citizens of Chicago.

It's no coincidence that this particular photograph came to fame during the mid-1950s, only four years after Mead photographed the clearance of the designated blighted areas around IIT in the South Side of Chicago for the Metropolitan Housing and Planning Council's (MHPC's) photographic collection of the city's reconstruction and clearance projects and one year after the federal government implemented the federal Housing Act of 1954. Like the Housing Act of 1949, this Act extended the unprecedented powers and public funding to purchase and demolish or revitalise large tracts and sell it to private developers for redevelopment. As opposed to the total demolition and rebuilding of the Housing Act of 1949, the 1954 Act demolition was only employed on 'a limited, surgical basis' in order 'to preserve and revitalize existing neighborhoods as physically and socially viable units'.[11] As part of a workable programme, required under the new legislation, the local agency was obliged to submit a detailed report on property improvements and 'the methods to be used in eliciting community cooperation for neighborhood conservation activities'.[12] This meant that the local agency must explain the objectives of rehabilitation, offer information and counselling services, develop organised neighbourhood support and maintain a continuing action programme to involve neighbourhood owners, tenants and business concerns.[13] As the photograph emerged more prominently on the scene at a moment when these acts were implemented,

Mildred Mead, *Urban Decay and Rebirth,* 26 September 1951. Source: University of Chicago Photographic Archive, Special Collections Research Center, University of Chicago Library. Photo: University of Chicago.

30 → 249

17 ↑ 147

we can ask if and how this particular photograph assisted in gathering support to apply for Housing Acts funds; in other words, to combat blight versus the 'run away' strategy.[14]

Chicago's dominant urban renewal narrative is depicted in the pictorial space of the photograph by the juxtaposition between old and new, between a Victorian house on the left and the newly built student residence at IIT on the right. It is the juxtaposition as a visual technique used by Mead, and further exploited in the use and dissemination of the image, that determined the iconic qualities of the image and subsequently its impact on the minds of the Chicagoan. From the nineteenth century onwards, juxtapositions have been a recurrent stylistic device in all genres of photography (and drawing, such as in Augustus Pugin's *Contrasts*, 1836) — and are affective in that sharp contrasts can create implicit statements and conclusions. This is specifically evident in how the viewer is guided in her reading of the image which moves from the centre of the pictorial space, in this case located on the left side in the dilapidated house where a lady in the doorway peeks into the house, to the newly built block in the second plane, placed deeper in the pictorial space. Because of this diagonal reading, and the placement of the newly built student residence in the second plane, at the end of the perspectival line, the residential block becomes an object the viewer longs for. She is forced to see the new through the old and is, as such, persuaded that the new can only be achieved through the erasure of the old. The other citywide campaigns mostly organised by the MHPC in cooperation with Chicago's housing coordinator and the City Plan Commission provide clues as to how to get from point A to point B, from old to new, from decay to rebirth.

The visualisation of this movement from old to new was exploited in the Housing Exhibit of 1954 in the Chicago Public Library, organised by the Housing Coordinator, D. E. Mackelmann, in cooperation with the MHPC, between two highly constructed photographic panels: 'This is our problem' on the left, aligned with the dilapidated house, versus 'This is our pride' on the right, adjacent the IIT student housing.[15] Because of the centrality of the *Urban Decay and Rebirth* image, the two panels on the left and right appear to extend and emphasise the juxtaposition represented in the photographic frame of the old-and-new photograph. 'This is our problem' is presented by images of dirty bathrooms, dangerous alleys filled with garbage, playgrounds and traffic congestion, categories the city defined further in the exhibit as 'blight'. 'This is our pride' was presented by modernist construction. This was the first attempt to load the old and the new of the image in a library. The second attempt followed quickly in 1955 when the photograph was enlarged and suspended above the main speakers of the MHPC's annual luncheon on the belvedere of a large ballroom next to the American flag, visible to all invitees from the city's administration and neighbourhood groups.[16] Written at the bottom of the photograph were the words, 'The challenge ... and the response', re-emphasising the juxtaposition of the old and the new. The presence of the American flag adjacent lends some authority to the photograph, symbolising a demand for unification under the flag and, as such, the urban-renewal projects presented in the photograph. The quest for a community of blight-fighters is extended with the words 'Chicago All-American Cities' placed on the other side of the photograph. It refers to the 1954 All-American Cities Award Chicago received 'in recognition of progress achieved through intelligent citizen action'.[17] The prize was awarded for the community efforts of Hyde Park — Kenwood Community Conference and the South-East Chicago Commission in the '56 square miles of "middle-aged" neighborhoods [that] are fast becoming slums'.[18] Although not directly related to conservation efforts of community groups, the redevelopment of the IIT was linked to the award here. The first time someone linked this award to the IIT redevelopment was the *Chicago Daily News* by featuring the photograph as the headline for the All-American City award article in the *Daily News*, 'Chicago Slum Clearance, An ... Example for the Nation'.[19] Other links were also suggested by offering flyers to the guest at the annual lunch in which a large map was included showing blight in the city of Chicago. The photograph became, as such, a visualisation of the mapped blighted areas. Linking national pride through the award and the American flag enforces the idea that citizens could indeed 'stand and fight' and clear the blight made visible in the map.

From 1955 onwards, the picture featured most prominently in the slide programme *This Is My City* composed, distributed and screened by the Women's Council for City Renewal, a citywide non-profit organisation working together with MHPC. As the opening slide, *Urban Decay and Rebirth* conveys a message of hope and progress and urges the many local community leaders and other city officials to act fast.[20] Sixty-eight slides with matching commentary, launched at schools, community centres, conferences and public libraries projected what kind of a city Chicago was and could be in the future and how the activities of government agencies and citizen groups contributed to better and 'decent' housing.[21] This was the second time that 'the courageous "stand and fight" policy' of the IIT to battle the spread of blight and slums was praised by the MHPC, thus demonstrating that if communities came together as requested by the 1954 Housing Act it was possible to 'save the city'.[22] In Mayor Daley's 1956 housing exhibition, *Chicago's Roads to Renewal*, the image becomes the principal hangout board.[23]

Although *Urban Decay and Rebirth* is only one of the many blight and success photographs collected and classified during urban renewal by Mead and other Chicago photographers for citywide groups such as the MHPC and the Women's Council for Urban Renewal, it is one of the most iconic. By tracing the social life of *Urban Decay and Rebirth*, the purpose of my contribution here is to highlight what one can unearth about a much discussed programme of urban redevelopment when the focus of the research shifts attention towards the photographs and their use in campaigns to gain political power. The timing of the photograph's success, its particular framing and use of juxtaposition, its dissemination in various events addressing each time different audiences, all gave agency to the photograph and forced Chicagoans to see the city as a place in need of redevelopment and thus to stand up and take up arms against blight. For that purpose, the city needed to be seen as divided into blighted and non-blighted areas, which is what the photograph does so strikingly.

1 Gillian Rose, *Visual Methodologies: An Introduction to the Interpretation of Visual Materials*, 2nd edn (London and Thousand Oaks, CA: Sage, 2007), 142.
2 Victor Burgin, *Thinking Photography* (London: Macmillan, 1982), 11. For a discussion on the different cycles of production, circulation and consumption, see Rose, *Visual Methodologies*.
3 For a discussion in these two modes of using visual imagery representing and evoking the city, see Gillian Rose, 'Visual Culture, Photography and the Urban: An Inerpretive Framework', *Space and Culture, India*. http://spaceandculture.in/index.php/spaceandculture/article/view/92 (accessed 14 October 2015).
4 The first time she photographed this house on the future IIT site was on 26 March 1951. She stored two of the photographs in an archive and classified them as 'Slum Contrasted with New Housing'. See Metropolitan Planning Council Records, '3115 Wabash Avenue, Referred to as S-1-200 and S-1-201'. Not dated, Box 703, Photographs, The Special Collections and University Archives, University of Illinois at Chicago. Although Mead wrote on the backside of the photographs 'From 32nd and Wabash to Michigan Ave., IIT dormitory', I will refer to the photograph as *Urban Decay and Rebirth*. See University of Chicago Photographic Archive, Special Collections Research Center, University of Chicago Library.
5 Arnold R. Hirsch, *Making the Second Ghetto: Race and Housing in Chicago, 1940–1960* (Cambridge: Cambridge University Press, 1983), 118.
6 Women's Joint Committee on Adequate Housing, *Annual Report*, Chicago, IL: The Committee, 1947–9, 7. The Women's Joint Committee on Adequate Housing changed name in 1954 to Women's Council for City Renewal. See Metropolitan Planning Council Records, 'Tomorrow's Chicago', vol. VIII, no. 2. 1954, Box 108, Folder 982, The Special Collections and University Archives, University of Illinois at Chicago.
7 Claudia Strauss, 'The Imaginary', *Anthropological Theory*, 6 (3) (2006): 322–44, 322. For 'the urban imaginary', see Alev Cinar and Thomas Bender, *Urban Imaginaries: Locating the Modern City* (Minneapolis, MN: University of Minnesota Press, 2007); Sharon Zukin, *Landscapes of Power: From Detroit to Disney World* (Berkeley, CA: University of California Press, 1991). For 'place imaginaries', see Ben Campkin, *Remaking London: Decline and Regeneration in Urban Culture* (London: I.B.Tauris, 2013).
8 Charles Taylor, *Modern Social Imaginaries* (Durham, NC: Duke University Press, 2007), 23.
9 Elizabeth Edwards, 'Material Beings: Objecthood and Ethnographic Photographs', *Visual Studies*, 17 (1) (2002): 67–75, 73.
10 Edwards, 'Material Beings'.
11 Columbia Law Review Association, 'Citizen Participation in Urban Renewal', *Columbia Law Review*, 66 (3) (1966): 485–607, 487.
12 Columbia Law Review Association, 'Citizen Participation in Urban Renewal'.
13 Columbia Law Review Association, 'Citizen Participation in Urban Renewal', 496–7.
14 In the end, it boiled down to what Henry T. Heald, the Director of IIT responsible for the construction of the new campus, had preached in the mid-1940s: 'We have two choices – either to run away from the blight or to stand and fight' (newspaper article). Thomas Buck, 'Heald Proposes 4 Steps to End Chicago Slums', *Chicago Daily Tribune*, 18 October 1946.
15 See Archival Photographic Files. Mildred Mead Photographs. 'Housing Exhibit of 1954'. 1954, Box 2, Folder 11, Special Collections Research Center, University of Chicago Library.
16 See Archival Photographic Files. Mildred Mead Photographs. 'Housing Council Luncheon for People Important in Housing'. 1955, Box 3, Folder 1, Special Collections Research Center, University of Chicago Library.
17 See Pamphlet 'Preventing Tomorrow's Slums'. Metropolitan Planning Council Records, 'Preventing Tomorrow's Slums'. 1954, Box 115, Folder 1075, The Special Collections and University Archives, University of Illinois at Chicago.
18 Jack Star, 'The National Municipal League and Look Salute the All-American Cities', *Look*, 8 February 1955.
19 Chicago Slum Clearance, an ... Example for the Nation', *Chicago Daily News*, 17 January 1955.
20 Metropolitan Planning Council Records. 'Slide "This Is My City"', 1955–62, Box 723, Series VIII: Audio/Visual, The Special Collections and University Archives, University of Illinois at Chicago.
21 Metropolitan Planning Council Records. 'Script for Slide Program "This Is My City" Set 1'. 1955–62, Box 722, Series VIII: Audio/Visual, The Special Collections and University Archives, University of Illinois at Chicago.
22 Metropolitan Planning Council Records. 'Script for Slide Program "This Is My City" Set 1'.
23 Archival Photographic Files. Mildred Mead Photographs. '1956 Mayor Daley's Housing Exhibit'. 1956, Box 2, Folder 12, Special Collections Research Center, University of Chicago Library.

19

WE THOUGHT WE WERE MAKING THE CAR BUT IT WAS THE OTHER WAY AROUND

Historical pathways and the ecology of the street network in industrial and post-industrial Detroit

Sophia Psarra

Computer modelling Mapping Morphology

In the early 1920s, Detroit was a boomtown propelled by innovations in the car industry, which transformed the city, and Western societies for that matter, through mass production. After Henry Ford's development of the Model-T in Highland Park, the standardised assembly line revolutionised industrial manufacturing. The economic and institutional innovations triggered by these transformations meant a break with the past, radically reshaping space and society. Fordism also came along as a new way of life: cars brought the prosperity that enabled people to move out of the city seeking a 'better' life. In the 1950s, Detroit pioneered the construction of motorways, which cut through urban neighbourhoods, connecting the city centre with the growing suburbs. With time, however, the relocation of Detroit's commercial activities, factories, businesses and shops to the city's periphery left an impoverished urban core, with unemployment, vast wastelands and industrial-age ruins behind. Fordism was followed by post-Fordism, spawning a period of more diversified industrial production and the rise of the services and knowledge economy, combined with the emergence of global markets.[1] Even though these changes affected many Western cities, they were most powerful and consequential in the 'motor city'. After its population peaked at nearly 2 million in the 1950s, Detroit has lost over 60 per cent of its inhabitants. In 2013, it became the largest US city ever to file for bankruptcy.[2] Today, the fate of public services for the 700,000 residents of Detroit remains uncertain. Urban decay gives an impression of large-scale destruction, with ruins, empty plots and decrepit infrastructures.

From academic articles to newspapers reports, Detroit's predicament is depicted as a total catastrophe brought about by diverse social and economic factors: this is what happens, they say, when mono-industries collapse and severe deindustrialisation takes its toll. Car ownership becomes the only type of transport, access to the housing market becomes racialised, and car dependence produces forms of spatial segregation between privileged and unprivileged neighbourhoods across the urban–suburban divide.[3] But to consider Detroit's trajectory as solely determined by socio-economic decline means to ignore the network of streets and its generic ability to provide access to a whole range of services and enterprise.

The analysis I present here stems from this realisation that all accounts of Detroit neglect the evolution of incremental systems of physical, economic and social infrastructure.[4] Like every urban process, industrialisation and suburbanisation in Detroit was facilitated by the street network, an interface that connects every building to a plot of land, to a street, to other buildings, other blocks and streets proceeding hand in hand with railways, freeways, commercial exchanges, corporate enterprises, municipal taxes, regulations, services and the ideologies that motivate the spatial distribution of resources and people. The argument that we develop through the Detroit study is that while capitalism drove the city, it was the infrastructural ecology of its streets that provided the foundation for changes to occur throughout the phases of Fordist growth and post-Fordist decline.

In our exploration of Detroit, we intertwine two types of research: one follows the history of Detroit's urbanisation in the first half of the twentieth century, and its suburbanisation between 1952 and 2010; the second is an analysis of the street network and socio-economic activity facilitated by it through computer modelling and digital mapping (Depthmap software used in space syntax research and GIS).[5] The purpose of the combined historical and morphological analysis is to avoid simplistic notions of causality, exploring instead the complexities

Detroit 1921, industrial distribution, streetcar system and main arteries of movement, 'choice' network analysis at radius 1,000 metres. 'Choice' is a space syntax measure also known as 'betweenness centrality' in graph theory, and it captures through-movement, that is, the simplest paths that are most frequently used in order to move between any pair of streets in an urban complex.

that link the specific urban morphology with the industrial, economic and social histories of the city. From an epistemological point of view, the combined study moves away from a priori concepts of capitalism, modernity, Fordism and the like, learning to read the street network as an infrastructure through which such phenomena were shaped in their territorial context. Our work's originality is, first, that it offers an analysis of the evolution of infrastructural networks in the Fordist and post-Fordist city of Detroit, which has not been previously analysed; second, it explains these networks in the context of historical and socio-economic information; third, and more generally, it establishes multiple connections in the fields of architecture, planning, social science and space syntax as a way to describe the ontological status of cities.

13 ↑ 117

Detroit 1952, 'choice' network analysis at radius 1,000 metres with industry superimposed.

Our analysis reveals that in the 1920s, industry, streetcar transportation and retail settled along global arteries of movement linking the city core with the expanding urban fabric. These routes formed the interface between industrial development, commercial activity and the streetcar system, which transported Detroiters to factories for work and to downtown districts for shopping and leisure. From the 1950s, the street network increasingly lost its capacity to integrate urban social and economic functions. Streetcars were eliminated while the freeways enabled industry, retail and housing to relocate. Despite this relocation, industrial zoning did not change, consolidating itself into linear zones that were multiple blocks wide.[6] The motorways and the industrial landscape

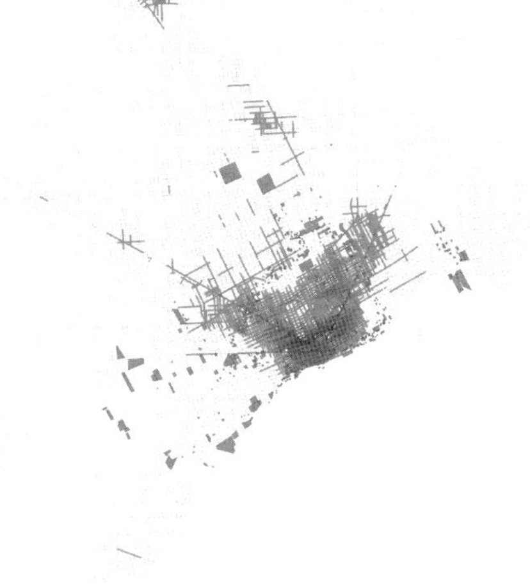

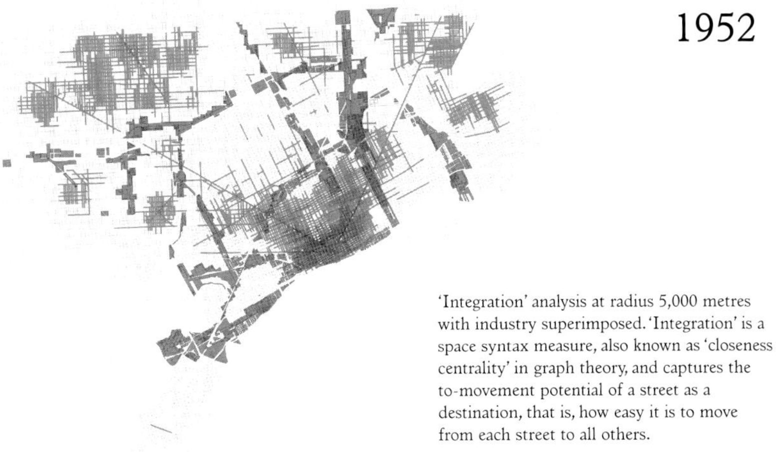

'Integration' analysis at radius 5,000 metres with industry superimposed. 'Integration' is a space syntax measure, also known as 'closeness centrality' in graph theory, and captures the to-movement potential of a street as a destination, that is, how easy it is to move from each street to all others.

13 ↑ 117

Detroit 2010, metropolitan region, 'choice' network analysis at radius 10,000 metres with commercial land uses superimposed.

disrupted the street network, breaking local neighbourhoods and segregating them from one another.[7]

Looking at the distribution of retail in the second period of study, we see two patterns emerging: first, commercial strips along the Jeffersonian supergrid, which is a consistent typology across the American landscape; second, large shopping malls and 'edge cities' (business centres) within a short distance from freeways. These patterns of distribution show an emergent social geography of discrimination and mass consumption based on large-scale traffic.[8] This is because shopping malls and business centres are accessible only by car owners and are located in the larger metropolitan region outside the city. As a result, a large percentage of deprived populations currently living inside Detroit have limited access to services and retail. As to the street network in the city of Detroit, this is broken by industrial ruins

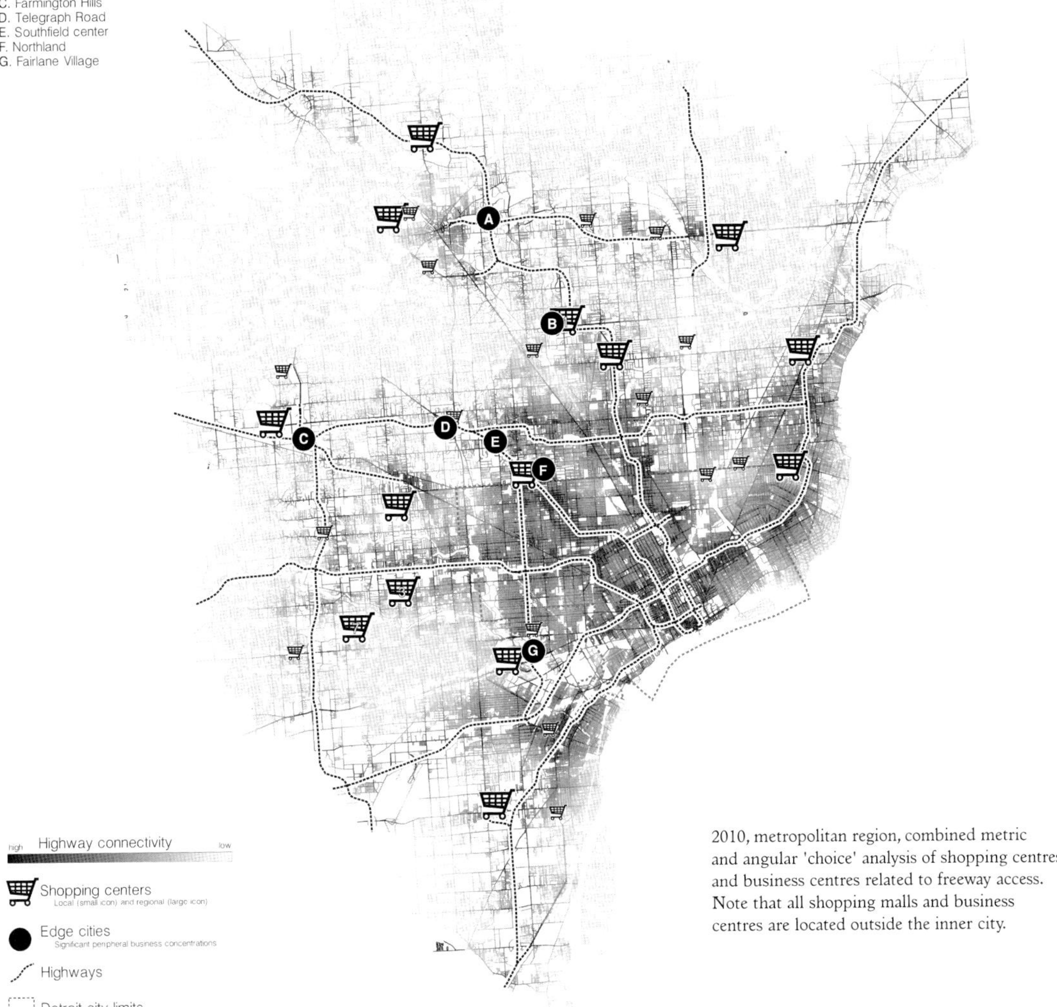

2010, metropolitan region, combined metric and angular 'choice' analysis of shopping centres and business centres related to freeway access. Note that all shopping malls and business centres are located outside the inner city.

and freeway conduits of high velocity movement. It has gradually lost its social and economic functionality, a fact that manifests itself visibly through disused infrastructure and obsolescence.

At the turn of the twentieth century, Detroiters thought that they were making the car. A few generations later, they discovered that it was the other way around: the car was making them, and their city. To discover Detroit as it once was is like the job of an archaeologist; one needs to imagine what once stood on empty land and abandoned industrial grounds. By looking at the evolution of infrastructural networks and the ways in which they formed an interface for social and economic activity, our analysis resembles archaeological work. We 'excavate' the spatial morphology of the city, its environmental data and physical remains in a way that allows us to explain society and human activity in the past and the present.

Our assumption is that the traces of the former city are embedded in these networks, and our job is to reveal them.

Yet, more important than to excavate the city as it was is to imagine its future through the insertion of new productive economies, new buildings and forms of inhabiting. Space Syntax modelling reveals the social and economic potential of the street network through its capacity to form an interface between generic movement and movement-seeking activities, that is, those activities that benefit from 'passing trade'.[9] Thus, it points to steps on the design process that can enable individuals and social groups to obtain better access to resources. However, Detroit's challenges are not just problems to solve, they are also design opportunities for the city to learn from. Grass-roots initiatives currently taking place in the city provide possibilities for people to reimagine Detroit in informal and co-operative ways.[10] The street network discussed here is part of a larger ecological network in which human and spatial parameters fuse and shape the city through practices and strategies of interaction, from citizen participation, urban planning and spatial organisation to real-estate regulation, and so on, mutually constituting each other.[11] Architects, planners, Space Syntax researchers, communities and organisations, spaces, buildings, technologies, documents, formulae and tools are all active participants in the networks and processes that make up the city and its social fabric. For us, the challenge for future work is to follow the interlinked trajectories of the street network with other networks so as to describe identities, occurrences, events and operations in a fine-grained dynamic cartography, making the spatial and social distribution of resources (and hence, power) representable, shareable and debatable.

1 Peter Drucker, *The Age of Discontinuity: Guidelines to Our Changing Society* (New York: Harper & Row, 1969). David Harvey, *The Condition of Postmodernity* (Malden, MA, and Oxford: Blackwell Publishing, 1990).
2 Jonathan Schifferes, 'Political Geography Bankrupted Detroit'. http://www.rsablogs.org.uk/2013/social-economy/political-geography-bankrupted-detroit (accessed 24 July 2014).
3 As Reinhold Martin explains, developers in partnership with government imposed deed restrictions to housing markets. Reinhold Martin, 'Fundamental #13: Real Estate as Infrastructure as Architecture', *Design Observer*, 12 May 2014, accessed 24 July 2014. https://placesjournal.org/article/fundamental-13/?fb_action_ids=10200886370481359&fb_action_types=og.likes&fb_ref=.U4h0HDCM1Ng.like (accessed 23 November 2015). Sprawl did not occur naturally. It was subsidised and legally mandated, the result of zoning, legislation and lobbying. Charles Montgomery, *Happy City: Transforming Our Lives through Urban Design* (London: Penguin Books, 2013).
4 The work was initiated in collaboration with Conrad Kickert in the University of Michigan but was first presented in Cities Methodologies, 2011 in London. Subsequently, it was extended in conjunction with Conrad Kickert and Amanda Pluviano through two publications.
5 Alasdair Turner, 'Angular Analysis', in John Peponis, Jean Wineman and Sonit Bafna (eds.), *Proceedings of the Third International Space Syntax Symposium* (Atlanta, GA: Georgia Institute of Technology, 2001), 30.1–11; Bill Hillier and Julienne Hanson, *The Social Logic of Space* (Cambridge: Cambridge University Press, 1984).
6 Amanda Pluviano and Sophia Psarra, 'Turin and Detroit: The Role of the Road Network in the Evolution of the Industrial and Post-Industrial City, 1920–2010', in *New Urban Configurations*, edited by Roberto Cavallo, Susanne Komossa, Nicola Marzot and Meta Berghauser Pont (Amsterdam: IOS Press under the imprint Delft University, 2014), 393–401.
7 Sophia Psarra, Conrad Kickert and Amanda Pluviano, 'Paradigm Lost: Industrial and Post-Industrial Detroit – An Analysis of the Street Network and Its Social and Economic Dimensions from 1796 to the Present', *Urban Design International*, 18 (4) (2013): 257–81.
8 Psarra et al., 'Paradigm Lost'.
9 The argument put forward by Hillier and colleagues is that in contrast to the idea that land uses are the sole attractors of movement, the urban network privileges certain spaces over others for through-movement and flows. Combined with the street network, retail land uses, which take advantage of the opportunities offered by passing trade, act as multipliers of movement. Bill Hillier, Alan Penn, Julienne Hanson and Tadeusz Grajewski, 'Natural Movement; or, Configuration and Attraction in Urban Pedestrian Movement', *Environment and Planning B: Planning and Design*, 20 (1) (1993): 29–66.
10 Andrew Herscher, 'The Unreal Estate Guide to Detroit', *Design Observer*, 27 November 2012 (accessed 14 September 2014). https://placesjournal.org/article/the-unreal-estate-guide-to-detroit (accessed 23 November 2015).
11 We derive inspiration from actor network theory, which suggests that non-human actors such as spaces and spatial networks play an active role in cities and the world. See Bruno Latour, *Reassembling the Social: An Introduction to Actor-Network Theory* (Oxford: Oxford University Press, 2005).

V

Embodied Cartographies

20

LEBENSRAUM | LIVING SPACE

Diary writing   Public reading   Mobile performance

Ger Duijzings and Rastko Novaković

3 ↑ 35

Lebensraum/Living Space was an exchange between an anthropologist and an artist, a three-year long experimental project which we carried out between 2007 and 2009. It was based on the diary Ger had kept in 1992 while doing fieldwork in war-torn Yugoslavia, which through a creative process initiated and moderated by Rastko evolved into an eighty-minute experimental movie exploring the themes of war and displacement, private and public memory, geopolitics and the everyday. The film is based on Ger's public reading of his diary (that is, a stripped-down version of it), while walking the streets of London. It is edited from seven continuous and simultaneous video-recordings of that single performance. Originating in experiences of violence and war in another part of the world, the performance was by the same token a public commentary on London as a site of geopolitical conflict.

One of the film's key features is the radical disjunction between the soundtrack and the moving images, between what one hears (fragments from a diary relating to events in the former Yugoslavia in 1992) and what one sees, the route taken by the performer through the urban and physical landscape of an area around central London's Euston Station in 2008. The work breaks with standard practices and conventions of how wars are represented in the mass media, academia and film, through the typical (and iconic) images and stories of horror and suffering that ultimately distance voyeuristic (including academic) audiences from the traumatic impacts of these events. It also breaks with the conventions of media and film production that compartmentalise pre-production, production and post-production: Ger, as the author of the diary, becomes performer of the script and is also involved in the film's editing, roles which are normally carried out by different sets of people.

Here we describe the stages of this project: the reading of the diary, the writing of the script, the soundscape research, the call for participation in filming, how we determined the route of the performance, the rehearsals, the filming and editing process, the various modes in which the script and the audio and visual material from the shoot were exhibited and used at screenings and during re-enactments, provoking diverse responses from different audiences. We stress the open-ended and visceral character of the project,

Stills from the film: different ways of organising video and textual material.

and we also show how London, itself scarred by violence in its own recent and more remote past, became the canvas on which it inscribed itself. This essay makes explicit our critique of conventional practices of representation of wars and cities, and of wars in cities, applying methods and protocols that are marginal in anthropology and film-making.

It all started when Rastko approached Ger with the proposition of exploring material that had not made it into a book Ger had written, *Religion and the Politics of Identity in Kosovo*.[1] Hence we agreed to take a detailed look at his diary, covering six months of anthropological fieldwork from March to August 1992, a small black hardcover notebook packed with neat (mostly Dutch) script. The reading of the diary, in Ger's office and in other locations across London, took several months. The result was twenty-five hours of sound recordings.

The diary is horizontal in character and displays a paratactic syntax, a presentation side by side, in short and simple sentences without order or hierarchy. It is written in the first and third person as there are dozens of people figuring in the diary, the people Ger meets or hears about during his fieldwork itineraries. It tells their stories from the perspective of an outsider who is part insider as he speaks the language (Serbo-Croatian). It makes the everyday of the violent break-up of Yugoslavia tangible through the experiences of random individuals, encountering a host of stories and destinies to which the overarching hegemonic historical accounts are usually indifferent.

Rastko wrote a transcript of the recordings and cut the text down to 7,500 words. He kept an entry for each day and changed the names to protect identities. The script moves between mundane (domestic and public) environments, police checkpoints and academic institutions. It describes Serbia's descent into militarisation and war, the growing paranoia and intolerance and, last but not least, the involuntary displacement of the majority of the population of the Croat village in which Ger was doing his fieldwork in the summer of 1992. The diary is brief and matter-of-fact, it does not dramatise things. It touches on the snippets of the everyday life of around 170 distinct people Ger encounters. The narrator himself is an everyman who is gradually emptied of his own story to let others in.

After Ger polished the script, he began rehearsing it on London's streets. The route was determined through an urban sound map created by sound designer Mark Durham that captured the metropolitan hustle and bustle and paid attention to sites of violence that had affected London in the past: Tavistock Square (site of one of the 7 July 2005 terrorist attacks), Euston station (hit by a German bomb in 1940), Drummond Street (the heart of the Asian community with a legacy of police brutality, gang violence and racist attacks) and Regent's Park (where the Provisional Irish Republican Army blew up a bandstand in 1982, killing six soldiers from the Royal Green Jackets). The sound research and the choice of the route along these locations cancelled the idea of the city as a silent and empty stage or neutral backdrop for Ger's performance: as Ger was to step out of his office to testify about violence in former Yugoslavia, he followed the grooves of war and conflict in London.

Next, Rastko sent out a closed call for participation to film-makers, film historians, theorists, curators, archivists, critical theorists, publicists, photographers, researchers, architects and psychoanalysts to participate in the filming of the performance. The call included a copy of the script, an outline of the process so far and the instruction to shoot the performance along the route for one hour continuously. Eight people confirmed, seven were to shoot video and one photographs. Rastko instructed participants to focus on a number of features and themes: first, devices and structures employed to control urban flows, on architectural rhetoric and surveillance structures; second, on the camera, the audio-visual record it produces and its potential non-human agency; and third, on the gestures, movements and rhythm of bodies, of the group filming and of those encountered on the way. He also prohibited the use of zooming so as to preserve the physical and spatial relationships between the cameras and impressed upon the participants the idea that there is not one focal point or 'stage'. The negotiation of traffic, pedestrians and officials was left to their initiative and judgement.

If you went to an actor and said, 'Here is a script and you are going to do it in one take, one chance to get it right, 75 minutes', he or she would say: 'You are crazy. This is impossible.' Since Ger is not a performer, he was able to do it, on a second-by-second

22 → 187

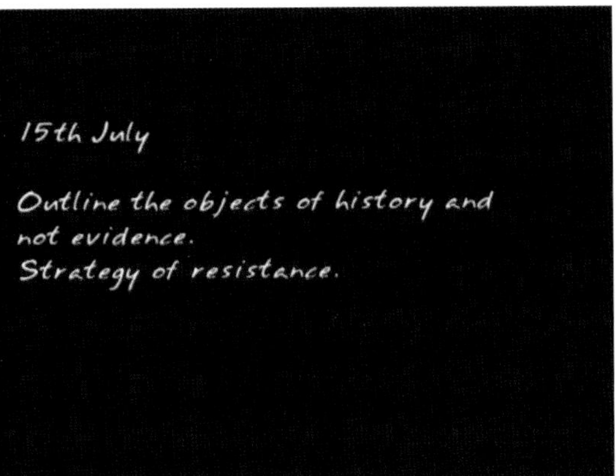

tightrope with all its stutters, mistakes and epiphanies, switching between immersion in the peripatetic reading of the script and his gaze focusing on something in the surrounding space. The dates in the diary provided the punctuation. Ger focused on reading the text and navigating the traffic without getting run over (although he once hit a signpost). The filming of the actual performance was akin to a procession, a paparazzi fest or SWAT team moving through the city, provoking different responses from the confused public, some of whom 'recognised' the celebrity that passed by surrounded by cameras.

With the rehearsals and the performance in public space, we turned to the procedural register of reading out loud and walking. It triggered in Ger memories which had not been there during his first reading of the diary in the office and other venues across London. Walking as a form of embodied and tactile understanding brings new, previously hidden, memories to the surface. Ger leaves his office, a sensory-deprivation chamber where he keeps his books and fieldwork archive, and confronts Londoners with the war he carries in him through an embodied act of walking and speaking. He articulates his experiences, which influences the ways in which he moves through the city, perceives the city and interacts with people in the city. He turns his internal archive of memories inside out.

The viewer who watches the movie makes his or her own associations; in the end, it is the same reaction we ourselves have when walking through an urban environment, recalling our memories, responding to spaces we inhabit and through which we transit, giving meaning to them on the basis of previous experiences and recollections, many of which may take us beyond the immediate context of London. While taking in the material images of London, what one realises is the utter physicality of London's urban fabric. The multiple simultaneous images of pavements, streets and walls seem to belong to a fly's eye or a number of tentacles feeling their way through a strange and outlandish landscape. Watching the film is a physical experience: you feel sick and want to close your eyes. As the images do not relate to the places mentioned in the script, you can only fully concentrate on what is spoken when you shut your eyes. There are many ways of sitting through this film.

3 ↑ 35

We do not use the conventional techniques of transporting the viewer into another world, through 'local' music, for instance, or the use of archival material. We made the decision not to use any images of the places about which Ger talks. Yugoslavia's dissolution (and London's history of conflicts) are not represented through archival images nor images or sounds from these instances of violence. The work gives no historical information or context. For those who know the context, it adds an extra dimension; for those who don't, it leaves them with snippets of disconnected events.

The defining aspect of the movie is the incongruous juxtaposition of sound and image, the radical disjunction or apparent disconnect between what you hear and what you see. You hear about a past war somewhere else in the world and see the normality of a large city (albeit with a laden past of conflict itself). The tension in this act of dis-location invites the viewers to make 'connections' themselves. The film's intention is indeed to trigger these associations. It breaks the connection between sound and vision and invites the viewer to build them up from scratch, inserting the war-torn Yugoslavia of 1992 and the splinters of its mundane everyday life into the mundane London of 2008.

The paratactic syntax of the diary is retained in the film's form: text, sound and image exist side by side. On the soundtrack, equal importance is given to Ger's voice and breathing, the traffic, the wind and the music in someone's car. On the image track, there is the equality between two (or more) camera viewpoints, one and the other footage running simultaneously, and being switched off and on. Initially, the seven cameras filming continuously and simultaneously are introduced, each camera representing a perspective of its own. There are moments when one camera films another, so you see the construction of these perspectives, takes on takes on takes. Part of the concept for the film was to make the equipment and the process of shooting completely visible. You do see the microphones mounted on Ger's spectacles and all the image-making equipment. The excess of criss-crossing shots is dizzying, a kaleidoscopic experience.

Rastko and editor Owen Saward were then faced with editing seven hours of synchronous footage. Over six months, they sketched out different ways of organising the

22 → 187

Images from the film shoot by Aubrey Wanliss-Orlebar.

raw material: in grids, wipes, layered and in different spatial configurations. A structure of ten sequences emerged. An introductory sequence, then a layout with a six-way grid which is brought down to three images (a split screen against one large background image), then two (layered), then one, then a black screen with dates, then two frames meshing, and then a gradual build-up to seven images, a pixellation sequence and a black screen with only text at the end. The movie is gradually reduced to only the narration, and it builds itself up again, and then once again is reduced to Ger's voice. This process reflects the key central idea behind the work: the tension between the One and the Multitude, between the many voices represented in the diary and Ger's own narrative. The pixellation sequence emerged as a visual summary of the break-up of Yugoslavia: from a complex and pulsating patchwork of colours to the Manichean flaring and flickering of black and white. The repetition of dates on screen reminds the viewer of the diary's pages, a relentless punctuation and visual magnet.

The project was presented at different occasions in various formats, for different audiences, in a variety of different renderings of the material: a collective re-enactment of the script in Kentish Town with a group of rotating performers (Zabludowicz Collection, London, 18 January 2009), a sound piece (Kunsthalle Exnergasse, Vienna, 2010) and screenings of the final movie at Cities Methodologies (2009) and Cities Methodologies Bucharest (2010). This essay seeks another connection with the audience. We are interested in the conversations to be had, breaking down commonplaces and challenging our sense of the spaces around us, our comfort zones.[2]

Finally we come to the highest level on which the work operates: on the level of Lebensraum and living space. The movie can be seen as juxtaposing geopolitical spaces (backed up by armies) where populations are cleansed from territories that are projected to become the Lebensraum for others, with the (unarmed) mundane, personal and subjective places of ordinary people. This dual notion is reflected in the title: Lebensraum (a political territorial project, claiming space) and living space (an inhabited world). The film is necessarily also about dis-placement and dis-location. The diary represents a world in shatters, not a single story but a multitude

3 ↑ 35

of stories. There is no attempt made to 'make up a story' out of what is not a story after all. Here we find Laurence J. Kirmayer's notion of 'landscapes of memory' useful: memories are lived in, offering vistas that reveal and conceal.[3] The metaphor of landscape is relevant as it signifies the immediate physical and social environment inhabited by people. A landscape of memory may inhibit and silence or allow and validate individuals to remember and retell. It determines what is possible and acceptable to speak of, what are the available contexts and templates for stories to be told and retold, and what must remain hidden and unacknowledged because of forced 'amnesia' or indifference. It is the difference between a public space of solidarity and a private space of shame.

1 Ger Duijzings, *Religion and the Politics of Identity in Kosovo* (London: Hurst, 2000).
2 We invite you to watch the film online: https://rastkonovakovic.wordpress.com/2015/02/18/lebensraum-living-space/ (accessed 14 October 2015); or to download the film here: https://archive.org/details/LebensraumLivingSpace (accessed 14 October 2015).
3 Laurence J. Kirmayer, 'Landscapes of Memory: Trauma, Narrative and Dissociation', in *Tense Past: Cultural Essays in Trauma and Memory*, edited by Paul Antze and Michael Lambek (London and New York: Routledge, 1996), 173–98.

21

ABDICATION AND ARRIVAL

Using an open-ended, collaborator-led ethnography to explore constructions of newly encountered cities

Open-ended ethnography   Listening   Embodied practice

Andrew Stevenson

6 → 59

This essay tells the story of what happened when I abandoned my initial research method of choice, that is, participatory photography, to explore the narratives of migrants arriving in a city.[1] Over a period of eighteen months I collaborated with a cohort of six international new arrivals to Manchester and engaged with their processes of making the city meaningful. On researching the question, 'How do new international arrivals develop knowledge of and meaningful attachments to a new city?', I elected, on the advice of one of my participant collaborators ('not everyone takes photographs'), not to impose a photographic method as I had planned. I chose to invite my collaborators to go beyond a pictorial telling of their stories, should they wish. After this abdication of responsibility, the sensory, technological and aesthetic preferences of my collaborators determined the nature of their engagement with my project. An ethnography led by collaborators emerged wherein Manchester, a newly encountered city, was subjectively constructed through mobile, multisensory engagement.[2] As we will learn, the newly arrived collaborators I worked with for this project variously engaged with their new city through sound (listening and recording), images (taking photographs) and embodied practice (walking). The stories I relate in this essay show how two of my collaborators in particular, Alyssa and Bina, used methods of engagement that encompass taste, olfaction and performance — choices based on their own sensory and aesthetic preferences.

This emergent, collaborator-led, ethnographic method saw my collaborators tell stories of arrival using their favoured technologies and methods of getting around. Febi, for example, an acoustician from Indonesia, engaged with Manchester through sound recordings.[3] Andrada, a documentary film-maker from Romania, primarily used pictures, taking photographs and working in a documentary film about the city. By accompanying my collaborators on mobile interviews around the city (on foot, on buses, even on a bicycle in one case), stories emerged in the context of collaborators' preferred method of travel. What follows are two of these arrival stories.

POSTCARDS FROM MAN-TUNIS

Although resident of Manchester for three years, Alyssa spoke fondly of Tunis, her previous home city. In a Mancunian café, she recounted memories of Tunis, evoking a handful of sites in her new city that reminded her of her former home. She offered to walk me through these evocative sites that seemed to join two cities. A fruit market, a Mediterranean restaurant, a doughnut shop and a retro clothes emporium were among the locations we visited. This string of half-Mancunian, half-Tunisian sites led us to coin the term 'Man-Tunis'. So many of these evocations were olfactory.[4] As we wandered, smells and tastes brought memories of Tunis to the surface.

28 → 231

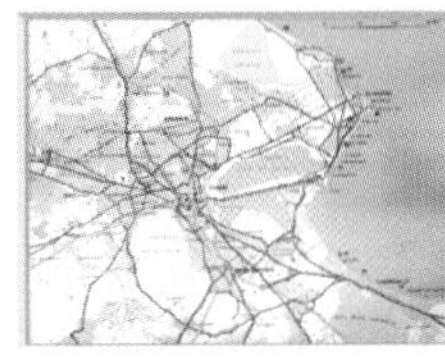

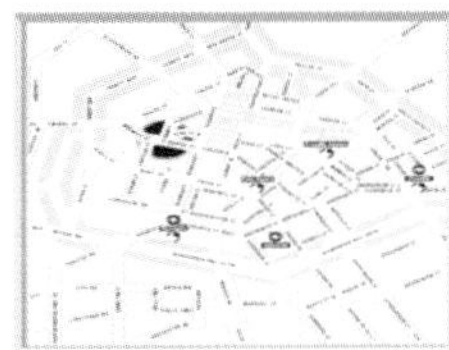

Dmitris, Man-Tunis

I first came to Dmitris the winter before last. It was quite cold and they had these lamps on and you felt like you were in the Mediterranean because you were eating outdoors and you were hot. It was so warm in this little alleyway, which is another thing that is very Mediterranean. In between buildings, it's literally a place between two places, all cobbled alleyways. You get tons of those in Tunis. Places that you walk through to get somewhere else, and in the meantime you can stop in them. You don't get this a lot here. Places are very much separate. This is this shop. This is this thing. You don't get the making use of the alleyways

Alyssa Ordu, *Postcard from Man-Tunis*, 2013. Dmitris Restaurant, Manchester. Alyssa describes the similarities between Dmitris (photographed), Manchester and Tunisian sites she knows.

Man-Tunis, an imagined, memorial city, is commemorated here in a series of picture postcards. Alyssa took the pictures during our walk, and her descriptions of Tunisian sites adorn the reverse of the cards. The postcards deliberately confuse memories and conflate stories. Manchester and Tunis coexist in pictures, words and multisensory (olfactory, gustatory) evocations from sites along our journey. They are a creative engagement with a new place, borne of Alyssa's own memories and her love of food and walking.

MEMORIES OF MAINZ AND MANCHESTER

My collaboration with Bina, from Mainz, Germany, also emerged from emplaced memories. On the day before she left Manchester, where she had been living for six months, she told me she wanted to place three mnemonic objects from Manchester along her return route to Mainz, for me to recover after she had left. Though an unusual idea, my collaborator-led method obliged me to go along with her suggestion and to retrieve Bina's mnemonic objects.

As she promised (see below) Bina buried her first memory of Manchester in Bloomsbury, London, her first port of call on her way home. 'I'm going to leave tomorrow to go to London to visit my friend there, and

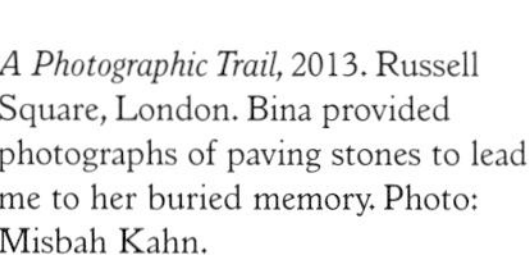
A Photographic Trail, 2013. Russell Square, London. Bina provided photographs of paving stones to lead me to her buried memory. Photo: Misbah Kahn.

then I'm going to go to Germany. So when I'm in London I'm going to bury the first item, near the Gandhi statue. It's sort of a treasure hunt,' she wrote. She provided photographic clues to guide me towards the burial site. The paving-stone trail began at Russell Square underground station. For the purpose of this performative, memorial enactment of place, a small part of Bloomsbury was transformed into a place of bounty, an archive of material memory.[5]

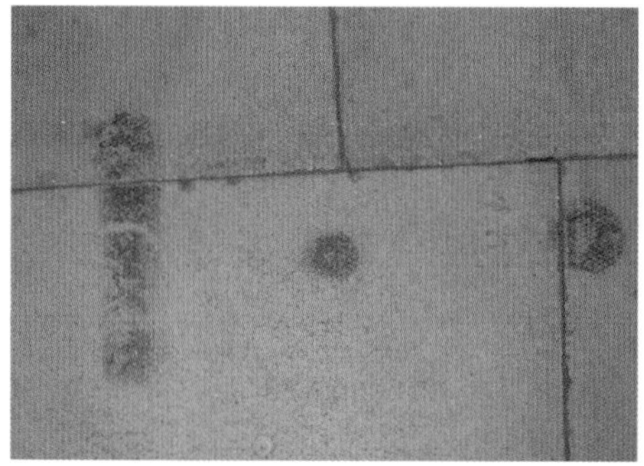

Eight days later, I excavated Bina's first memory. Concealed under a plant pot was an envelope containing a short, melancholy message, telling of experience Bina wished she had had in Manchester, ending with 'I loved travelling around the UK and exploring cities but sometimes I felt sad because I saw a wonderful place alone.'

A Memory of Manchester, 2013. Russell Square, London. I found Bina's buried memory under a plant pot in Russell Square Gardens, London. Photo: Andrew Stevenson.

Bina and I agreed to meet on German soil a few weeks later. I told her when I would arrive in Mainz. Beyond this, the arrangement was loose. I wanted Bina to organise things. This excerpt from my field notes explains what happened next.

> Although she knew my train was due to arrive into Mainz at 16:15, she hadn't actually said she would be there to meet me, so when I didn't see her on the platform, on the escalator, in the subway, in the station forecourt, or by the meeting point under the destination board, I wasn't surprised.

I approached my arrival in Mainz in a spirit of deliberate, contrived unknowing. My method dictated that events should be beyond my control: 'I stood at the main entrance to the station, as disoriented as any new arrival to a city might be, looking out onto Bahnhofplatz for the first time, when a voice over my left shoulder said "Excuse me, this is for you."'

Excuse Me, This Is for You, 2013. Russell Square, London. I received the envelope from a stranger at Mainz railway station. Photo: Andrew Stevenson.

Bina's orchestrated non-appearance was an ingenious performative re-enactment of a memory of her own arrival in a new place. It was delivered by a stranger and received in the form that it was experienced, as Bina explained to me later. She told me how confused and disoriented she had been on arriving in Manchester for the first time and that the only way I could really understand how this felt was to experience it for myself.

Using a map contained in the envelope, I tracked Bina down to one of her favourite cafés, a few blocks away. On the table in front of us were some of the objects Bina had used to construct her Manchester: a photograph of the Bloomsbury package, the envelope from the railway station and a small parcel, wrapped in brown paper, which Bina now presented to me. It contained a brightly decorated egg painted with yellow and black hoops to make it look like a bee. There were two eyes, a little red smile and a hole in the top where the contents of the egg had been blown out to preserve the shell before painting.

Egg Bee, 2013. Mainz, Germany. Bina's decorated egg shows a symbol of Manchester's industrial past: the busy bee. Photo: Andrew Stevenson.

The busy bee, a symbol of Manchester's industrial history, was perhaps the happiest of Bina's three memories. Distancing herself from the city enabled her to construct her own, more positive history of Manchester.

COLLABORATOR-LED ETHNOGRAPHY

The methods I have used during this project emerged from creative, diverse forms of engagement my collaborators used to get to know new places.[6] The essence of the method involves listening and following rather than speaking and leading. It involves the collaborative making of images rather than mere observing and photographing of a passive subject. It requires the collaborator to initiate the work based on their expressive preferences and habitual modes of engagement with place.

Collaborator-led ethnography requires the pursuit of unfamiliar embodied routes and practices. The abdicating ethnographer who expressly invites methods of engagement initiated by the other is committed to following them into new and unfamiliar (if not unknown) places. For example, the busy-bee symbol and the Man-Tunisian postcards were all examples of collaborator-led emplaced knowledge that added to my own engagement with, and de-familiarisation from, Manchester. My own use of this method facilitated more than just my researching of the arrival of my collaborators in their new city. It ushered me into a new approach to research and into the multisensory worlds of others.

1 Sarah Pink, *Doing Visual Ethnography* (London and Thousand Oaks, CA: Sage, 2007).
2 Tim Ingold, *The Perception of the Environment* (London and New York: Routledge, 2000); Sarah Pink, *Doing Sensory Ethnography* (London and New York: Sage, 2009).
3 Andrew Stevenson, 'Manchester through the Ears: Soundscape Compositions by a Newcomer from Bandung', *The Senses and Society*, 8 (2) (2013): 209–22.
4 Jon Holtzman, 'Food and Memory', *Annual Review of Anthropology*, 35 (2006): 361–78.
5 Alan Latham, 'Research, Performance and Doing Human Geography: Some Reflections on the Diary-photograph, Diary-interview Method,' *Environment and Planning A*, 35 (11) (2003): 1993–2017.
6 Latham, 'Research, Performance, and Doing Human Geography', 1993–2017.

22

LEARNING TO WALK

On curating a walking-methodologies programme

ThienVinh Nguyen

Walking Wayfinding Getting lost

20 ↑ 173

When I first moved to London, I explored the city by walking. For my first few weeks, without the use of a smartphone and GPS map app, I relied on drawing maps and writing down directions to get from place to place. In minimising my writing efforts, I would leave out plenty of details, like when one street merged into another with a different name. This practice did fail me on a number of occasions. I also realised that I could not trust the London tube map to provide me with an accurate sense of place in terms of scale, distance or detail. I appreciated stumbling upon public city maps, usually located near hire stations for bikes sponsored at the time by Barclays bank, since they provided me with approximations of time by foot.

In experiencing the city this way, I discovered that it could be magical getting lost: it was through trying to find my way from Liverpool Street station to Islington that I stumbled upon Exmouth Market, with its twinkling Christmas lights, charming brick buildings with big bright windows, and bustling food market. It was then that I learned to appreciate the romantic beauty of London, on a brisk cold day when I started off miserably lost. It was through this practice of walking to explore, and by getting lost, that I learned about the contours and intricacies of the city. This vignette speaks to my initial engagement with philosophising about urban walking.

According to Rebecca Solnit:

> the history of walking is an unwritten, secret history whose fragments can be found in a thousand unemphatic passages in books, as well as in songs, streets, and almost everyone's adventures ... To make walking into an investigation, a ritual, a mediation, is a special subset of walking ... [and] is, in some sense, about how we invest universal acts with particular meanings.[1]

The meaningful act of walking, and its 'intuitive connection' to thinking and writing, has been affirmed since the time of peripatetic Greek philosophers, who walked among the architectural marvels of Athens.[2] This scope of walking to think and then to think deeply about walking as both a methodology and field of study continues to resonate with philosophers, researchers and artists alike.[3] Walking can be employed in many different ways in urban research from walking alone (with a purposeful route or wandering) to walking with others ('go-along' or in organised educational tours) to walking with tools (maps, guidebooks, cameras, camcorders, biometric monitors and journals for writing). In this essay, I analyse some of these methodologies to expand on how these walking approaches contribute to new understandings of cities and everyday life.[4]

Home to restaurants and small shops, as well as a street market during the week, Exmouth Market is a pedestrian-friendly and quaint London street. Photo: Fi Williams.

WALKING ALONE

Walking is a creative and contemplative act and is a practice that allows our minds to wander freely. In walking through space, we reflexively allow our minds to impart thoughts and feelings onto the world as our bodies experience and are stimulated by a kaleidoscope of sights, sounds and smells around us. There is a certain freedom, as Frédéric Gros argues, in our ability to think while being able to set our own tempo, rhythm and directionality.[5]

The act of walking alone, whether during the day or at night, allows one to 'lose oneself in the city', as posited by Walter Benjamin, one of the greatest writers on cities and walking.[6] This idea of 'losing oneself' — in contemplation and in one's surroundings — stems from a Romantic tradition that values exploration in the pursuit of the sublime. Indeed, this form of walking productively combines experience, movement and thought. Moreover, Benjamin, paying homage to Charles Baudelaire, advocated for a particular poetic form of walking: *flânerie*, or the practice of drifting or wandering. As a solitary *flâneur* (albeit a privileged male during Benjamin's time), this form of walking celebrated the empowered stroller, who, with his knowledge of the city, can travel incognito among the crowds and through the dark labyrinths of the city.

20 ↑ 173

Feminist critiques of *flânerie* contend that it is a concept that privileges and celebrates the *flâneur* (male stroller) and fails to recognise the walking histories and challenges to the practices of the *flâneuse* (female stroller).[7] In this vein, the novelists Vita Sackville-West and Amantine-Lucile-Aurore Dupin, best known by her pseudonym George Sand, disguised themselves as men in order to walk freely through the streets of London and Paris, respectively.[8] Indeed, a deconstruction of the *flânerie* with a critical lens that pays attention to gender, race and class is important for understanding social difference within a context of unequal urban spaces.

Taking this theory one step further and with an activist agenda, Guy Debord and Situationalists argued that the *dérive*, also a form of wandering, enables the stroller to not only territorialise unknown spaces of a planned city but also allows them to 'awaken' the city. In waking up the city, they are able to project their own desires for a city to come, a city with potential to change. Thus, the Situationists recognised the need not only for critical reflection when one is drifting (the *dérive*) but also for a 'playfulness' in creating and charting new and multiple routes and spaces as they critiqued the rigidity of city forms and institutions and their attendant social constraints.[9]

Indeed, the city became a 'New Theatre of Operations', and walking became a political act. In this regard, the Situationalists played a prominent role in the events leading up the May '68 protests in France, whereby they realised that radical thinking is made possible through walking and changing the technocratic formulations of a built city. As Michel de Certeau argues, walking in the city is an everyday practice, which contributes to the making of 'urban life' that contradicts and counterbalances the 'city as [being] a totalising and mythical landmark for socio-economic and political strategies'.[10] Expanding on de Certeau's argument, cultural-studies scholar Simon During posits that walking 'individuates and makes ambiguous the "legible" order given to cities by planners — revealing gaps of and values in larger power-structures taking place'.[11] Walking challenges the programmed and rationalised 'concept-city', as walkers reinvent the city, drawing on memories of the past and hopes for the future through their paths and experiences in the city. Thus, walkers are 'researching' and producing their own space through the tactic of walking as they bring to life a city that is migrational, metaphorical and full of possibility.

WALKING WITH OTHERS

Another methodology we can apply to walking is walking with others, from the 'go-along' walking interview to walking as a pedagogical practice, where one teaches others while walking (e.g., the tour group). In social science research, particularly in sociology, there has been a need to identify research methodologies with a 'phenomenological sensibility', that is, research that allows us to better understand the subjective experience and perspective of another person. Margarethe Kusenbach contends that there are limitations to solely relying on the two core methods predominately used in ethnographic research, namely participant observation and interview. Kusenbach advocates for a 'go-along' method, whereby researchers are able to explore the environmental perceptions, spatial practices and biographies, and social architecture and social realms of their interviewees by walking with them.[12]

These social approaches to walking are found in ethnography and the arts where they include sharing and going along with participants on walks and potentially writing narratives or comments on unfolding walks. In their research on doing 'fieldwork on foot,' Jo Lee Vergunst and Tim Ingold observe how walkers tend to share a rhythm when they walk, providing them with a mutual space for discussion.[13] This mutual understanding between walkers, which could feature a researcher and an interviewee, allows the researcher to build rapport and to be more embedded within the local context of understanding the interviewee's everyday life, full of embodied experiences and routes.

This place of mutual encounter, not only with the built environment but also with people and the social fabric of the city, is a key factor in the choice of walking as a pedagogical or guiding practice. In historian Tom Bolton's River Fleet Walk, his purpose was for participants to learn about the history of the 'lost' and hidden river Fleet, which runs for four miles from Hampstead Heath to the Thames, flowing beneath the streets of central London. With the river underneath participants' feet, the walk meanders the river's route. Although it was once a major river that flowed into the Thames, by the thirteenth century it was polluted, and industrial use greatly decreased its flow. As London grew, it increasingly became a plague-infested sewer to the houses, businesses, pubs and prisons that sat along its banks, until it gradually become fully covered. Walking in this manner allows ones to learn about particular histories and about urban change so that while the river Fleet is hidden beneath the streets of London, its history is not lost.

Indeed, this walking to learn and to remember involves imprinting knowledge and memory to a series of loci or places. Solnit contends, 'Memory, like the mind and time, is unimaginable without physical dimensions, to imagine it as a physical place is to make it into a landscape in which its contents are located, and what has location can be approached.'[14] One of the best forms of walking that taps into this method of loci or memory palace is the architectural walk.

Architectural walks are a fundamental part of architects' education and inform their understandings of built form by contextualising it within urban social, economic and political structures. For example, in Money Walks, architectural historian Amy Thomas guides students through the labyrinthine City of London, highlighting how changing financial practices throughout time have shaped the built environment. For instance, paper messengers were instrumental until 1992 and the advent of new communication

20 ↑ 173

Behind the forecourt of Rothschild Bank in London – completed in 2011 by Ellen van Loon and Rem Koolhaas of OMA – stands Christopher Wren's landmark St Stephen Walbrook church, built in 1680. While planning restrictions required that the view be made public, visitors are not allowed to walk from the bank's forecourt to the churchyard. Photo: Fi Williams

technologies as they had specialised knowledge about how to navigate the dark confusing alleyways between financial institutions and firms quickly. In the desire to further the efficacy of walking in the City of London, a short-lived elevated pedestrian walkway system was constructed.[15]

Moreover, through walking, students experience the highly securitised and patrolled nature of the area at first hand. For instance, behind the forecourt of Rothschild Bank headquarters in London (completed in 2011 by Ellen van Loon and Rem Koolhaas' of OMA) stands Christopher Wren's landmark St Stephen Walbrook church, built in 1680. While planning restrictions required that the view be made public, visitors are not allowed to walk from the bank's forecourt to the churchyard. There is a locked gate and security guards barring public access between these two iconic buildings. Such discoveries are best understood by a double awareness of seeing and experiencing it while being 'taught' the knowledge about these particular places.

Group walks can also bring out new visions for urban places. In 'Invisible Londons', a walk devised and led by Sabeth Tödtli, Nina Lund Westerdahl and Cecilie Sachs Olsen, participants walked in teams on a curated scavenger hunt. They went out to look for envelopes with riddles and clues that tied into this theme of discovering 'invisible Londons'.[16] Not only did these clues include questions that required individual reflection and group discussion, they also directed individuals and groups to create 'artefacts' (i.e. doing drawings or collecting materials from the different sites) that went into a growing museum exhibit. Inspired by Italo Calvino's novel, *Invisible Cities* (1972), these urban 'invisibilities' are rooted in ideas about taken-for-granted elements of the city as well as newly imagined ones. For instance, during the London walk, participants uncovered a clue that led them to an old cemetery near Euston station that will be affected by the construction of the planned High Speed 2 (HS2) rail line. The clue asked participants to visualise the future of this site due to HS2 and then to draw these futures on paper, incorporating whatever materials they could find around them. Further clues followed, leading participants to explore and interact with other areas of the city. The created and collected 'artefacts' were brought back into the exhibition space to be discussed and displayed with the entire group, and gallery goers got a chance to learn about new urban critiques and visions.

Organised urban walks can be conducted in silence as well. In A Silent Circle, led by the artists Tilly Fowler and Anna Hart, participants walk for two hours in London's King's Cross area, starting at Central Saint Martins School of Art and Design in the newly regenerated privately owned and managed public space, Granary Square. What is unusual about this walk is that, although it is curated, with all of the walkers keeping in pace with each other, everyone remains silent. In a sense, this walk subverts traditional walking tours, with these walkers reflecting how this silent group walk heightens their senses to their social and material surroundings, as they are fully confronted by the city itself, one that's going through profound change.

WALKING WITH TOOLS

In order to encompass other walking methodologies, this last section focuses on walking with tools such as journals, maps, cameras, camcorders and biometric monitors. The use of these tools, which form new walking methodologies, can be utilised while walking alone or with others. While the use of maps and guidebooks typically allows walkers to spatially locate themselves and provides information for a personalised journey, other tools serve as a form of knowledge-creation or data-collection. Indeed, walking with a journal or camera in hand allows one to add permanence about a specific experience and context to a particular moment in time.

Following walking traditions that encourage wandering and getting lost, artist Jennie Savage challenges the notion of using a guide for locatedness in her interactive audio piece, *A Guide to Getting Lost* (2013). In her piece, she describes her movements to the listeners, and the sights and sounds on the streets of Marrakech. She invites the listener to leave the comforts of the exhibition space by intentionally getting lost by putting on a pair of headphones and following her audio directions. Those who experience this encounter a dissonance, being dislocated between the environment of Marrakech and their own immediate environment, as they follow directions that lead them to getting lost.

Visual ethnographers employ many of the following methods, from the use of photography to film to spatial mapping. Interesting to note here is that while there is a strong acknowledgement of the visual (perhaps as a remnant of walking traditions that valued the sights of picturesque landscapes), these artists recognise the need to elaborate on their embodied experiences while walking.

Urban photographer David Kendall utilises walking as a practice in his photography in pedestrian-unfriendly Doha, Qatar. In *Material for Reconstruction* (2013), Kendall comments on his experience of walking in areas full of exhaust and noise as he photographs the material conditions of a place that consists of twenty-four-hour construction works, traversing spaces unintended for pedestrian circulation. In reading these descriptions, there is an understanding that the spatial layout of the city and its physical infrastructure affects the conviviality of walking. However, paradoxically, perhaps it is only through walking that such realisations can be made, and it is also through further walking that can we create more pedestrian-friendly cities.

In *Walking with Video* (2008), Sarah Pink, a Professor of Design and Media Ethnography, elaborates on the contention that researchers who walk with video produce not only empathetic and sensory embodied understandings, but also audio-visual texts for particular moments in time, inviting viewers later on to share in such 'emplaced experiences'.[17] Pink advocates for recording not only the fleeting visual moments but also the embodied reactions from a walker, thus capturing a particular experience in time. Indeed, her work has moved from an overt focus on visual ethnography towards sensory ethnography.

Expanding on visual studies and walking, in a composition of frame-by-frame photographs, artist Alexandros Pissourios' films provide unusual perspectives which are evocative of embodied experiences of the city. In *Underwater: Dalston to Bethnal Green* (2014, 21 seconds), we see a rhythmic series of manholes, one after another, as Pissourios transverses the streets of London. In *1001 Feet* (2014, 67 seconds), we see, again, a rhythmic series of Pissourios' right leg passing through differently coloured and textured streets of London. In both of these paired pieces, they speak to the symbolic nature of the 'seen' unknown, of a city that lies beneath us our very feet—a city that inspires urban exploration. Here, his work speaks to a whole other world that services the city above. Moreover, both of these short films mimic walking motions and the transitions through space and time, again with a focus on urban details, which are lost with other modes of movement, such as being in a car or even bicycling through the city.

Aside from walking with video and photography, other urban researchers, such as designer Christian Nold, use GPS and location-based technologies in their work. In mapping two areas, Greenwich and Stockport, aided by a bio-mapping device he created, Nold is able to measure a walker's emotional arousal in conjunction with their geographical location. In both areas, walkers who wore the device also noted down their whereabouts and experiences. Despite using the same technology, the visualisations of the two areas are quite different. The Greenwich visualisation is a heat map (on a gradient from green to red) that focuses on the intensity of areas to which people congregate, with select comments about these areas. In the Stockport project, the map's focus is on participant drawings commentary, with the participants' emotional arousal illustrated by cylinder-shaped icons. This form of emotional cartography helps us to visualise how our bodies, which radiate heat and emotion, along with our experiences, create a 'lived' city beyond just the physical infrastructures around us.

ON WALKING MORE

My walking journeys and practices have varied over time as I continue to explore new walking methodologies and as those methodologies continue to be refined and developed. My walking repertoire now includes creating walking routes for tourist friends, knowing where I should walk for the best chances of finding edible plants and fungi, figuring out where to wander (*dérive*) when I need thinking time, and going on organised themed walks. I have also escaped London by walking to Oxford, a walk inspired by many others before me, including the travel writer Hilaire Belloc, who, rumour has it, walked the fifty-four-mile journey from Oxford to London in a record eleven and a half hours.[18] In comparison, it took me two full days, and this city-to-city walk required a different set of walking methodologies. I had to learn how to interpret Ordnance Survey maps to walk on open pastures (under the Public Right of Way) and to avoid the major roads suggested by Google maps. It is through these walking journeys that I have come to the conclusion that the more I walk the more I learn about the city and the more I learn about the city, the more I walk.

DAVID KENDALL, WALKING AND PHOTOGRAPHING IN GULF CITIES

My interest in walking started when I was a teenager. I grew up inside the 'Metropolitan Green Belt' on the edge of Greater London. At weekends I would walk east along the A40 into the City of London, and I was captivated by the layers of architectural and social history encountered en route. When I studied design, I used photography to discover inner-city and suburban London, looking for relationships between communication design, architecture, signage and topography. I was fascinated by visual research and photography. As an urban photographer, I use film grammar and site-specific techniques to inspire and present photographic ideas. Walking is an important component in my artistic practice and is used to explore the built

20 ↑ 173

environment and to generate creative projects.

A number of years ago, I visited Dubai and became interested in the early stages of architectural development and the construction of roads. It was difficult to walk in a city designed for motor vehicles. I was preoccupied by the climate. Wandering around, I located different routes and accessed private and public spaces via motorways, flyovers and slip roads. Often, I'd spend half an hour to an hour dodging cars and lorries, trying to cross the road, thinking about navigation, time and space.

My work in progress focuses on climate and how atmospheres affect walking and restrict access to Gulf cities. This project is about being alone, drifting through cities. In Doha, Qatar, roaming around congested roads for eight hours was an unhealthy experience. It is gruelling to walk in outdoor spaces due to high temperatures and pollution. So I've developed a sensory research practice that moves beyond photography. I'm introducing sound recording and film-making methodologies into my workflow and wish to produce audio-visual work inside and outside architecture. I aim to direct projects that investigate human mobility and spatial interaction in fluctuating environmental conditions along Arabian coastlines.

JONATHAN HILL, PICTURESQUE WALKING

My interest in walking really started, very much, because of where I grew up. I grew up in Somerset, and I was always interested in walking as a way of thinking. It was partly stimulated by what I found around me. It was also through reading Thomas Hardy's novels and the idea of landscape and weather representing fate. I was very much intrigued by this Romantic landscape tradition. Another influence was that my grandfather was an architect. In his late eighties and early nineties he lived in Dorset, where Hardy set his novels. My grandfather's home was on some cliffs, and there were woods between him and the beach. He would walk every day down to the beach to keep fit. As he did this for three years, he scattered bluebell seeds in the woods. After three years, the woods were full of bluebells in the spring. That was very interesting to me because it suggested that walking was a creative act, not just a contemplative one.

My interest in theorising walking does primarily come from the picturesque. I think that the picturesque is misnamed really because it is not only about pictures. Visual images are just a small part of the picturesque, which is very much a practice of walking. If you go to eighteenth-century picturesque landscapes, only one or two of them have an intended route, while in the most interesting ones there are endless ways in which you can construct alternative routes and endless ways for you to negotiate them.

GABRIELA GARCÍA DE CORTÁZAR, ON WALKING IN THE CITY AND ARRESTED MOVEMENT

One part of my research has to do with studying different guides and maps for walking in London, from the eighteenth century to the twentieth, and how they describe movement. I have basically found four kinds of records: the map, where you can trace the route you want to follow; the street finder, where you check a list and find the place you are and the place you want to go—with this, you never see the whole, you see an abstract representation of the city; then, commercial guides that weren't abstractions of the city but instead tried to emulate the way the city looked by incorporating ads, for example, proposing not a text but a texture. And the fourth kind of guide, which I found very interesting, was a rural guide that used texts and drawings. The text was written instructions telling you how to walk, and the drawings were little strip maps — not a picture of the whole but just your walk.[19] Not surprisingly, however, this last kind of more textual guide was for walking in the outskirts of the city: it's almost as if the city is represented by the map, by a view of the whole that is essentially abstract, whereas the outskirts allow for a more narrative representation.

These guides and maps for walking suggest that there are some rules for how to walk; they set out a guide for acceptable walking. We might think that we walk freely and that we own the way we walk, but in reality how much of it is informed by external abstract systems? Here I look at other forms of movement in London in the same period, mainly the train, the car and the Tube, asking how much of our understanding of London is shaped by these systems, for example, through representations such as the tube map — that is, how much of our knowledge of London is informed by the tube diagram. All the representations associated with these technologies (maps, guides, road signs, diagrams) perform an arrest of movement and not only describe space but prescribe a way to move. In this way, I ask, how much of the ways in which we walk the streets is informed by, for example, the bus routes or plans, if we tend to follow the big roads and avoid the little ones? A final question I pose in my thesis is to what point this normalising and capturing of movement and experience also generates the will to subvert it, to find the glitch in this fixed way of seeing the city. By understanding how our movement has been prescribed by these descriptions, we can find a way to subvert them.

AMY THOMAS, ON WALKING AND PEDAGOGY

I'm currently teaching first-year architecture students at the Bartlett, but in the past I've also taught at Queen Mary University of London in the History Department and also in the UCL History of Art Department. So, I've often had to deal with non-architects and think about how the architectural tour could be used as a way to teach in a more effective capacity. And actually, the memory palace and the method of loci (the technique of remembering things as spatially aligned to places) has played a huge part in the way in which I go about these walks. I quite often think about the best way to structure information around a specific set of places; in fact, I recently gave a talk to some heads of secondary-school art departments, teaching them how to choreograph architecture, or, rather, how to choreograph knowledge around architecture, in a very specific way. In relation to this, I was also involved in the production of an app called Edifice: London, written by Sandy McCreery, Daniel Wilkins and myself. The idea was that it would be the first architectural guide to London for smart phones, and so the way we wrote the different entries was organised to suit the walker. We were approaching from a very experiential level; using the app you can geo-locate different buildings on a map, near to you and so on and so forth. So I suppose that, before I came here, I wondered if walking really made any difference in what I do ... and I now I realise it does. It's inherently in every aspect of my academic life. So that might broadly help answer the question of architectural teaching and how it's informed by walking.

1 Rebecca Solnit, *Wanderlust: A History of Walking* (New York: Penguin, 2001), 3.
2 Ferris Fabr, 'Why Walking Helps Us Think', *The New Yorker*. http://www.newyorker.com/tech/elements/walking-helps-us-think (accessed 8 June 2015).
3 Philosophers and writers who have written about the importance of their walking practice include Jean-Jacques Rousseau, Henry David Thoreau, Emmanuel Kant, Friedrich Nietzsche, Charles Dickens (particularly night-walking), Walter Benjamin, Guy Debord, Michel de Certeau, to name a few. For more historical accounts of these walkers, see both Solnit, *Wanderlust* and Frédéric Gros, *A Philosophy of Walking* (London: Verso, 2014).
4 Some of these methods are drawn from the Learning to Walk programme, Cities Methodologies, 2014.
5 Gros, *A Philosophy of Walking*.
6 In *Nightwalking: A Nocturnal History of London* (London: Verso, 2015), Matthew Beaumont elaborates on the 'shadowy perambulations' of poets, novelists and thinkers alike: Geoffrey Chaucer, William Shakespeare, William Blake, Thomas De Quincey and Charles Dickens. Beaumont contends how writings about night-walking provided understandings about a feature of urban life that's often overlooked and how through walking at night our concept of urban nightlife has changed from one that was criminalised to one that's more accepted.
7 Deborah L. Parsons, *Streetwalking the Metropolis: Women, the City and Modernity* (Oxford: Oxford University Press, 2000); Aruna D'Souza and Tom McDonough, *The Invisible Flâneuse? Gender, Public Space, and Visual Culture in Nineteenth-Century Paris* (Manchester: Manchester University Press, 2006).
8 Deborah Epstein Nord, *Walking the Victorian Streets: Women, Representation, and the City* (Ithaca, NY: Cornell University Press, 1995).
9 Guy Debord, 'Theory of the Derive', *Les Lèvres Nues*, 9 (1956): 50–4.
10 Michel de Certeau, *The Practice of Everyday Life*, trans. Steven Rendall (Berkeley, CA: University of California Press, 1984), 95.
11 Simon During, introduction to Michel de Certeau, 'Walking in the City', in *The Cultural Studies Reader*, edited by Simon During (London and New York: Routledge), 151–60.
12 Margarethe Kusenbach, 'Street Phenomenology: The Go-Along as Ethnographic Research Tool', *Ethnography*, 4 (3) (2003): 455–85.
13 Jo Lee Vergunst and Tim Ingold, 'Fieldwork on Foot: Perceiving, Routing, Socializing', in *Locating the Field: Space, Place and Context in Anthropology*, edited by Simon M. Coleman and Peter Collins (Oxford: Berg, 2006), 67–86.
14 Solnit, *Wanderlust*, 77.
15 See Chris Bevan Lee's documentary, *The Pedway: Elevating London* (2013).
16 An unrelated methodology for discovering the invisibilities of cities includes the urban exploration or 'urbex' movement, in which participants explore 'unseen' man-made structures, like abandoned ruins and underground tunnels.
17 Gros, *A Philosophy of Walking*, 250.
18 See also Iain Sinclair's (2003) book *London Orbital: A Walk around the M25*. Edwin Valentine Mitchell, *The Joys of Walking: Essays by Hilaire Belloc, Charles Dickens, Henry David Thoreau, and Others* (New York: Courier Corporation, 2013).
19 Strip maps such as Ogilby's *Britannia Depicta* (1675): this is a pre-modern mode of representation.

23

I HEAR SOUNDS INSIDE MY HEAD

Constructing situations Autobiography Intuition

Joanna Rajkowska

I am stone deaf in my left ear and see practically nothing through my left eye. Therefore, I do not have stereophonic hearing; all sounds from the outside world reverberate inside my own head. I internalise most stimuli, including visual sensations.

As a child, I learned to react like a seismograph, that is, to sense the energy of places. My mother suffered from progressive psychoses, and I was taught to constantly differentiate between places that constituted a threat for her and would certainly send her into a panic, and those that allowed her a momentary respite from her anxieties. I had to learn to decipher the language she read the landscape with, carefully registering every change in mood. Every mundane stroll turned out to be a nightmare. We were always going out and about, but we never got anywhere. When we were at the ends of our tethers, exhausted by her relentless anxieties, attacks of paranoia and attempts to unravel conspiracies, we thought we found the right place to sit down, such as the edge of a forest. Yet it turned out that we always chose the worst and ultimately the most hostile place. The edge of the forest turned at once into something demonic.

I recall the mysterious evolution of an ordinary field into a wild, deserted space bristling with thickets, a space where strangers lurked behind every crooked blade of grass. Returning to familiar places was a little easier. Everything Mother's sight had absorbed ceased to be so terrifying. But sometimes a place that had slowly, arduously, been tamed and neutralised suddenly revealed a monstrous and incompatible element, and Mother would immediately be forced to get up and move on.

Today, I choose to make public art in places that are missing something. My instinct takes me to them: places with absent memories, with no sense of belonging, places weighted by isolation or trauma. If it is at all possible, and if people feel tied to these places, I try to transform these sites together with them. I have nothing against modifying my projects, because they are no more than a pretext for building a new and different relationship between people and such burdened places. And they often know better than I what should be done. If the edge of the forest is demonic, you create a situation to lift the curse once and for all, or to make the demon show himself and speak.

I depend on animal instinct, which generally concerns the collective: what people dream of in a given place, what they instinctively want to avoid, what they fear. I don't send out 'messages' with my artworks. I only produce a frame in which various groups, communities or individuals can start to formulate their own messages. My task is to give the frame coordinates that are as relevant as possible. You could call it the establishment of a certain field: a field of intensity, a field of relationships or a field of games of all kinds, which is, in itself, initially empty.

Top *Oxygenator*, 2007, photo: Joanna Rajkowska. *Oxygenator* was a public project within the boundaries of the former Jewish ghetto in Warsaw: a pond with a cloud of oxygenated and moist air hovering over it. This man was an *Oxygenator* visitor. He found this chair that had been left by someone at the edge of the pond, but it was crooked and the man was hunchbacked. He spent a good five minutes trying to position the unstable chair so that it would stand, and then he attempted to sit on it, while it was moving. I never saw his face, as I was filming behind him. He spent a lot of time there, very quietly.

Bottom *The Peterborough Child*, 2012, photo: Joanna Rajkowska. This photo was taken during the production of *The Peterborough Child*. It depicts a fake archaeological site with a little burial site of a girl. The project was designed for Peterborough in east England, but it was never realised due to protests by representatives of the local Muslim community. The plaque that was going to stand next to it read, 'The Peterborough Child was a girl born 3,500 years ago and found here during a 2012 excavation. Tests indicate that her mother came from the East, but that her father was a local man. It would appear she migrated for reasons unknown to us. Analysis of bone tissue shows that she suffered from a very rare DNA mutation. Her thirteenth gene was slightly damaged, which produced a genetic form of eye cancer, retinoblastoma. It is thought that a child like this was valued by the community and was considered to have shamanic powers. The site of her burial was carefully chosen to ensure it brought blessings to the land. Evidence of her special status can be seen in the objects her grave contains, among them a beaker, a fawn skull and deer teeth. Some were presumably gifts for her to take into the afterlife, but others seem to be invocations. Apparently, the donations continued throughout the centuries, as the most recent objects date from our times. The distinctive container next to her was fashioned from deer nostrils and holds her two well-preserved eye tumours.'

Born in Berlin, 2011. This is me photographed by Sławomir Bergański, pregnant, diving in the famous swimming pool where Leni Riefenstahl filmed Olympic divers in 1936. I subverted the image of an ideal, trained and disciplined body, core to Riefenstahl's film, turning it into a clumsy and disproportioned pregnant body of a woman who is just about to give birth. The scene is part of the film *Born in Berlin*, in which I give birth to a baby girl, Rosa. The film intends to bring life to a city from which (at least for my country and for my family) destruction would have traditionally come. Rosa, when being asked where she was born, will have to say, 'Berlin'.

16 ↑ 139

The moment you have to decide how to be with someone is the moment at which politics begins. Politics begins with the body. My projects attempt to reduce this political moment to a situation of ignorance and awkwardness and to the need to reconstruct 'togetherness' from this base of unease. I begin with body positions and hand gestures, provoking intimacy and vulnerability, the elimination of all rituals of behaviour and social hierarchies. My work is utopian: it consists of mirages that fade as soon as they are set in motion.

My projects live, grow and age like organisms. Their lives germinate in urban legends, debates and seminars, as well as whispers, snapshots and press clippings. Only a narrative is able to rehatch them, assembling hundreds of scraps of information into an entirety that lets us see them as a story and understand what really happened. Writing is my most precise instrument of analysis, it reveals the project by translating it through language and, surprisingly, through my own body. What is missing in the immediate experience presents itself through language.

I am a woman and a mother, and I come from Poland, where I grew up under communism, a different orbit. My entry to public space was an entry into the post-communist realm, deeply politicised and traumatised. Recovery from historical trauma and the necrosis of the urban fabric required a return to the most primal phenomena of bodily coexistence: sharing our breathing, situating our bodies together in relation to each other. I didn't address my projects to communities — they no longer existed — but to individuals. I was building unfamiliar, sometimes rather alienating or estranged points of reference so that people could finally relate to each other, often non-verbally. I didn't have the ambition to solve conflicts or provoke debates. On the contrary, I blurred their identities as much as I could and generated new problems for them to deal with and new lines of division. One thing was certain: I shared their fear of reality.

Coming from a historically traumatised region, I know that the world is not a complex mechanism that can be repaired or fixed; it is not architecture which can be rebuilt. The world is a monster, unpredictable in its actions. Even if we humans believe that we are able to control its movements, we are under an illusion. This is why art in public space can not and should not be seen as a set of social tools. It has the power to reset the existing political and social coordinates, and it can build an image of a new, utopian realm.

24

CHARTING SMELLSCAPES

Smell mapping Chemical analysis Olfactory design

Mădălina Diaconu

21 ↑ 181

The most immediate experience of cities is their synaesthetic perception in which we are immersed via all of our senses. These multimodal sensescapes require specific methods of investigation. Whereas visual and acoustic cityscapes can be designed, recorded and even reproduced, tactile and olfactory qualities resist a systematic approach and are difficult to describe, record and replicate.

In what follows, I discuss a collaborative interdisciplinary research project exploring the haptic and olfactory topographies of the Austrian capital Vienna, with a special focus on its public spaces.[1] Our aim was to establish which perceptual aspects confer a specific 'atmosphere' and 'flair' to Vienna and to identify locations that, in these aspects, would benefit from design interventions. We also endeavoured to sensitise decision makers, architects and the general public to the non-visual dimensions of the public spaces we inhabit and to draw attention to citizens' collective responsibility for shaping, deliberately or not, the olfactory profile of a city.[2]

The various methods we used for the investigation of smellscapes included chemical analyses of samples collected indoors and outdoors using gas chromatography and mass spectrometry, the interpretation of the psycho-physiological and emotional effects of odours and a new botanical classification of fragrances. We also tried to develop practical applications of our research so that it could be used, for instance, in the design of coffeehouses as well as making recommendations as to which fragrant plants are suitable for the Viennese climate.[3]

My own research focused on the phenomenological description of smells and on the possibilities of using odours positively through urban design interventions. The intention was to counteract the strategy of modern urbanism and architecture to overlay bad odours, to suppress smells and to create sterile 'blandscapes'. My methods combined a hermeneutic exploration of historical treatises on aesthetics with phenomenological descriptions of olfactory experience. The latter emerged from first-person testimonies, questionnaires and in-depth interviews with various age groups, with subjects with visual impairments, residents who were born in Vienna and those who had settled or visited the city later in their lives, including migrants and tourists.

In order to test and raise awareness of the smellscapes as a part of everyday urban environments, I asked my students and some of the interviewees to draw two categories of 'smell maps': mental maps and monitoring maps. First, fifty-six students were invited to draw a map of Vienna and to locate on it the smells that occurred to them spontaneously by using symbols or colours to be explained in a legend. Further parameters, such as how to draw the map, which symbols to use and how to describe the odours, were deliberately left to the students and research subjects in order to heuristically test possibilities for the visualisation of smells. Second, we selected thirteen relevant areas in the city and asked students to choose one of them and to explore or monitor it at least once a month, to download

Cognitive map of the smellscapes of Vienna, Mădălina Diaconu, Kristina Schinegger, 2009.

27 → 225

Smell Maps – Mind Maps (2007, 2008)

Gerüche/Gesamt–Wien

GRÜNE GERÜCHE

1 Gras, Wiese
2 Blumen, Blüten
3 Bäume, Laub, Holz
4 Wald, Waldboden
5 Erde, feuchte Erde, Moder
6 Dünger, Felder
7 Wasser
8 Frische Luft

ESSEN

9 Früchte, Obst
10 Gemüse
11 Fisch
12 Käse, reifer Käse
13 Bäckerei, Pizza
14 Gegrilltes Fleisch, Kebab, Würstel
15 Frittiertes, Frittierfett, Schnitzel
16 Gewürze
17 Kaffee
18 Schokolade, Süßigkeiten

ORGANISCHE GERÜCHE

19 Abfall, Verfaultes
20 Kanal, Abwasser, abgestandenes Wasser
21 Urin
22 Tierkot, Hundekot
23 Pferdemist
24 Schweiß, Körpergeruch
25 Erbrochenes

VERKEHR/INDUSTRIE

26 Abgase, Staub
27 Öl, Diesel
28 Hafen, Fischgeruch

ANDERE

29 Steine, Mauern, Beton
30 Alkohol, Bier, Brauerei
31 Rauch, Zigarettenrauch
32 Parfum, Raumparfum, Seife
33 Desinfektionsmittel

21 ↑ 181

its map from the municipality website and to register on the map whatever odours they encountered during their walks and trajectories, using freely chosen symbols that they had to explain in a legend. A few subjects kept a diary of smells in a particular area, for example along an underground line. The data gathered from these maps was then grouped into four categories of smells: natural odours (mentioned by 82 per cent of the subjects), food odours (75 per cent), exhaust fumes and industrial smells (63 per cent) and smells produced by organic waste (59 per cent).[4]

The research showed us the impact of social practices, particularly cooking and transport, and of cultural history (for instance, popular films) on the subjects' sensory perceptions of Vienna. Their hedonic evaluation of smells also depended on their narrative identity: the smells of their childhood in rural or urban areas, for instance, in Austria or elsewhere. It was also influenced by specific memories of spaces, the macro- and micro-histories of public squares and of coffeehouses. In more general terms, we learned that the atmospheres that emanate from places may depend on the constructed image of the city, but they may also diverge from it.

The difficulties in exploring this topic derive from peoples' underdeveloped verbal or written competence to describe the olfactory experience, the widespread lack of sensibility to odours and the challenge of visualising smells. In addition, the task of designing and controlling smellscapes, and, thus, of shaping, indirectly, atmospheres, comes up against the unplanned and protracted emergence of smellscapes as a result of the accumulation and repetition of practices in a city. This accretion of smellscapes escapes regulation and evolves through an interplay between calculated decisions concerning the selection of materials and their spatial arrangement in the urban built environment and public spaces on the one hand and contingent or highly complex and almost unpredictable factors, ranging from social practices to the weather, on the other.

The design of atmospheres can only succeed when taking into account anthropological insights regarding the social lives and lifestyles of individual people and urban communities. As for the suitability of methods, I found that in-depth interviews work better than questionnaires, yet they imply a need for 'experts' who manage to verbalise their experiences and thus interpret the experiences of others. In general, the interdisciplinary exploration of sensescapes still needs to agree on a minimal set of common methodological and terminological tools beyond the specific research instruments of each discipline.

After the completion of this project, I repeated, on a small scale, the experiment of drawing mental maps with participants in Bucharest.[5] Many of the resulting twenty-one 'smell maps' of the city mentioned food, including the international and the local, fast food and home cooking. There was also a high frequency of vegetal odours and the smell of water (connected to the lakes in the northern part of the city), as well as traffic odours. A specific 'humid' smell was associated with the underground, like in Vienna. Organic

Monitoring smell maps for selected areas in Vienna, Mădălina Diaconu, Kristina Schinegger, 2009.

27 → 225

Monitoring Smell Maps (2007, 2008)

Überblickskarte Wien, Innere Stadt

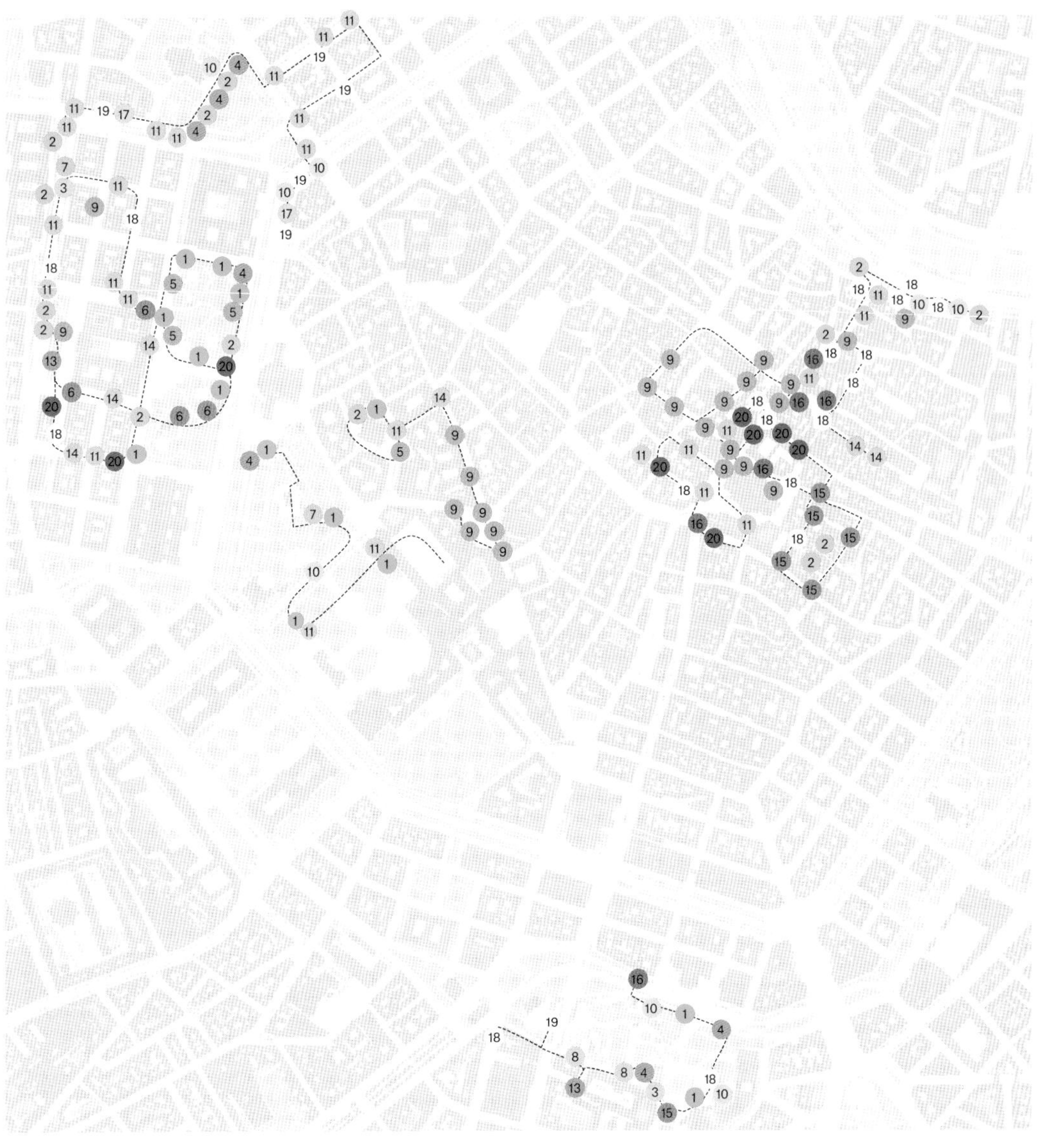

1 frisches Gras, Wiese
2 Sträucher
3 Blumenduft
4 Rosenduft
5 Fliedergeruch
6 feuchte Erde, modriger Geruch
7 Baumrinde, Holzgeruch
8 Düngemittel
9 Pferdemist, Pferdeurin
10 Urin
11 Tabakgeruch, Zigarettenrauch
12 Verkehrabgase
13 verbrannter Gummi
14 Staub, Baustaub
15 Stein, Mauergeruch
16 Kaffeegeruch
17 Eisgeruch
18 Pizza, Gasthaugeruch, Bratwurst, Kebab
19 Brot, Bäckereigeruch
20 Parfum, Raumparfum

21 ↑ 181

human smells and animals, such as urine, were also conspicuous. Unlike in Vienna, however, a prominent role was played by the smell of dust from a variety of sources — traffic, building sites, industrial areas — and the persistent, hard-to-describe odours of fish, wastelands and voids, stale water and sewage. The olfactory profile of Bucharest was also dominated by the dampness of the ubiquitous old, abandoned buildings.

The 'localisation' of these odours often lacks precision in terms of a close association with specific zones or city districts. As is the case for the Danube in Vienna, the river Dâmbovița is almost absent from the mental image of Bucharest's inhabitants, but, unlike Vienna, which has a clear nucleus (St Stephen's Cathedral), Bucharest lacks such a symbolic centre. Stronger than in the smell maps of Vienna were the symbolic codes of social stratification: in Cotroceni (a wealthy district) and along the Dacia and Aviation Boulevards, one can smell 'money and power', linden trees and car air-freshener, while poorer neighbourhoods such as Rahova and Ferentari, Crângaşi and Pantelimon reek of homeless people and rotting garbage. Bucharest is a city where 'clean', 'corporate' smells mix with those of fish from the chaotic and unpredictable suburbs. The exercise carried out in Bucharest, although done in a tentative fashion, confirmed that smellscapes are closely connected to social practices and hierarchies as well as to individual and collective narratives.

1 Between 2007 and 2010, I led a research team that carried out the programme *Haptic and Olfactory Design: Resources for Vienna's Creative Industries* as a cooperation between three Viennese universities (two departments from the University of Vienna, the University of Applied Arts and the University of Natural Resources and Applied Life Sciences) and ZOOM-Children's Museum Vienna.

2 Tast- und Duftdesign: Ressourcen für die Wiener Kreativwirtschaft. http://www.univie.ac.at/tastduftwien (accessed 3 September 2014).

3 The results were gathered in *Sensorisches Labor Wien: Urbane Haptik- und Geruchsforschung*, edited by Mădălina Diaconu, Gerhard Buchbauer, James G. Skone, Karl-Georg Bernhardt and Elisabeth Menasse-Wiesbauer (Berlin, Vienna and London: Lit, 2011).

4 Mădălina Diaconu, 'Mapping Urban Smellscapes', in *Senses and the City: An Interdisciplinary Approach to Urban Sensescapes*, edited by Mădălina Diaconu, Eva Heuberger, Ruth Mateus-Berr and Lukas Marcel Vosicky (Berlin, Vienna and London: Lit, 2011), 223–38.

5 The participants were drawn from those who attended the Bucharest edition of Cities Methodologies, 2010.

25

CONTRA BAND

Cross-continental performance

Music exchange

Live-stream

Leah Lovett

As host cities to the 2012 Olympic and Paralympic Games and 2014 World Cup, both London and Rio de Janeiro witnessed an intensification in performance practices and urban interventions. While in sporting stadia, the bodies of athletes and performers stood in for and reinforced different national identities, activists and artists took to the streets and social media to unsettle those national imaginaries and identifications. If international sporting events put into motion processes of urban restructuring and securitisation with lasting implications for the ways in which host cities are performed by their citizens, then performance art can also be a methodology for challenging those authorised performances.

Contra Band was a cross-continental, inter-urban performance commissioned for the Floating Cinema (London) and CASA 24 (Rio de Janeiro), presented on six occasions between 28 June and 30 August 2014 and streamed live via the Floating Cinema website.[1] Conceived and orchestrated by artist Leah Lovett, the project linked up musicians Raphael dos Santos (Rio de Janeiro) and Nicholas Underwood (London) and their audiences for a live set comprising songs censored in both countries between 1964 and 1985, the years of the Brazilian military dictatorship. The musicians took turns to sing songs written in their non-native language and to accompany the other. The link was established via Google+ Hangouts, a full-duplex video-conferencing system freely available in both locales that enabled them to play together even as it frustrated their attempts to do so by introducing a three-second delay.

The promulgation in Brazil of Institutional Act 5 (AI-5 1968), an anxious piece of legislation that made provision for the surveillance and censure of artists, resulted in creative forms of self-censorship and, for many artists, exile to the UK and Europe to escape violent forms of repression. Brazilian musicians targeted by and subverting state censors included Chico Buarque, Gilberto Gil, Caetano Veloso and Tom Zé. Meanwhile, in the UK, musical censorship during this period was an effect of a conservative broadcast media, with songs by the Beatles, Frankie Goes to Hollywood, Ian Dury and the Blockheads and the Sex Pistols all falling foul of BBC censors on grounds of indecency. Notwithstanding the very different contexts, censorship played a role in the construction of public space in both countries by demarcating political and moral limits, which is to say the political identities and moralities that could be represented to the public.

Bringing the offending music together, Contra Band invited audiences to consider how limits on artistic freedom of expression have necessitated different ways of seeing, experiencing and communicating. A case in point is Chico Buarque and Gilberto Gil's poignant song, 'Càlice' (1973), which eluded censors who were reading rather than hearing the lyrics because of a homophone. When written, *càlice* translates as 'chalice', but it also sounds as the imperative *cale-se*, meaning 'shut up', or 'silence'. What appears on paper to be a song about Jesus in Gethsemane is therefore heard as a criticism of the military regime's violent silencing of political opposition.

The song includes the lyric, 'In the city, silence is not heard,' words that seem to suggest the city itself as resisting censorship. It was performed by Buarque and Gil as part of the Phono 73 Festival (1973), a mass event staged in a city-run convention centre in São Paolo. While they were playing, the military police came on stage to unplug their microphones.[2] This spectacle of censorship took place as a spatial and political effect of Buarque and Gil's deceptive play on words. By demonstrating the critical message of 'Càlice' to a mass audience, the censors unwittingly cemented its status as an iconic protest song.

In paying tribute to artists who have creatively subverted censorship in this way, I do not mean to imply that censorship is creatively desirable. Indeed, the years following the introduction of AI-5 in Brazil are usually referred to as *os anos de chumbo* (the leaden years), a term that describes the suffocating effects of censorship on critical art practices.[3] Rather, my intention is to highlight how strategies for closing down critical forms of expression have tended to produce potent counter-strategies. The question that concerns me is whether and how these creative cultural counter-strategies might be recovered and redirected to challenge the political and social limits of public space in another place or time? How did songs censored in such different circumstances resonate in London and Rio de Janeiro, as host cities to recent international sporting mega-events?

One possible answer came in an email from the artistic director of CASA 24, Filipe Espindola, written a few days after the first performances of Contra Band. In it, Espindola reflects:

> We are experiencing a difficult period in terms of police oppression here in Rio, because of the World Cup. Our street theatre and performance group was arrested on the day of the game against Mexico. ... We hadn't committed a crime, so they couldn't charge us with anything, but it was a moment of tension in a difficult period. Participating in Contra Band feels important, because we don't want to be silent at this time, like [artists] during the dictatorship of 1964.[4]

For my part, what remains is the capacity of performance as a medium for connecting across territorial space and national boundaries, as a means of making connections that cut across the interests of powerful stakeholders intent on stifling critical interventions into the urban during the 2014 World Cup in Rio de Janeiro and the 2012 Olympic Games in London.[5] With Contra Band, these connections dropped out at times, leaving audiences in either city with a fragile voice or a voiceless accompaniment. What I realised, however, is that these moments of technological interruption only intensified the musicians' and audiences' desire to reconnect, an echo perhaps of the ways in which censorship made resistance more urgent. If it is, as Buarque implies, that the city resists censorship, then this is surely because cities are places where people amass and therefore where connections between

1 ↑ 23 10 ↑ 87

many and diverse people can occur. With the increasing accessibility of communications technologies, there are more possibilities for multiple, varied and challenging connections that extend beyond the territorial boundaries of any one city.

Performance view of Contra Band from the Floating Cinema, London, 2014.
Photo: Nina Pope & UP Projects.

1 Contra Band was commissioned by UP Projects, Somewhere and the Live Art Development Agency as part of the Floating Cinema's Extra-International season, 2014. For more information, see Floating Cinema, '2014 Commissions: Live Art Commission 2014 with Live Art Development Agency', 26 June 2014. http://floatingcinema.info/commissions/live-art-commission-2014-with-live-art-development-agency (accessed 14 October 2015).
2 For an extended discussion of 'Càlice' and censorship under the Brazilian military regime, see Christopher Dunn, *Brutality Garden: Tropicália and the Emergence of a Brazilian Counterculture* (Chapel Hill, NC: University of North Carolina Press, 2001), 161–3.
3 See Claudia Calirman, *Brazilian Art under Dictatorship: Antonio Manuel, Artur Barrio, and Cildo Meireles* (Durham, NC: Duke University Press, 2012), 5.
4 Filipe Espindola, email message to author, 1 July 2014 (author's translation). Reproduced here with permission.
5 See Wail Qasim, 'London 2012 Protests: Heavy-Handed Policing Is an Affront to Rights', *The Guardian*, 30 July 2012.

VI

Fabric and Fabrication

26

THE TWIN SISTERS ARE 'ABOUT TO' SWAP HOUSES

Displacement and the bordering practice of matching

Multi-media installation Bordering practices Swapping

Mohamad Hafeda

3 ↑ 35 20 ↑ 173

Q. COULD YOU DRAW THE ROUTE MAP TO YOUR TWIN'S HOUSE?

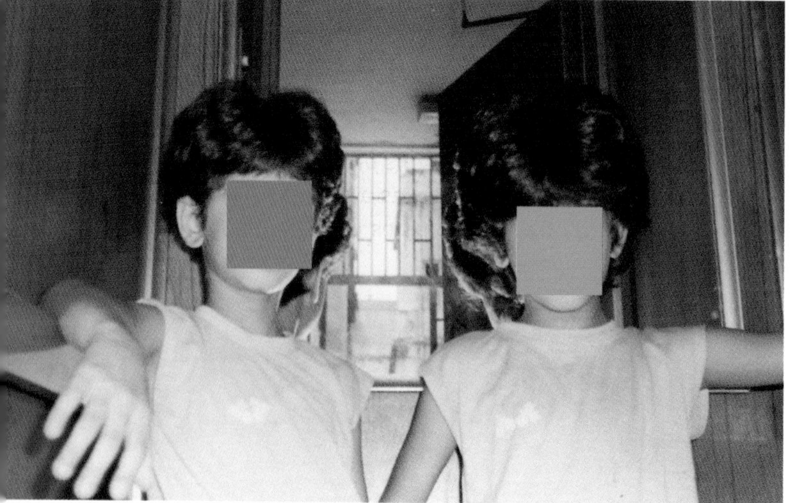

Photograph taken in the lift of the twin's childhood house, summer 1986, Beirut.

Map of the geographic location of R. and L. houses. The blue and green squares refer to the colours of the political parties with which their husbands are affiliated.

The Twin Sisters Are 'About to' Swap Houses introduces the act of swapping as a voluntary and non-violent act of displacement, a bordering practice across geographies configured along the political and sectarian tension that has resurfaced in Lebanon since 2005. It is a research project and an associated gallery installation through which I worked with twin sisters I have known since childhood who had decided to swap their houses, respectively in Tarik el-Jdide and the adjacent Mazraa area in Beirut. The two areas have witnessed violent clashes and temporary demarcation lines (borders) on the Mazraa main road separating both.

The sisters were married to men of different political allegiances, and, by residing with them, their husbands were living in the 'wrong' areas — that is, neighbourhoods at odds with their politics. The sisters thought that by swapping houses they could match the political affiliation of their husbands with the political affiliation of the areas in which they lived. At least, this was their intention. Their decision to swap houses came in the wake of the armed clashes of May 2008 between the Mustaqbal movement and Hezbollah in Beirut and the harassment their husbands experienced in the streets where they lived following these clashes. However, although they had intended to swap, further changes in the political situation in Lebanon around the time I worked with them (2010 and 2012) meant that they put their plan on hold, and the swap has yet to take place. I was nevertheless intrigued by the idea that one might alleviate political tensions by swapping houses and so provide

27 → 225

a safer home and protection for one's family. The proximity of the houses the sisters wished to swap, and their state of being 'about to' swap and 'on hold', are spatial and temporal aspects characteristic of processes of displacement as an everyday activity within Beirut and determined by a fast-changing political situation.

The research project explores the interplay between material and immaterial borders. It is my attempt to move away from defining borders as things and objects and towards understanding and producing borders as processes and practices embedded in the everyday lives of city-dwellers, an alternative to a focus on the physical divisions of walls and fences. Thus, the investigation follows the shift from 'border' as a noun to 'bordering' as a verb, as suggested in the field of borders studies by Alexander C. Diener and Joshua Hagen.[1]

In my research, I consider bordering as a set of spatial practices, particularly those negotiated among residents, militias and politicians whether as tactics or strategies following Michel de Certeau's definition,[2] and situating my analyses through the concept of everyday life as a site of resistance following Henri Lefebvre's theory.[3] I propose negotiating and narrating as two main aspects of bordering practices in Beirut today in order to account for the relational and (im)material aspects. Specifically, I explore the bordering practices of art and research activities in their capacity to negotiate conflicts existing in urban space, starting from residents' interior spaces, and to operate as sites of resistance. In this respect, the bordering practices of art and research are critical spatial practices that, following Jane Rendell's definition, have the potential to transform and displace the materiality of borders and operate across the borders between different sites, such as the urban site I am researching and the gallery space in which the work is installed.[4] In the twins' narrative, the bordering practice is the act of swapping with the intention of matching, of moving in order to be blend in and make the same, and this is the bordering practice I project in the installation *The Twin Sisters Are 'About to' Swap Houses.*

DISPLACEMENT AS SWAPPING

The twins' narrative echoes the current subtle and invisible movements of residents and the demographic changes experienced in the city and its peripheries that have prompted residents to prefer living in areas which are either of a homogeneous sectarian nature (in order to avoid the possible clashes that might arise from mixing) or in totally heterogeneous mixed areas where no political party has dominance. These movements are not publicly announced, and they happen through normal real-estate-market mechanisms of exchange and within families' social networks. They are invisible in comparison to the displacement of refugees and other migrants.

20 ↑ 173
3 ↑ 35

For example, the Syrian refugees in Lebanon since the outbreak of the Syrian war in 2011 are forced into mobility, through which, as the geographer Alison Mount has noted, they 'are sighted, marked, [and] coded', particularly pertaining to their legal status.[5]

In comparison to other types of displacement, the sisters' swapping is an act with agency, a chosen rearrangement to achieve balance and order, with each filling the space of the other through the exchange process they propose between the two respective areas. The sisters' swapping is a form of control that they decide to perform on their own domestic lives, as a response to the political situation forced upon them. This provides an alternative to the forced and violent displacements that Lebanon witnessed during its previous civil war (1975—90), comprising chaos and imbalance. The displacement that occurs across close proximity is a strategy mobilised and indirectly suggested by political parties to achieve division and social segregation across sectarian lines, and it is applied and practised by residents as a precautionary and pre-emptive measure to avoid being forced to move by violence.

DISPLACEMENT AS MATCHING

In *The Migrant Image* (2013), T. J. Demos presents modernity through the lens of the exile, echoing Walter Benjamin's and Edward Said's views on modernity as 'the age of the refugee, the displaced person' and of 'mass immigration'.[6] Demos does this through the work of artists who have dealt with the issues of refuge and migration and who have changed and challenged the use of (moving) images in the documentary art of films and photography.[7] Demos suggests that by 'mobilizing the image as much as imaging mobility',[8] such artists have invented representation strategies that adopt displacement as a language and 'disrupt the purity of film and language alike. As a result, the categories of the visual, the auditory, and the scriptural are rendered insufficient on their own, as necessarily dialogical and stranded in their incompleteness and therefore contingent on contextual determinations for their meanings'.[9]

The mobility involved in the twin sisters' displacements, their plan to swap, suggests the need for a mobile investigation that analyses and constructs the sites of potential displacement as an extended spatial and social arrangement of people, their belongings, homes and lives, spanning from the interior spaces inhabited by the twins to the urban context in which both houses are located. I wanted to investigate and to image (as well as imagine) the swapping site and to perform the process that would be involved in the swap. At each house, I carried out a photographic survey of the floors and ceilings of their houses that present fixed structures, the location, as well as the departure and destination points for the

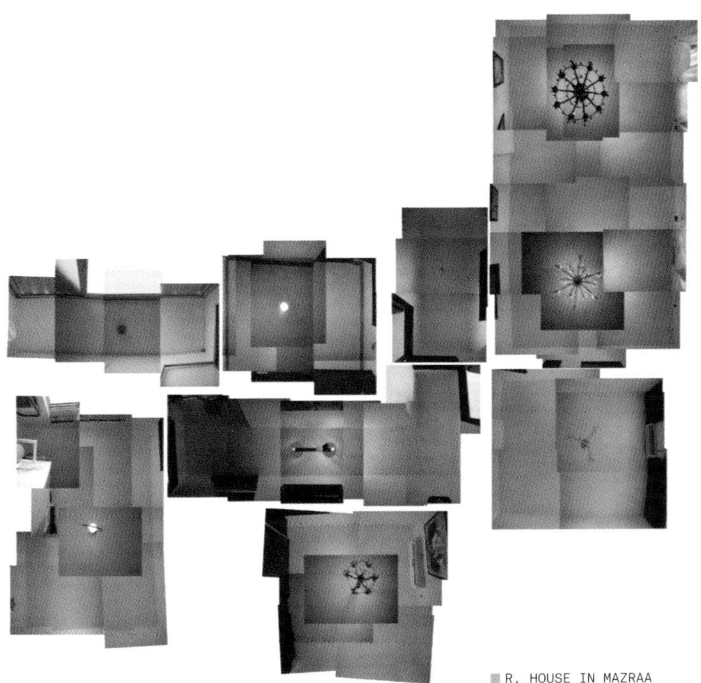

Photographic survey of the floor and ceiling plan of R. and L. houses.

3 ↑ 35 20 ↑ 173

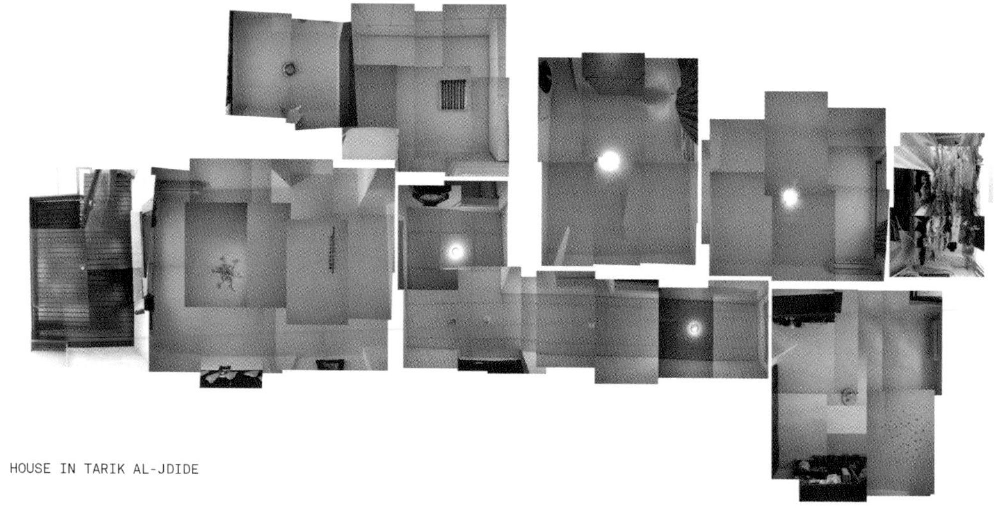

■ L. HOUSE IN TARIK AL-JDIDE

displacement. I also asked each of the sisters individually to draw the route map from one house to the other, and I video-recorded the drawing process. I also asked each sister to track this route on the city skyline and to locate the other sister's house from her high-level balcony, using a small video camera. These simple mapping exercises aim to mobilise and visualise what the sisters wanted to avoid in their voluntary displacement, which is invisible and silent. The exercises perform this act of swapping and investigate the possibilities that might be generated out of these actions.

In the gallery installation, I responded to the sisters' swapping decision by suggesting spatial moments of matching and twinning in the footage

27 → 225

Stills from *Finding Houses, The Twin Sisters Are 'About to' Swap Houses,* 2012.

20 ↑ 173
3 ↑ 35

obtained from the two exercises performed with them. The viewer is located in a space of swapping: a negotiation of continuous matching that aligns geographies across the visual horizon and through lines drawn while narrating a journey on a map, captured at a moment of time that is 'about to' swap.

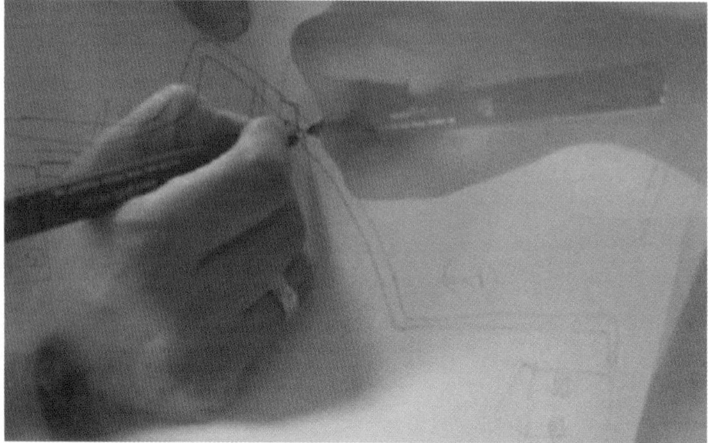

Stills from *Drawing the Route Map, the Twin Sisters Are 'About to' Swap Houses*, 2012.

The Twin Sisters Are 'About to' Swap Houses, gallery installation, Cities Methodologies, London, 2012.

1 Alexander C. Diener and Joshua Hagen, *Borders: A Very Short Introduction* (Oxford: Oxford University Press, 2012), 59.
2 Michel de Certeau, *The Practice of Everyday Life* (Berkeley, CA: University of California Press, 1988).
3 Henri Lefebvre, 'The Everyday and Everydayness', in *Architecture of the Everyday*, edited by Steven Harris and Deborah Berke (Princeton, NJ: Princeton Architectural Press, 1997), 32–7, 34.
4 Jane Rendell, *Art and Architecture: A Place Between* (London: I.B. Tauris, 2006), 8.
5 Alison Mountz, 'Refugees: Performing Distinction – Paradoxical Positionings of the Displaced', in *Geographies of Mobilities: Practices, Spaces, Subjects*, edited by Tim Cresswell and Peter Merriman (Farnham: Ashgate, 2013), 255–68, 255.
6 Edward W. Said, 'Reflections on Exile', *Granta*, 13 (autumn) (1984): 159–72, 159. Quoted in T. J. Demos, *The Migrant Image: The Art and Politics of Documentary during Global Crisis* (Durham, NC: Duke University Press, 2013), 1.
7 Demos, *The Migrant Image*, 255.
8 Demos, *The Migrant Image*, xv.
9 Demos, *The Migrant Image*, xv.

27

CITY SHAPES AND URBAN METAPHOR

Visual comparison Sand sculpture Watercolour

John Aiken

24 ↑ 205 26 ↑ 217

My research and practice exploring the paradox of the objective and subjective nature of mapping in relation to shifting boundaries often takes the form of drawing or large-scale installations that have strong physical and temporal aspects. The work is concerned with ideas about how we, as visitors to urban environments or public, museum or gallery spaces, inhabit or occupy space in a temporary or transient manner and the ephemerality of habitation and occupation.

City as Shape in Time is a series of apparently abstract watercolour drawings. These were based on a number of copperplate prints of maps published by Baldwin & Cradock during the 1830s for the Society for the Diffusion of Useful Knowledge.[1] The maps and the drawings based on them show a range of notable world cities as shapes defined by the cities' boundaries. They reveal in graphic form the comparative development of the cities subject to differing social and economic conditions at transitional points in their history. The drawings were drawn to scale and supported by statistical information about the area of each city and the density of its population at the time the corresponding map was drawn.

Watercolour drawing of the land area of Amsterdam based on *Amsterdam 1835*, published under the superintendence of the Society for the Diffusion of Useful Knowledge, drawn by W. B. Clarke, engraved by B. R. Davies, 16 George Street, London University. Published by Baldwin & Cradock, Paternoster Row, 1835 (London: Chapman & Hall, 1844).

Watercolour drawing of the land area of Stockholm based on *Stockholm 1838*, published under the superintendence of the Society for the Diffusion of Useful Knowledge, drawn by W. B. Clarke, engraved by B. R. Davies, 16 George Street, London University. Published by Baldwin & Cradock, Paternoster Row, 1 July 1836 [*sic*] (London: Chapman & Hall, 1844).

During the 1830s, many densely populated European cities were constrained within increasingly redundant defensive perimeters. Other cities had already broken out of these constraints, their urban expansion fuelled by economic development and the rise of industrialisation in Europe and the USA. For instance, in Baldwin & Cradock's city maps, Amsterdam, Hamburg, Genoa and many other European cities were still defined by the geometric regularity of their city walls. But others, like Dublin, Berlin and, of course, London, had already developed into expanded urban areas and suburbs.

Amsterdam, with a population of over 220,000, occupied an area of only 1.7 square kilometres, producing an extraordinarily high population density of 122,000 people per square kilometre in 1835. By comparison, Stockholm in 1838 had already expanded extensively from its defensive centre into a suburban sprawl. With a population of 88,000, it occupied an urban area of 12.4 square kilometres, resulting in a population density of only 7,100 people per square kilometre.

The shapes and forms of these cities were, of course, a consequence of multiple factors — the topographic nature of the sites, the economic, social and cultural ecology of each place and their demographic profiles — and they were undergoing a continuous process of change and transformation. The maps documented a particular moment in time. Although rapidly out of date, they were nevertheless important images to help understand change. They are now valuable as historical documents, and comparison of consecutive editions reveals the ephemeral nature of the layout of the cities. The watercolour drawings act as historical 'snapshots' in the form of shapes, exemplifying the fast-changing landscapes of cities from the nineteenth century onwards.

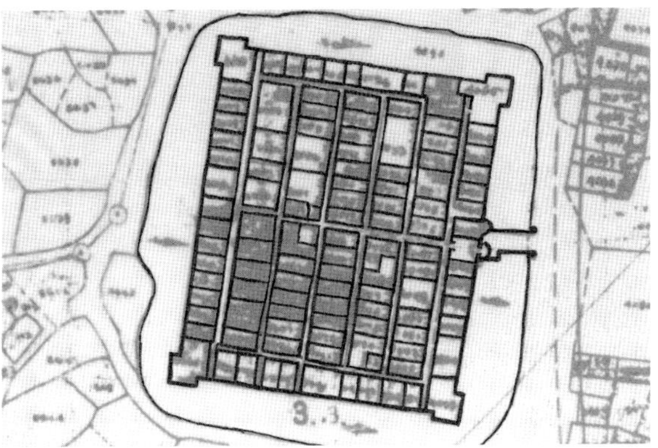

Plan drawing of a walled and moated village in nineteenth-century Kowloon, Hong Kong.

I am now based in Hong Kong, and my interest in urban spaces and the mapping of cities has focused on the historical, clan-based, small walled villages, which were common in southern China before the colonisation of Hong Kong by the British in the nineteenth century. Many still exist and are accessible. The best known of these villages is the once notorious Kowloon Walled City, which, prior to its demolition in 1994, had a population of 33,000 living in an area of 0.26 square kilometres. This was the equivalent to an astonishing 1,255,000 people per square kilometre and was the result of

24 ↑ 205 26 ↑ 217

decades of uncontrolled and unregulated building construction.

The surviving villages are located in what were formerly sparsely populated rural areas in Kowloon and the New Territories. These walled villages are now often absorbed into new urban developments, either in the city itself, in new satellite towns or within the many ever-expanding and urbanising village communities. Some of these historically significant villages are in danger of being demolished to facilitate large-scale urban regeneration and development. Some have lost many of their historic buildings due to wilful neglect, the lack of an effective system of preservation or the desire of the residents to build new homes with improved facilities.

A recent work, commissioned for an exhibition at the Kaohsiung Museum of Fine Arts in Taiwan, is a development of an installation completed in Belfast in 2010 at the Golden Thread Gallery.[2] The installation in Belfast was concerned with mapping my experience exploring the urban spaces of Rome when I was a student there in the 1970s. This was a counterpoint to my prior and subsequent experience living and working in Belfast during a period of intense social and political upheaval that dramatically reshaped the urban environment. The installation took the form of a series of low linear walls formed in moulded soft sand. The temporal nature of their construction and the memories that informed them simultaneously represented solidity and fragility, acting as a metaphor for the temporary and often fragile manner in which the casual visitor occupies the volume of a public space.

Sand installation based on a walk through the city of Rome in *Art Beyond Ulster: Collective Histories of Northern Irish Art* exhibition at Golden Thread Gallery, Belfast, 2010.

Drawing for the installation at Kaohsiung Museum of Fine Arts, Taiwan, 2014.

The work I made for the exhibition in Kaohsiung represented a linear walk around and through the surviving structures of one of the historic Hong Kong villages, Nga Tsin Wai, located in an area dominated by high-density commercial and residential multi-storey buildings in Kowloon.[3] Nga Tsin Wai village has a 650-year history and dates from the Yuan Dynasty. It still maintains an identity and some structural integrity but is compromised by a lack of amenities, a dwindling population and crumbling infrastructure. Pressure from high land prices and its potential for commercial development threaten its very existence as a coherent village community.

The installation, made from moulded soft sand, echoed a type of adobe or taipa system employed in historic village-house wall construction. The work revealed a meandering passage through the distinct urban grid of small streets and alleyways. The form and physical substance of the low walls represented the 'volume' of the passage and direction of the pathway. The 'volume' of the street is the only space the casual visitor can inhabit and temporarily own. Over the three-month period of the exhibition, the sand walls dried out, lost sharpness and crumbled. Visitor interaction left its mark, and, ultimately, the only record of the work's existence is in the memories of those who experienced it and through documentation. Similarly, the commercial imperatives of Hong Kong may well consign Nga Tsin Wai and other inner-city historical village communities to little more than memories.

The sense of dynamic renewal in Hong Kong is ever present. Like all cities, it is in a state of perpetual change, reshaping itself daily through

Sand installation based on a walk through the village of Nga Tsin Wai, Kowloon, in *Voices Travel: Conversation between Two Harbours* exhibition at Kaohsiung Museum of Fine Arts, Taiwan, 2014.

24 ↑ 205 26 ↑ 217

land reclamation, construction of new commercial, residential and cultural buildings, the extension of its rail and road infrastructure, including new links to mainland China and Macau, and the revitalisation of selected historic buildings. A rapidly developing agenda that forefronts the role of arts and culture in the future economic development of the city includes a limited acknowledgement of the importance of cultural heritage and its preservation. The ephemerality of the city's shape and infrastructure is exemplified by the temporary transformation and repurposing of key parts of the city, particularly the Admiralty district, by the Occupy Movement in the autumn of 2014.[4]

1 From the 1836 edition of *Maps of the Society for the Diffusion of Useful Knowledge published under the superintendence of the Society for the Diffusion of Useful Knowledge, drawn by W. B. Clarke, engraved by B. R. Davies, 16 George Str., London University. Published by Baldwin & Cradock, Paternoster Row, 1835* (London: Chapman & Hall, 1844).

2 *Art beyond Ulster: Collective Histories of Northern Irish Art*, Golden Thread Gallery, Belfast, 1 October–13 November 2010.

3 *Voices Travel: Conversation between Two Harbours*, Kaohsiung Museum of Fine Arts, Taiwan, 21 June–21 September 2014.

4 http://blogs.wsj.com/chinarealtime/2015/02/23/hong-kong-government-soffice-architect-reflects-on-occupy-movement/ (accessed 22 March 2015).

28

(IN)VISIBLE BODIES

Migrants in the city of gold

Johan Thom

21 ↑ 181

Migration, as the movement of bodies from one place to another, is a useful framework through which to think about the visible and invisible symbolic, economic, political and historical dimensions of the city of Johannesburg. A number of Johannesburg-based artists have recently produced work that encapsulates otherwise overlooked realities of living and working in the city for immigrant communities, in varied ways.

Artists, entrepreneurs and people of vastly different interest and backgrounds from all over Africa and the globe flock to Johannesburg in search of the reward and recognition it promises. In this regard, it may be argued that the fact of the discovery of gold in 1886 remains ever present in the Johannesburg's contemporary status as a highly sophisticated, economic metropolis, one that is often locally referred to in Zulu as *aseGoli*, the 'place of gold'. Today this idea is largely symbolic with the depletion of the gold reserves fast becoming a reality. It is estimated that up to 40 per cent of the world gold reserves have been unearthed in and around Johannesburg. However, in its stead, the world of corporate business, global banking, sports and electronic media continue to make Johannesburg the largest business centre in South Africa and arguably all of Sub-Saharan Africa. In this way the city continues to engender a sense of hope and possibility, one, it is argued here, that is underpinned by the possibility of 'becoming visible' by and through one's belonging to it.

Short commentaries follow on three projects curated to suggest different ways migration and immigration have been explored in art practice through a common motif: the movement and visibility of bodies. These are the Hillbrow/Dakar Project (2007–8) by Stephen Hobbs and Marcus Neustetter (Hobbs/Neustetter), Trolley Works (2007) by Ismail Farouk and *Challenging Mud, after Kazuo Shiraga* (2008) by Johan Thom. Together, they allow a complex, multifaceted vision of the city of Johannesburg to emerge, one defined as much by the corporeality of the body and its movement through Johannesburg as by the various socio-historic and economic meta-narratives more commonly associated with the city.[1]

All three artworks contain trace elements of the material movement of bodies within, into and from the city of Johannesburg: the physical act of carting over-sized baggage from the taxi rank in modified supermarket trolleys; using hand-drawn city maps to go searching for long-lost friends, family or familiar places located elsewhere in Africa; or witnessing the slow process of burying a body covered in gold. Each of these works was made possible by intimate, personal exchanges between the artists and the different communities and familial structures they engage as part of their production.

Together these artworks prompt us to recognise how the movement of bodies actively shape and reshape the city of Johannesburg and actively contribute to its prominent place within Africa and the world. They also allow for an understanding of the city to emerge beyond the familiar post-Apartheid South African narratives of race, exploitation and poverty. In retrospect, the miracle of South Africa's peaceful transition to democracy under the banner of the 'New South Africa' in 1994 seems largely premised upon the fulfilment of a multi-racial vision rather than the recognition of multicultural strata of ever-changing 'migratory bodies' through and by which a city like Johannesburg first came into existence. Today, the relative invisibility of the huge African and other immigrant communities in Johannesburg bolsters the possibility of their systematic economic, political and cultural exploitation.

TROLLEY WORKS
ISMAIL FAROUK

Push-trolleys designed by Ismail Farouk as part of the *Trolley Works* project, 2009.

This project sought to address the plight of informal community of trolley-pushers (or luggage-porters) in and around inner city Johannesburg. Commonly, trolley-pushers congregate near the taxi ranks where they are likely to find customers. However, the trolley-pushers are often subject to exploitation, legal persecution and police brutality: trolley-pushing is an unregulated activity, and the trolley-pushers mostly use stolen shopping trolleys to cart luggage around the inner city.

The project sought to regulate and decriminalise trolley-pushing activity in central Johannesburg in order to mobilise support for the formalisation of a representative trolley association body; define particular safe routes for trolley-pusher activity within the city; forge formal partnerships with the police and city administrative bodies; change perceptions about trolley-pushers as contributing to crime in the city; provide trolley-pushers with a legal trolley alternative to the stolen shopping carts by way of the design and manufacture of a custom trolley specifically suited for their purposes; and empower undocumented migrants, refugees and informal traders about their rights through the distribution of education material located on trolleys.

21 ↑ 181

URBANET—HILLBROW/DAKAR, 2007
HOBBS/NEUSTETTER

During site research for an urban-regeneration project on the border of Johannesburg's Hillbrow neighbourhood, artists Stephen Hobbs and Marcus Neustetter were confronted by two Senegalese immigrants who warned them that entering Hillbrow with a camera was not safe. African 'foreigners' in South Africa are often blamed for the high crime rate, and yet, as this encounter clearly illustrated, things are not as simple. The artists initiated a more in-depth, albeit informal conversation with the Senegalese African immigrant community in Hillbrow, visiting local eateries and other places of communal cultural significance (including social clubs and bars). The immigrant community voiced their serious concerns over their ongoing status as perpetrators of crime in the place they now call home, when, in fact, the opposite often holds true: owing to their status as immigrants, they are easy targets for economic exploitation, bribery and crime. The artists also found that owing to the unstable nature of technological infrastructure on the African continent, many of the Senegalese immigrants had effectively lost contact with their close friends and family in Dakar, thus exacerbating existing feelings of isolation, disconnect and loneliness in Johannesburg.

Drawing their inspiration from this encounter, Hobbs/Neustetter interviewed a group of Senegalese immigrants, asking them to draw maps of the city. The artists then used these hand-drawn maps to navigate the city of Dakar and to visit the friends and family of Senegalese immigrants in Johannesburg. The culmination of this project, a collaboration between the artists and those who had drawn them maps, comprised a series of wall-map-paintings and still photographic projections documenting interactions and engagements that resulted from these social visits.

The project returned to source as a social event at the Chez Ntemba nightclub in Hillbrow, where the documentation of the entire process was shown as a series of slide and video projections alongside informal talks between the artists and participants.

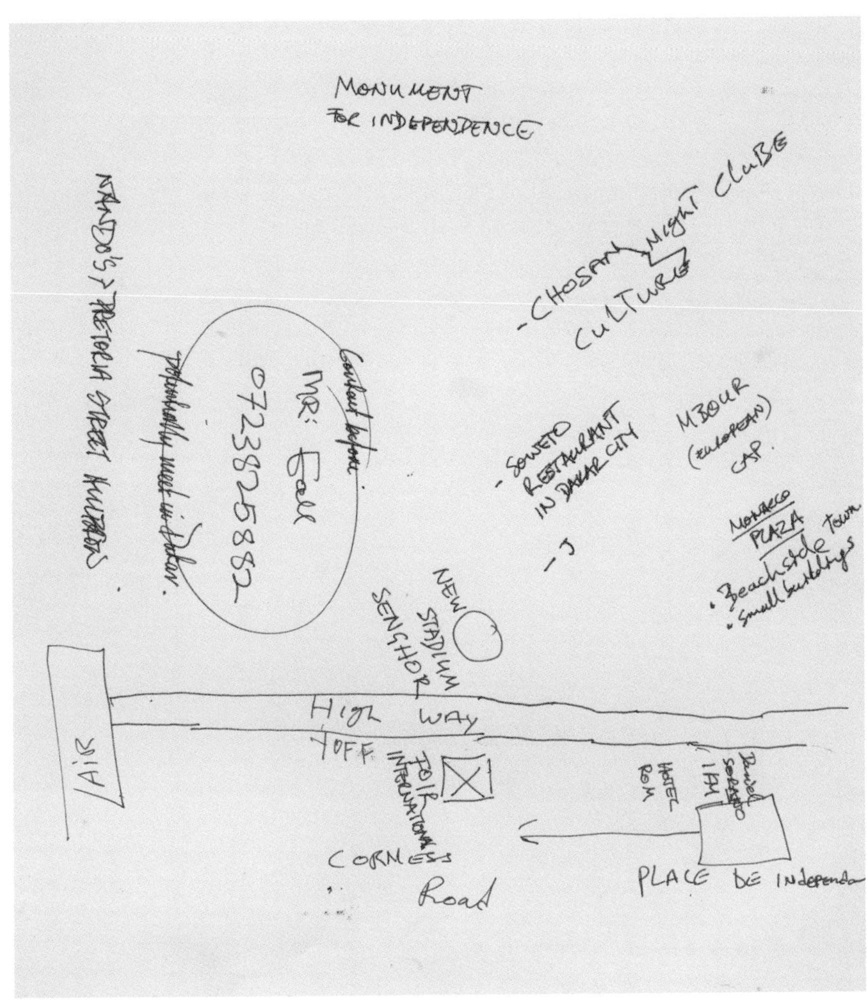

Digital scan of hand-drawn map of Dakar.

21 ↑ 181

CHALLENGING MUD, AFTER KAZUO SHIRAGA
JOHAN THOM

Video still from *Challenging Mud, after Kazuo Shiraga*, 2008, Johan Thom.

On Sunday, 23 March 2008, the artist covered his entire body with honey and gold leaf for a private performance in which he was to be buried alive by his wife and a close group of friends. In the resultant artwork, the viewer witnesses an unseen hand slowly covering a golden figure lying in a foetal position at the bottom of a full-scale grave. The work is strangely hypnotic, with the repetitive sound and motion of the spade and red soil creating for a meditative viewing experience, an effect accentuated by the slow transformation of the visual image. This serves for the emergence of a variety of interpretative strands though perhaps most prominently his difficult relationship with his place of birth, Johannesburg (also often known locally as the 'city of gold').

1 For further discussion of the relationship between these projects, see the full curatorial statement. http://johanthom.com/2012/07/04/invisible-bodies-migrants-in-the-city-of-gold-hobbsneustetter-ismail-farouk-johan-thom/ (accessed 14 October 2015).

29

NEGOTIATING SPACE

The artist as creator and enabler of spaces for working, thinking and meeting

Kieren Reed

As an artist who has worked on several projects that to different degrees see me giving agency over the artwork over to the different publics, participants and collaborators, it has become more apparent that I feel the need to maintain some control over the artistic outputs of the artwork both in terms of aesthetics and concept. If I hand over too much agency to the participants, then my position becomes precarious. This is not necessarily an issue or concern for the audience, but it is something that I, as an artist, have become very aware of in recent works. I am developing methods of managing that situation, whether that means being more in control, working slower to enable more time to see how the artwork develops, or ensuring a better understanding of the negotiation process as an integral part of the work. The art critic Claire Bishop has discussed the problematics surrounding the changing roles of:

> the traditional relationship between the art object, and artist and the audience. To put it simply: the artist is conceived less as an individual producer of discrete objects than as a collaborator and producer of situations; the work of art as a finite, portable, commodifiable product is reconceived as an ongoing or long-term project with an unclear beginning and end; while the audience, previously conceived as a 'viewer' or 'beholder', is now repositioned as a co-producer or participant.[1]

With this in mind, in my work it is also important for me to think critically about collaboration: where, when and how it actually happens, and how real it can be. Or if it is more often a popular word to use in artistic terms but is actually about the control and manipulation of others' experience within art practice and beyond. Both politically and personally I believe in the value of collaboration and in the idea that individuals are able to work together and act altruistically. But I notice increasingly that this is difficult to achieve. In my practice, when I am establishing roles in the first place, I try to remove myself and step back from things, but in actuality that is challenging. These are tensions that I constantly encounter and address, and, to date, I am working out what control mechanisms or solutions might be possible.

The opportunities of collaboration are also altered by the differences in types of audience. I see my practice as exploring the relationships between the different people who might experience it. As Claire Doherty discusses, site-specific and situation-based works operate differently in their 'originating context' — when they are created or when they 'happen', to how they function in their subsequent 'displayed context'.[2] The general public are the ones who I have the least level of engagement with, and perhaps the work is not necessarily made for them. They may simply view the work in its final stages. I am most engaged when working with audiences with whom you have the potential for more considerable impact or where the work has a didactic role and introduces something new. These are the participants I get to work alongside and, depending on the definition of the term, with whom I collaborate directly. My ambition in reality would be to introduce them to a completely new knowledge or a skill which could even in some way change the way they think, act or do and maybe even change an outlook and how they experience something. This works both ways, and I too learn from them. Then the work really is about having impact. As John Dewey discussed in his major writing *Art as Experience* (1934), art is rooted in specific experience, something that is unique and significantly separate from other things in life.[3] This is where I consider the work being at its most interesting, when one is able to pass on information and positively shape experience, be that between artist and participant or between co-participants. When working with small groups, you can teach skills and equip them with abilities to make and build and think, and through that they are able to pass these on to others. It is then about sharing and dispersing information and possibility. As Helen Chadwick discussed in conversation with Andrew Brighton at the 1996 Wimbledon and Tate education conference:

> The people who I have learnt most from in my life were technical people; they were makers. I was learning a kind of attitude in order to be able to make something ... a kind of empathy with making ... (meeting someone who) gives you a perception into things ... people who showed you things, not by telling you but by showing you.[4]

THE PHYSICAL SPACES OF ART PRACTICE

It seems artists are constantly searching for space: space to work in, space to exhibit, space for creativity, space for learning. In cities with booming property markets, studio space has become increasingly expensive. The act of actually making artwork becomes a luxurious activity and for many artists has to be part-time, in the evenings or around other forms of paid employment. The *Guardian* newspaper recently reported that nearly three-quarters of artists earn just 37 per cent of the average UK salary from their practice and so paying rent for a space to make artwork in exasperates the issue.[5] I am exploring this situation through my artwork, in creating and negotiating space for others to use. Through the idea in my practice of making spaces for other artists to inhabit or use, their search for space could become less of a bureaucratic activity for the artist.

I am also interested the physical spaces in which artworks come into being and that in many cities these are not as available as they once were. Often now the laptop acts as studio — a box, a panel, a screen, a space for artwork undefined by physical location. That is, of course, an obvious shift, a change towards much artwork today being mediated and viewed through the internet and other platforms for digital sharing, so artists already have

3 ← 35

a relationship with the virtual. This is a progression, but not necessarily one that is perhaps totally positive in terms of the visual. The internet itself is a vast immeasurable space. In contrast, the space of an exhibition or an event such as a biennale does have a set and confined boundary. It works within these terms. Like the studio space, it is where actual and real things can be experienced at first hand. I feel that the need to have physical space to make, to investigate and to touch, should not be underestimated.

FROM THE GROUND UP: A SOCIAL BUILDING

I was commissioned by the UK's Whitstable Biennale 2014 to create an architectural structure that would be a multi-use space, somewhere between a headquarters or base point, for the Biennale, and, for me, a sculpture. The artwork needed to explore the possibilities of creating a space for performance or screenings, a meeting point and a place to exhibit a collections of objects. I was very interested in creating this space for interactivity; however, this project was also very much about the fabrication of the building. As Neil Cummings and Marysia Lewandowska write, 'Objects — while acting as tools, products, works of art or commodities — are essentially vehicles for relationships between people.'[6] I saw the moment of my artwork being in the negotiation with collaborators and in the potential of bringing different people together to design and build a piece of functioning architecture-as-sculpture. As Duchamp said, 'The creative act is not performed by the artist alone, the spectator brings the work into contact with the external world by deciphering and interpreting its inner qualifications and thus adds his contribution to the creative act.'[7] Jacques Rancière also discusses the importance of the audience or spectator in the making of an artwork, arguing that 'the [e]mancipation [of the spectator] begins when we challenge the opposition between viewing and acting ..., when we understand that viewing is also an action that confirms or transforms this distribution of positions. The spectator also acts, like the pupil or scholar. She observes, selects, compares, interprets.'[8] The consideration of these relationships in connection to the 'object' of the artwork I was to create were essential to my research and thinking. Later, the artwork would tour to be shown in the grounds of the Red House, in Bexleyheath, a National Trust property that was once the home of William Morris. At both the Whitstable Biennale and the Red House the piece would explore its relationship with the people who encountered it on different levels, allowing its audience to have an involved and direct physical experience. In Whitstable, the structure was used as an education space, and in the Red House it was an artist-in-residence studio.

Through their network, the Whitstable Biennale introduced me to the University of the Creative Arts where I was invited to speak, and through

From the Ground Up: a Social Building, interior, Whitstable Biennale, 2014. Photo: Kieren Reed.

From the Ground Up: a Social Building, workshop, University of Creative Arts. Photo: Kieren Reed.

that I recruited participants for my project. Over a ten-week period, I led workshops designing the structure, and these participants, who were drawn from higher education, further education and the general public, were involved in every aspect. The learning environment was clearly set out in both my verbal description of the project to the group and in the physicality of how I set up and wanted the learning space to be used. I was very interested in the dynamic of the working group, trying to create an environment that was very nurturing and appreciating the strengths of each participant, attempting to make opportunities for us all to gain new experiences and creating networks and relationships through shared meals and friendships.

Curator and writer Emily Pethick presents the idea of 'conversation' within the making of artworks: 'Conversation generates forms of exchange that are not fixed or static but rather sustain ongoing processes of engagement, responsiveness and change.'[9] Our group used social media to 'converse' visually and to share design ideas, always meeting in a library so reference materials were easily at hand. I made as much information as possible available and introduced interactive sculptural elements for the participants to work with. Wooden blocks were provided to physically design

Liminal, Kieren Reed and Abigail Hunt. Tate Britain, 2013. Photo: Kieren Reed and Abigail Hunt.

Liminal, Kieren Reed and Abigail Hunt. Agency without Intention, Herbert Read Gallery, 2015. Photo: Kieren Reed and Abigail Hunt.

in three dimensions, and these linked to some of my previous projects, namely, *Liminal*.[10] Working from a brief and facilitating the participants in designing a building through research, I was using teaching techniques to create a shared learning environment making the most of the groups' diverse skill sets and previous experience.

In some ways, the process was instrumental in that I already knew that I needed to achieve a design for a structure that could be installed on the foreshore in Whitstable (a seaside town in Kent). But as much as possible I allowed the participants to work out what they could and wanted to do. And so, collectively, they designed it, sourced the materials and worked on the build itself. I also shared my knowledge of negotiating with the local authority to gain permissions and fulfil building regulations as I wanted the group to have an awareness of the challenges of producing artworks in public spaces.

Once the designs had been approved, we had a week-long build period to assemble the structure. The design chosen by the group was an A-frame formation, which was informed by my research into West Coast American counter-culture dwellings and vernacular architecture. These homes are interesting in amplifying the social culture in which they were built and in

From the Ground Up: a Social Building, Day 1, Whitstable Beach (raising), Whitstable Biennale, 2014. Photo: Kieren Reed.

that they didn't follow expected norms of society and architecture of the time. The build process had a very similar set-up to the design sessions. I was teaching people how to use tools, make joints and work with timber. Many of the participants had experience of making small-scale maquettes, but a live project, actually working on a real structure, was new to them. Tasks were kept short to enable exposure to a wider skill set of techniques (cutting, drilling, screwing, bolting, measuring, etc.), and I also introduced some thinking and discussion around the notion of labour within art practice. In my view, it is essential to gain a very intimate understanding of the materials one uses through touch and repeated processes. I am fascinated by how participants' haptic experience offers so much more than experiencing an artwork in a singular visual moment, through looking. Using your hands doesn't mean that one is not thinking and developing a conceptual frame to underpin to one's practice.

As with some of my previous artworks, I also discussed with the Biennale team my desire to hand over the finished sculpture for an artist or group of artists to use and that that they would take control of the space, determining its use during the festival. Through a selection process, CRG (Collaborative Research Group) was chosen, and they were very keen to be

3 ↑ 35

From the Ground Up: a Social Building, Day 1, Whitstable Beach (frame detail), Whitstable Biennale, 2014. Photo: Kieren Reed.

involved from the beginning. They were then seen as the client, so we really considered what they required from the space. I also wanted to build into it some features I had developed in earlier works. This included for example, functional social furniture with dual use (a seat, which is also a plinth, which is also a storage box, a stage, which is also an object for play), and these elements became integral to the design.

Eighteen A-frames were prepared at the University of Creative Arts, flat-packed for transporting and ready for assembly on the beach. The sculpture was raised very quickly on the site itself — in only three hours — and was then clad and covered in waterproof fabric. Every person involved in the project was paid for manual work as I felt it was key that the funding was distributed evenly. Again, the working process involved shared meals, and this became a way of bringing a community of people together to share and develop ideas.

Working in this way together as a group can be tricky. It introduces the idea of co-authorship, but the artist's name is on the wall at the end of the day (my name in this case), and that is something that I have thought a lot about as to how to determine. I struggle with the possibilities and differences between co-authoring and de-authoring. My ideas look around this and consider how much, if at all, I am trying to remove myself from the process.

I am interested in highlighting where the audience are, and I suppose that within *From the Ground Up: a Social Building*, they appear at different stages. There is the audience made up of the participants or collaborators who helped design and build the structure, and they are my key audience. They chose to be there, and they supported the project from beginning to end. Then the audience who came in to work within the structure — they were selected but were in some ways slightly more removed from the process of the project, and they did not necessarily have the same understanding of the intention of the space. And, last, the 'general public' of Biennale visitors who came in to see the work in its final stages, who had not bought into the process. This became very apparent to me when an artist colleague came to Whitstable but called me later to apologise that he missed my artwork as he had looked for it but couldn't find it. Playing along with the situation, I asked him where he had been, and he described being next to a building on the beach, looking on the map but not being able to find my work anywhere. Then he described *A Social Building* and the practice that was going on inside it, but in his description it was clear that he did not consider it to be an artwork.

The philosopher Jean Baudrillard, in writing about art and functionality, remarks that:

> Every object claims to be 'functional' ... The term evokes all the virtues of modernity, yet it is perfectly ambiguous. With its reference to 'function' it suggests that the object fulfils itself in the precision of its relationship to the real world of human needs. But as our analysis has shown, 'functional' in no way qualifies what is adapted to a goal, merely what is adapted to an order or system: functionality is the ability to become integrated into an overall scheme. An object's functionality is the very thing that enables it to transcend its main 'function' in the direction of a secondary one, to play a part, to become a combining element, an adjustable item, within a universal system of signs ... Every object thus has two functions — to be put to use and to be possessed.[11]

I feel that this artwork has a purpose. It has duality, it has function as well as being aesthetic as it is a sculpture. In Whitstable, my colleague had missed the aesthetic because he had focused on looking at the artwork's function. But this is not problematic as the function is the purpose. So it's an interesting play on not standing back to view and venerate the object but instead considering when it becomes an artwork and if and when it gets recognised as such.

There is a space between artwork which would be considered public art and my practice in the sense that my work is about the public and about the experience of the public but not about the permanent and not really

3 ↑ 35

SAVE
TODAY'S
SPECIAL EVENTS:
1pm FIONA JAMES
'The Incident: A
Diagram for Whitstable'
WB LAUNCH
performance HERE
2.30pm
'Letter of Complaint'
@ Sea Cadets Hall

From the Ground Up: a Social Building, Whitstable Biennale, 2014. Photo: Kieren Reed.

about the object (even though the object is a key element). It is about the experience of the event, about constructing and building, about the process of making the object and who that involves. It is also very much about audience. Marcel Duchamp theorised the significance of the audience in the making of an artwork. Believing that it was the viewer who brought an artwork into the external world, he saw the audience as being allowed to determine and refine the artwork through 'aesthetic osmosis' from simply being made up of materials, into art.

So, in some ways, it is public, and it is a public experience, but not all of the public can experience the actual moment of the work. It can therefore be compared to public art and also be compared to architecture. But it is not necessarily either one, instead sitting somewhere between the two. I hope then it explores a point of balance. I am not an architect, and I am not making a public artwork which has been dropped down into a place. I want to work directly with public participants, making relationships with my audience and with the building process.

Many artists have this continual negotiation with space, needing to make a consideration of where and how they want their work to exist. Time itself is also relevant here: the importance of the moment in time when the artwork is created and the value of that moment. I am also questioning the role of the 'real' object and the relevance of that object within an artwork as a whole, or whether it is what happens in the time and space around and as a result of that object where the essential aspects of the work happen. I do of course make objects, but as those objects are often buildings or functional pieces, they have a real use value. The situations I create within and because of them question the moment at which the art happens. I look to explore if that is a moment I have created or caused to happen. And if yes, then this is then me as artist, as curator, as facilitator, and as one who brings objects into question.

1 Claire Bishop, *Artificial Hells: Participatory Art and the Politics of Spectatorship* (London and New York: Verso, 2012), 2.
2 Claire Doherty, *Contemporary Art: From Studio to Situation* (London: Black Dog, 2004).
3 John Dewey, *Art as Experience* (New York: Putman, 1934).
4 Helen Chadwick and Andrew Brighton, 'In Conversation', in *Issues in Art and Education: The Dynamics of Now*, edited by William Furlong, Polly Gould and Paul Hetherington (London: Wimbledon School of Art and Tate, 1996), 77–85, 81.
5 Susan Jones, 'Artists' Low Income and Status Are International Issues', *The Guardian*, 12 January 2015. http://www.theguardian.com/culture-professionals-network/2015/jan/12/artists-low-income-international-issues (accessed 14 October 2015).
6 Neil Cummings and Marysia Lewandowska, *Capital* (London: Tate, 2001).
7 Marcel Duchamp, 'The Creative Act', Session on the Creative Act, Convention of the American Federation of Arts, Houston, Texas, April 1957. http://ubu.com/sound/duchamp.html (accessed 10 November 2015).
8 Jacques Rancière, *The Emancipated Spectator*, trans. Gregory Elliott (London and New York: Verso, 2009).
9 Emily Pethick, 'Resisting Institutionalism', in *Documents of Contemporary Art: Education, edited by Felicity Allen* (London: Whitechapel, 2008), 193–6.
10 Commissioned by Tate and created in collaboration with artist Abigail Hunt, *Liminal* (2010) is an eighty-piece wooden sculpture of varying geometric forms. The artwork is only 'activated' by a relationship with its audience who interact with it physically through touch, movement, composition and looking.
11 Jean Baudrillard, *The System of Objects* (London and New York: Verso, 1968), 63.

30

25 DEMOLISHED HOUSES

Mircea Nicolae

Spatial appropriation Photo matrixes Documenting demolition

8 ↑ 77 18 ↑ 155

My installation, *25 Demolished Houses*, portrayed here, was the second iteration of a work, shown at a site-specific exhibition organised for Cities Methodologies, Bucharest, 2010. It took place in Casa Scarlat-Ghica, a typically old and neglected villa in the courtyard of the National University of Arts, which was being emptied out for future use by the university. Formerly an artist studio, it became a large, unused space, vacated by its former inhabitants.

Each exhibition room has its own requirements. My intention was to try my best to adapt the display to the room, in order to use both the objects and the general ambiance to communicate my research on demolitions in the city. The room itself was barren and dusty, which is why I decided to use a form of presentation that blended the geometric purity of objects with the fragility and precariousness of their materials and with the crumbling environment. To take these matters further, I chose to show the production process as well as the end product in order to arrive at a more unfinished look and feel for the whole installation.

A map of the demolition sites was placed on the wall. A crate was placed in a corner, containing the bricks that had been cut in order to extract small, house-like fragments which I had inserted into the glass globes. A billboard showing a new, typical high-rise development was also displayed, along with a hand-made sign that signalled a 'demolition by the owner' of one of these old houses. A matrix of twenty-five photos of the demolition sites was placed on the other wall. A binder containing a photographic documentation of the production process of the objects was included at the end.

Demolition fragments, location information, the photographic documentation of the demolished sites and of the production methods as well as the final artwork were all shown at the same time, in the same space. They made the trajectory from the issue of urban demolition as a research question to a physical artistic form clearly visible. The experience of the installation could be one of aesthetic pleasure or one of acquiring knowledge and information on demolition and renewal, or it could be both. There was the possibility of seeing how the objects came into being and of oscillating between a known urban reality and an aesthetic experience.

The run-down look of the room enhanced a strong familiarity between the final product of the production process and the site, thereby enhancing the aesthetics and effects of the room itself. In turn, the aesthetic experience of the room made the larger question of demolition more present, tangible and urgent.

Installation shot of *25 Demolished Houses*, Cities Methodologies, Bucharest, 2010.

DEMOLITION: THE URBAN ISSUE

Beginning in the 1990s and gaining momentum after the year 2000, a large-scale process of destruction of the built heritage of the city of Bucharest started to make its presence felt. Private homes built between the 1850s and the 1940s in the centre of Bucharest were demolished and replaced with high-rise office buildings and residential complexes. Often, these changes in the aspect and height of these neighbourhoods were carried out illegally, with the support of the local administration. The City Hall was interested in colluding with the developers while at the same time disregarding the existing urban heritage legislation it was meant to protect. Large parts of the city completely changed face.

8 ↑ 77 18 ↑ 155

A HISTORY OF BRUTAL MODERNISATION

Generally speaking, the destruction of buildings is an ordinary occurrence. Old houses crumble. Their shabby walls fall down into the dust. However, historically speaking, Bucharest seems to have a certain specificity with regard to its cyclical processes of destruction. In this city, at least since the nineteenth century, urban and architectural modernisation have been implemented in abrupt waves of demolition and reconstruction, on a large scale, following the trends of the day, with little respect for or interest in the preservation of the previously built space.

This view is supported by the demolition campaigns of the 1850s, the 1980s and the 2000s. This is how the Ottoman and Byzantine cities

32 ↑ 259

Photos of actual sites of demolition in Bucharest from where brick fragments were collected.

of the 1800s and then the Bourgeois and the Modern cities of the 1900s and 1930s were dismantled. These transformations were extensive and sometimes exhaustive, completely removing large parts of the city in a matter of a few years. In this context, demolition acted as a way to quickly catch up with the external forms of progress of the prevailing empire of the day. In its turn, the act of building architecture became a driving force for the blunt modernisation of Romanian society. With little time on their hands, however, the demolition men and builders neglected some of the complex laws that allow for the very development of society and architecture.

Urban continuity, as well as the reappraisal and exploitation of the

8 ↑ 77 18 ↑ 155

past as a resource of knowledge and identity were not considered valuable endeavours, a statement that rings true today as well. To fully understand this we only have to go back to the issue at hand, which is the large-scale demolition of nineteenth-century private homes from the historical centre of Bucharest. This can be said to be the most recent phase of the process of modernisation and self-colonisation.

In this most recent case, what is being flushed out is the old city, with its one-story bourgeois homes surrounded by private gardens. In its place, the builders implement a city of cramped, gated communities in the shape of towering concrete and glass structures. There is also the option of different arrangements of prefabricated urban offices along with all the corresponding behaviours associated with the new market economy.

The developers make big money out of contracts that often take the shape of speculation. The local administration profits as well as permits are given in exchange for bribes. Quite often, legislation or building-regulation maps are changed to favour the builders. The final product is an urban context scarred by petty interest and short-term gain. Cheap architecture triumphs over heritage, the street is patchy and poor, and the city itself feels dysfunctional, somewhat repulsive, broken.

THE MOTIVATION BEHIND THE PROJECT

When one is confronted with the form of the city of Bucharest, marked by its transformation processes, and their dysfunctionality, one is prompted to search for clues as to what caused each rupture. Finding out what some of those causes were and critically engaging with them by focusing on specific case studies, rendered through particular symbolic gestures, was the main motivation behind this project. Although limited in capturing the complexity of demolition and renewal, the installation makes this issue present on a material and sensorial level, sustaining contemplation as well as communicating knowledge gained through research.

In so doing, the project does not shy away from its own potential futility to alter destructive processes. Yet, rather than give up on the issue, it aims to educate those who visited the installation about the state of the city, through aesthetic means and through shaping their embodied experience of a semi-derelict space.

31

THE BRIDGE OF SIGHS

'Happy are those who see beauty in modest spots where others see nothing. Everything is beautiful; the whole secret lies in knowing how to interpret it.' *Camille Pissarro* (1893)[1]

Temporary installation Documenting immateriality Memory transmission

Simson&Volley

12 ↑ 109

The Bridge of Sighs was part of a series of temporary installation works that consider the overlaps and associations between memory and place. It alludes to a landscape in which inner and outer worlds interact and the poetic possibilities in recognising these relations are brought together.

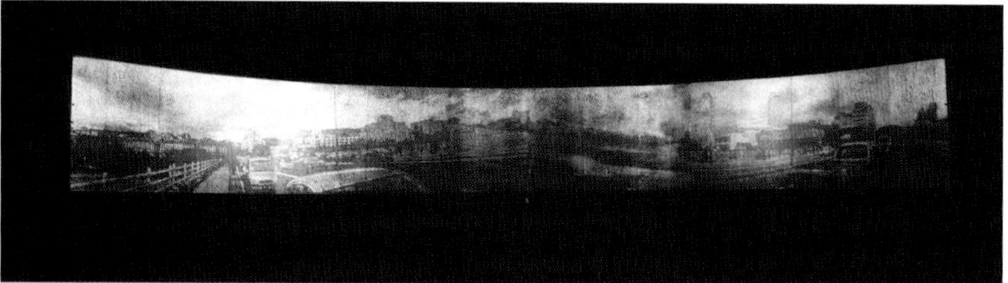

The installed work consisted of a gilded arch placed above and spanning the framework linking two gallery spaces with a panoramic image of London's Waterloo Bridge projected from the floor onto the gilded surface.[2] The arch was a literal reference to the shape of the bridge, a physical connection between two things. By passing through the arch, the viewer was offered a visual, tactile and sensuous experience of 'transmission', the eternal energy of the gold leaf reconciled with the transient and ephemeral quality of light from the projected image. The piece took an everyday urban scene and a familiar architectonic form, and through their association and juxtaposition suggested a narrative. The familiarity of Waterloo Bridge was framed by the archetype of a golden arch: a portal for exiting reality or an entrance to the metaphysical.

The Bridge of Sighs, installation view, Slade Research Centre.

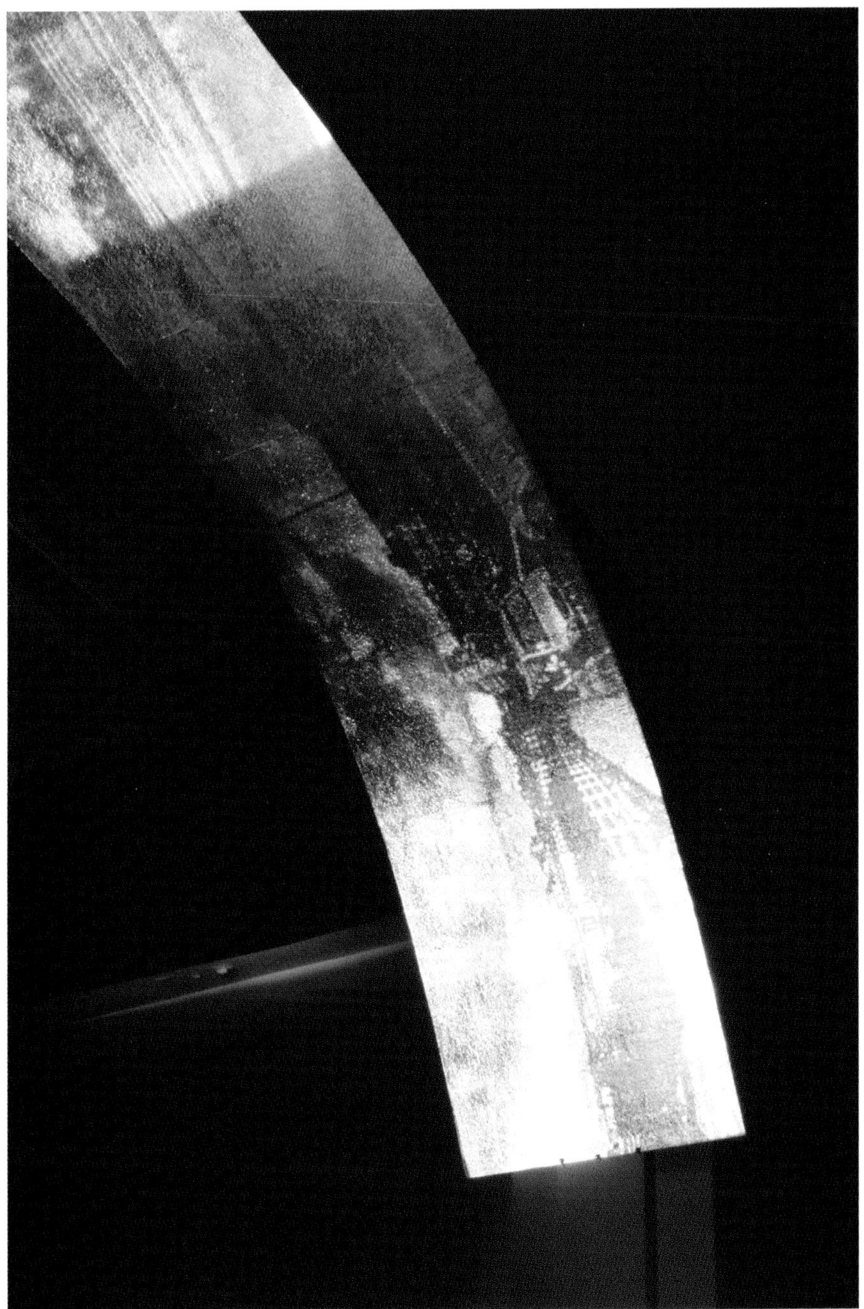

The Bridge of Sighs, left-hand detail.

12 ↑ 109

The Bridge of Sighs draws attention to the beauty of the ordinary. There is also the underlying claim that, in the daily cut and thrust of the city, art practice, and its use of forms, media and materials can help, through its sustained and critical interventions, to shape the public realm and force us to reflect on it. Also important is that the beauty of the work draws attention the poignancy of the place, which became a frequent site of suicides in the 1840s. The title, *The Bridge of Sighs*, refers to Thomas Hood's 1844 poem about the suicide of a prostitute there. The work raises questions about the dynamics between subjective human experience and the urban infrastructures that frame this experience. In what way do these interact and what traces do they leave on each other?

1 Quoted in Angela King and Susan Clifford, *Holding Your Ground: An Action Guide to Local Conservation* (London: Maurice Temple Smith, 1985), 251.
2 A site-specific work made for Cities Methodologies, Slade Research Centre, London, 2010.

32

MATERIALS. STORIES

Collaboration with materials Salvage Story-telling

Hilary Powell

2 ↑ 29 3 ↑ 35 11 ↑ 97 30 ↑ 249

This project examines the material components of the demolition site (from zinc to copper, steel, concrete, brick, asbestos, cement and slate). In direct collaboration with these materials, it explores their stories and adapts traditional printmaking techniques to create images of both demolition sites and those who work on them. Through imaginative salvage, the work explores regeneration and economic transition by putting the excess and waste products of transformation to artistic use. Creative production and the poetry and politics of place combine with the science, agency and political ecology of materials in this cross-disciplinary exploration of the lifecycles and micro- and macro-economics of the material culture of post-industrial urban landscapes. The project focuses on often overlooked and undervalued processes, materials, lives and livelihoods and questions the way we value, consume and waste materials.[1]

COPPER

In abandoned toilet blocks you come for me: crude tools wrenching cracked porcelain, tile shards revealing broken anatomy. Once coursing waters are unleashed from hidden reserves in geysers flooding dank basement grottos. Down distant corridors the contortions of electrocution resound. Flashlight on bright wire exposed, live scorched flesh, metallic surge. Am I so valuable to you?

High above, I am left to my own devices. Storms brood, and I conduct a symphony of cloud formations. Tarnished sentry of cities, I guard and protect utopian longing, glass towers of Babel and heavenly aspirations. I am struck: sparks fly, sheet rain and steeple-jacks fall, and I am in my element. Radiant machina metereological of turquoise azurite and remote grace.

I am at the centre of your electric age. I relay thought, speech, heat. Beaten and bruised I share my verdigris complexion with gods and heroes, many Venuses and Liberty herself. I endure domestic blows as the workings of the mundane are plundered in search of me. Find a penny, pick it up. ... I am prized amid plastic toys on pleasure piers fuelling low-budget gambling addictions. I make my way through novelty charity collection boxes, overflowing jars and drains and circuits.

From the enigmatic smiles of monarchs to ancient and modern mysteries encoded and encrypted I host multiple faces and forms. I am current and currency. Wash your hands after dealing in me, dirty lucre, invisible plague and pestilence. I repel such accusations with my touch. No need to cross your palm with silver. Why bastard, wherefore base. I am precious. I am part of you but take care. I am life- and death-giver. I poison the waters I carry, encase the ammunition that maims and burst the veins that carry me.

Do you value me so little? Is it because I am so malleable to your

Copper.

2 → 29 3 → 35 11 → 97 30 → 249

needs? On trading rings and telephone exchanges you speak of me in the language of zeros, risk and futures. What is my future? Far from here, desperate men queue to risk entry into claustrophobic earth, humanity's canaries feeding supply and demand. Listen to me: in the wires, earth, air, fire and water. What do I demand? Intergalactic, I come to you from beyond the skies and below ground. Blood mingles with earth's crust, through rescue and recovery life cycles continue, and I am remade, leaving a metallic taste in your mouth.

STEEL

I am warrior metal of sword and spear. Knife-wielding pyromaniac performing cosmic dance and meteoric fall. Hammer and sickle. Haematite and haemoglobin. Body and blood. I am forged from red ore mimicking the rusting planet above. Warlords and weapons of Martian and martial law abandoned to anaemic landscapes. Discovered in the embers of dying fires my metamorphosis was hard-fought. Iron Age origins of smelter and forge. Surprised by Vulcan into revolution. Destroyer and benefactor I am military might and munitions. Iron muse. With carbon, oxygen and belief I support the weight of wonder. Terra firma soars as superstructures and skylines rise. I traverse rivers, withstand oceans, shelter millions, cross continents.

Earth, air, fire, water. Molten rivers of flame and steaming muck of money. The price that we pay. Dead fish, rancid sweat and beer. Throw the bugger back. The Rother and Don. Afan and Ruhr. Jianhe and Yangtze. Going hammer and tongs. Thump. Thump. Thud. A maimed land vibrates. Scorched skin on calloused hands beat injury and lost time. Blinded eyes and deafened ears. Beating, shouting, but nobody hears. Song and story reverberate across a geography of inequality. Midwest to Midlands exhuming ancient and industrial ballads. Poems to freight trains and fire gods. Ode to the railroads. To motherfuckin' Detroit.

Black Monday. Fateful day at foundry and pit. Rebel songs of steel and struggle unite in crisis. Solidarity and solidity outmoded and overthrown. Division and derision. Scabs and cuts. Metallic veins and fresh blood. Oppressed northern soul and proletariat orchestra of crutches and frying pan, dustbin lid and oil drum. Strike. Strike. Strike. Sparks fly. Soot and sulphur snuffed out. Mothballed furnaces, steel towns and motor cities. Heavy industry, hearts and liver decline. The glittering dust settles. Deep breath. Swallow.

Bulk haulage. Strait of Malacca. Steel hulls hold iron ore and scrap, votive offerings to global behemoths. Tata. Mittal. Nipon. Wuhan. The future is traded. London. New York. Shanghai. Monopolies and cartels hide gouged mountain steppe and slag. Crucible and casualties of the Great Leap Forward. Downturns and dumping. Tundras of trash and everyday

Steel.

2 ↑ 29 3 ↑ 35 11 ↑ 97 30 ↑ 249

devastation. Dystopian districts and satellite cities of excess production, overburdened commodity and surging skyscrapers.

Lost cargo corroding in ocean depths. Rescue flare, salt water and air. Above ground, rust belts of Cadillac and collapsing mill, coke ovens and dismantled towers are recovered. Magpie magnates oversee industrial salvage while itinerant collectors press magnets to mangled remains. Site manager and demiurge reclaim my opus. With ferrous fatigue or fault line I am chewed, snipped, munched and made anew. White heat of electric arc transforms artefacts of an era as violent palimpsest. We have lived this before. Tool and truck reincarnate, cranes lifting, girders hanging, scaffolding ascending. I brace, fortify, fasten, buttress, strengthen and reinforce a civilisation in perpetual motion. Volcano sun rising on the pace of change.

ASBESTOS

Breathe in. Breathe out. Breathe in. Bombs drop. You hold me close. Smell of rubber and disinfectant. Breathe in. Breathe out. Respite from the chaos. Sound of siren and rattle. Breathe out. Breathe in. I wrap myself around you.

Firefighters enter the inferno. Inhale. Exhale. Smoke-eaters of inextinguishable flames. I am untouchable rock of ages and mortal grief. Ancient texts warned of my chronic brilliance, weaving a natural history of fire spirits, shape-shifting salamander and the disease of slaves. I am curiosity and wonder. Playing with fire and magic, purity and danger, I withstand purgatory. From rock vein to human tissue I have clothed popes and emperors. Mineral silk. Risk unravelled. Now naked torsos are hosed down in decontamination units. Vacuums of exposed flesh. Examinations and X-rays.

War and industry courted me. Shipments of progress. Cargos of resistance and reinforcement. Consumed and surrounded. Rooftops, walls, patented pipes, lagging and cladding, aircraft hangers and naval vessels, warships and armaments. I am strength and shelter, safety and security. A blessing on hearth and home. Tools for domestic goddess and practical man. Insoles and underwear, baking paper, tobacco filters, iron holders, curtains and covers in a variety of patterns. On 54th floor or Route 66 I bring you to a sure safe stop. Cessation of breath.

I am Marvel comic villain succumbing to reality. An antihero of unfortunate surprises. Largely unseen and seldom recognised, take a punt on where I turn up next. I am carnival token and poker chip. Ship-breaking, demolition, decommissioning, removal and remediation. A rigged gamble of disturbance and disaster. The curtain calls but my glory days are fading. Fibres fall gently on the poppy fields of Oz awakening Dorothy from sweet forgetfulness. Show's over. Fields of remembrance. To the fallen victims of industrial negligence, denial and defamation. Factory-town children

Asbestos removal.

2 ↑ 29 3 ↑ 35 11 ↑ 97 30 ↑ 249

dreaming of a white Christmas as artificial snow drifts into nightmares.

Mines and mountains take my name. Dust-covered townships exploiting Apartheid and child labour. Scars of whip and lung. Black Lake. White Gold. Unquenchable desire for profit. Banned here, I arrive there. An elsewhere beyond corporate responsibility or care. Toxic trade in betrayal and hypocrisy. My lethal infrastructure is insured against. Compensated for. Lawsuits, litigation and libel contaminating lives.

Breathe in. Breathe out. Respire. Expire. I endure as exploited paradox. Indestructible stone. Imperial export. Exiled as dangerous goods. Transported in locked carriages. Committed to the earth. Secured in rock rooms and mineral museums. Molten miracle. Bruised lungs. Blue, brown, black and blue all over until lying white. I am shroud and sepulchral lamp. Eternal mourning flame.

1 The project began through artist Hilary Powell's ongoing work on demolition sites as part of an Arts and Humanities Research Council Fellowship in the Creative and Performing Arts at the Bartlett School of Architecture, UCL. It continued as she became Leverhulme Artist in Residence in the UCL Chemistry Department, collaborating with the Anthropology Department through a UCL Grand Challenge of Sustainable Cities award for the project 'Deconstructing Demolition: Journeys through Scrap and Salvage', working towards the production of 'Urban Alchemy' events, prints and book. For more information, see http://www.hilarypowell.com (accessed 8 August 2016).

33

BUILDINGS ON FIRE

Towards a new approach to urban memory

Stamatis Zografos with Edwina Attlee,
Eva Bachmann, Eleanor Dare, Robin Morrison,
Sotirios Varsamis, Eleni Zacharia

2 ↑ 29

Most major cities in the world have been partly or fully destroyed by fire. Urban fires are usually accidental but are sometimes deliberate. Cities in Egypt, Syria, Libya and Tunisia suffered fire destructions during the Arab Spring; parts of Athens have repeatedly been burnt during protests against austerity; London and other cities in the United Kingdom were severely affected by fires during the riots in 2011. Regardless of how an urban fire starts, buildings and the urban landscape are silent victims, and fire is the last memory.[1] The idea of 'fire as a methodology' stems from my research in which I examine the birth and evolution of architecture and the city in relation to this element and comment on how memory manifests itself in architecture and urban design.

Specifically, the primitive hut is believed to be erected around fire. The Roman architect Vitruvius, in his book *De Architectura* (27 BC), explains that the primitive man was initially terrified by accidental fires that started by branches of trees being rubbed together but slowly observed and appreciated the comfort of standing in front of the flames. He wanted to prolong his comfort, and this he achieved by adding more wood to the fire. The accidental discovery of fire was, according to Vitruvius, what 'originally gave rise to the coming together of men, to the deliberative assembly, and to social intercourse'.[2] More recently, the German architect Gottfried Semper confirms that the fire of the hearth is the 'first and most important, the moral element of architecture' around which three other elements came to emerge, namely the roof, the enclosure and the mound.[3] Reinforcing Vitruvius' description, Semper confirms that the fire of the hearth was the initial assembly point of primitive man.

Fire is intimately associated with construction in the myths of origin too. In Ancient Greece, Hestia was the goddess of the hearth, and her fire used to burn in the *prytaneion*, the town hall, as it represented the centre of city life. In Ancient Rome, the goddess was called Vesta, and 'ruled both the household fire of the individual family and the civic hearth of the city'.[4] According to the architectural historian and critic Joseph Rykwert, when Rome was initially erected, the city founders dug a round hole in the ground called the *mundus*. The mundus had a central position in the city and represented the mouth of the Underworld. On the top of this hole they built a stone altar, where a fire burnt constantly. Every time a new city was founded, they created a new mundus, which burned fire taken from the initial altar in Rome.

Fire symbolised the beginning of creation and always occupied a central position in space. In this sense, fire also comprises the first memory we have of the built environment. Before that, there is dark empty space and oblivion. Following fire's gradual proliferation in architectural space, one sees that the flames of the hearth once occupied a central position in space and functioned as a gathering point. During the first years of modernity, there was a shift. The centrality of the hearth was gradually replaced by fireplaces, radiators and under-floor heating. People found themselves surrounded by multiple centres, and fire was dislocated and confined in space (i.e. into the boiler room). In sustainable design, fire is 'out', and the space which it once inhabited is simply redundant (that is, because of the use of solar panels replacing boilers).

Fire is also one of architecture's biggest threats. It usually breaks out without warning and expands unpredictably. As a result, society has invested in various ways to tackle this threat. Today, buildings are protected with active and passive fire protection systems. Cities have organised fire-fighting forces and appropriate building legislation, and there is a constant investment in fire-prevention research, which is all fed by the imminent risk of urban fire and the traumatic memory of previous catastrophes.

Looking at architectural evolution in relation to fire, one finds that the element is present from the birth to the death of architecture. My research also explains how the memory of fire is absorbed, stored and externalised into the form, materiality and organisation of buildings and cities. It is in this sense, therefore, that fire operates as a methodological tool to access and explore memory. The following texts, projects and installations push this idea further and approach memory through multidisciplinary methods that expose fire's diverse, powerful, enigmatic and often catastrophic nature.

Fire as a methodology

Eleanor Dare, *Head on Fire: Burning Down Memory*. Model of a memorial made by the artist. Photo: Eleanor Dare.

BURNING DOWN MEMORY
ELEANOR DARE

The Burning Down Memory project aims to explore the nature of London's absent memorials via digital mediation, in particular the absence of memorials that significantly mark the many destructive fires London has endured, including the New Cross fire of 1981, which killed thirteen young black people at a time of intense racist activity in South London. (An exception is the monument to the Great Fire of London, more commonly known as 'the Monument'.) Marita Sturken's question, 'What is an experience that is not remembered?' (1999) is the starting point for a project that attempts to uncover the nature of London's absent memorials, asking how a medium that is implicitly representational and symbolic (e.g., binary computing systems) can adequately articulate the loss of representation in destructive fires. How can a computer program adequately convey the complex nature of urban fire? In response to these questions, the artist destroyed digital images of urban trauma sites by digitally burning and permanently destroying pixels when skin sensors detected her anxiety or stress. The artist explores Mieke Bal's notion of memory as an act that always takes place in the present, testing the idea that fire itself can represent a dynamic cultural memorial.

Jack Wates, Rocio Ayllon, Riccardo Vincentini, *The Falling House*. Stills from the film depicting the (reversed) construction of the building by fire.

THE FALLING HOUSE
JACK WATES, ROCIO AYLLON, RICCARDO VINCENTINI

The Falling House plays with notions of the absurd through the portrayal of a continuously changing burning building. The perception of time as a linear construct is altered as the house is first destroyed in flames and then, played backwards, the house is perceived to be constructed by the same flames that destroyed it. Fire is the catalyst for change and renewal but also becomes an integral part of the material fabric of this building.

FIRE ESCAPE/EXCESSIVE TO FUNCTION
EDWINA ATTLEE

Edwina Attlee presenting on Westhorpe House in Bethnal Green, Cities Methodologies, 2014.

Fire Escape/Excessive to Function is a reading of the space of the fire escape, the practice of the fire drill, and how both reflect the memory of architecture's destruction by fire. Thinking about the fact that these routes and exits are built in the hope that they will never be used, and the ways in which they *are* used, provokes questions about the radical potential of the useless, the empty and the wasteful. The fire escape invites subversive poetry, the poetry that aims to rebel and be controversial, permitting city-dwellers to play with the useless detail.

CITY THAT BURNS, FLOWER THAT BLOSSOMS
ELENI ZACHARIA

Eleni Zacharia's presentation, Cities Methodologies, 2014.

The paper 'City that Burns, Flower that Blossoms' is a psychoanalytic interpretation of the violent protests and demonstrations that took place and burnt down Athens in December 2008 after the shooting of a fifteen-year-old boy by a policeman. Drawing on psychoanalytic object relations theory, Zacharia's paper tries to explicate possible unconscious states of mind that directed these catastrophic protests and their interplay with the social, political and economic situation in Greece at the time.

2 ↑ 29

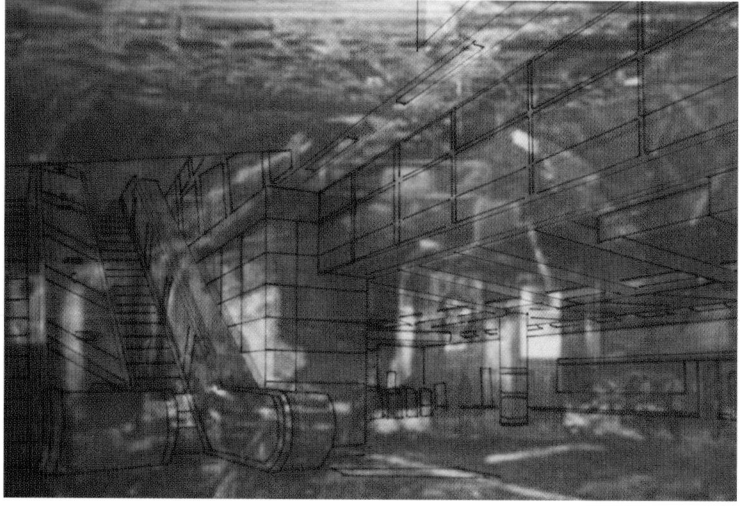

Eva Bachmann, *Tracing Memories 1* and *2*. King's Cross Fire.

TRACING MEMORIES
EVA BACHMANN

Tracing Memories is a visual exploration of the King's Cross Fire in 1987 and the architectural changes made after the disaster. The eerie impressions of the aftermath are drawn with charcoal, as the material itself is a product of combustion. The dark images of the fire are contrasted by the transparent, austere-looking interiors of the station in its reconstructed form. Like layers of time, or blurred memories, the multilayered images fade in and out, depending on one's view.

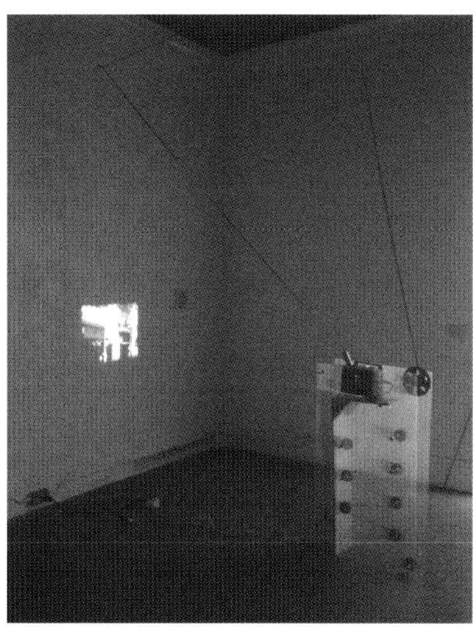

Stamatis Zografos, *Burning Seville: An Architectural Meditation 1,* Super 8 film installation. Photo: Stamatis Zografos.

Stamatis Zografos, *Burning Seville: An Architectural Meditation 2,* still from the Super 8 film. Photo: Stamatis Zografos.

BURNING SEVILLE: AN ARCHITECTURAL MEDITATION
STAMATIS ZOGRAFOS

This Super-8 film installation is generated by architecture students of Seville University and reflects their desire to 'destroy' buildings of a historically significant part of their city: Paseo de Cristóbal Colón in Seville and Calle Betis in Triana. According to theories of psychoanalysis, the expression of the desire to 'destroy', or of the death drive, is of vital importance as its repression can bring about masochism and self-destruction. The sublimation in this case is a conceptual artistic praxis that takes place through an in-camera editing technique that relies on sunlight's destructive capacity to burn the film's emulsion.

TOWARDS THE FLAME
SOTIRIOS VARSAMIS AND ROBIN MORRISON

In girum imus nocte et consumimur igni (*We enter the circle at night and we are consumed by fire*) is an ancient Latin palindrome that describes the action of moths which are consumed by their inclination to fly in circles towards the flame — a movement towards the light, the fire or en(light)enment that devours them.

Towards the Flame is the memory of death we all have while still being alive. It is a sound installation that brings to flame/light and simultaneously

2 ↑ 29

Sotirios Varsamis, Robin Morrison, *Towards the Flame*. Audience experiencing the sound installation. Photo: Ståle Eriksen.

burns a space, a room of thoughts. All of our friends were asked to read the Latin palindrome thirty times with their own personal way, accent, rhythm and style in the space of their choice. All these recordings, all these memories of voices and spaces are over-layered and move in circles of random combinations within the space of the installation, around the flame/light like moths. Some of these recordings were made in private spaces like in the bedroom, office or in one case under the duvet. Some other recordings were made in nature like next to a stream of water or by the fire in the moonlight, while others were made in public spaces like an open market or on the bus.

All these breaths/voices and spaces bring to flame/light this installation, this room of thoughts, while at the same time they burn/exhaust it by constant repetition. Breathing is the fire that keeps us humans alive. Breathing brings light to our memories, our relationships, and occupies our private and public spaces, while at the same time it burns them, carrying us closer to death in ways we cannot control and comprehend — like the moths in the Latin palindrome and like us in this installation.

1 This was the starting point of the event 'Buildings on Fire: Towards a New Approach to Urban Memory', which dealt with 'fire as a methodology'. The curation of this event, which was in collaboration with Elena Papadaki, consisted of artistic interventions and a series of one-day presentations by fire specialists, researchers, architects, curators and artists.

2 Thomas Gordon Smith, *Vitruvius on Architecture* (New York: Monacelli Press, 2003), 38.

3 Gottfried Semper, *The Four Elements of Architecture and Other Writings* (Cambridge: Cambridge University Press, 1989), 102.

4 Joseph Rykwert, *The Idea of a Town: the Anthropology of Urban Form in Rome, Italy and the Ancient World* (London: Faber and Faber, 1976), 104–5.

CONTRIBUTORS

Wes Aelbrecht
is a PhD candidate at the Bartlett School of Architecture, UCL. He holds an MA in Architectural History, a BA in Art History and a Diploma in Architecture. Before he turned to the history of cities and its architecture, he worked in architectural and urban practices in Rotterdam, Madrid and Brussels. Currently he is a teaching fellow at The Bartlett. Wes started pursuing his PhD in 2010, and he investigates the visual discourse of urban decline and urban redevelopment in three different reform moments in Detroit and Chicago, namely urban renewal, urban renaissance and urban shrinkage. He focuses on the use and abuse and the repression of urban decline in the construction of public discourse(s). In other words, his work focuses on the attempt to design the urban imaginary of a large section of the population and explores the role photographs play in the construction of the urban imaginary. The AHRC and Fulbright Fellowship fund his research.

John Aiken
was born in Belfast, Northern Ireland. He completed his undergraduate and graduate studies in London at the Chelsea School of Art and subsequently was awarded the Rome Scholarship in Sculpture at the British School at Rome. He works mainly in the field of sculpture and installation and has exhibited extensively in galleries and museums internationally. He has a strong commitment to public art and its interface with architecture and urban environments and has completed many collaborative projects and public commissions in Europe, the USA and China. He has lectured and has been a visiting artist at many universities and art schools in Europe, Australia, Asia, the USA and Canada. In 2012, he was appointed to his current position as Chair Professor of Fine Arts and Director of the Academy of Visual Arts, Hong Kong Baptist University. Previously, he held the Slade Chair of Fine Art and was Director of the Slade School of Fine Art at University College London (UCL).

Sabina Andron
is a lecturer in architectural history and a PhD candidate at the Bartlett School of Architecture, UCL. Her research focuses on city surface inscriptions such as graffiti and street art, in the context of a semiotics of the built environment. She holds a BA in comparative literature (2008) and an MA in visual culture (2011). Sabina has presented her work on graffiti and street art in the UK, USA, Australia and throughout Europe, has published articles in edited volumes and has shown photographic work in exhibitions in Philadelphia and London. She is also an arts advisor and facilitator. She runs the London-based arts organisation I Know What I Like, where she organises critical gallery visits and art walks, and curates exhibitions with work by international artists.

Sarah Bell
is an environmental engineer whose research relates to the sustainability of urban water systems. She is Senior Lecturer in the Department of Civil, Environmental and Geomatic Engineering at UCL. She is currently Director of Thek, which aims to improve engagement between local communities and engineering research. She is interested in policy and the social aspects of

sustainability and how they relate to new technologies and infrastructure. Her work addresses water efficiency, water recycling, green infrastructure and options for new water resources. Her ongoing research investigates how to engage communities in infrastructure design to meet needs for food, water and energy. She has led or co-convened projects including the UCLoo Festival of alternative sanitation and London 2062, which addressed the future of London. In 2015, she was a British Science Association Media Fellow, covering science, engineering and the environment for Londonist.

Camillo Boano
is an architect and urbanist. He is Senior Lecturer at the Bartlett Development Planning Unit, UCL, where he directs the MSc in Building and Urban Design in Development. He is also Co-director of the UCL Urban Laboratory. Camillo has over twenty years of experiences in research, design consultancies and development work in South America, the Middle East, Eastern Europe and South-East Asia. His research interests revolve around the encounters between critical theory, radical philosophy with urban and architectural design processes where collective agency and politics encounter urban narratives and aesthetics, especially those emerging in informal and contested urbanisms. He is the author, with William Hunter and Caroline Newton, of *Contested Urbanism in Dharavi: Writings and Projects for the Resilient City* (London: Development Planning Unit, 2013) as well as several journal articles.

Ben Campkin
is the author of *Remaking London: Decline and Regeneration in Urban Culture* (London: I.B.Tauris, 2013), which was awarded a commendation in the Royal Institute of British Architects President's Awards for Research (2014) and won the Urban Communication Foundation's Jane Jacobs Award (2015). Ben is also co-editor of *Dirt: New Geographies of Cleanliness and Contamination* (London: I.B.Tauris, 2012), and founding co-editor of the series *Urban Pamphleteer*. His essays have recently been published in anthologies such as *Forty Ways to Think About Architecture, Camera Constructs, The Art of Dissent* and *Urban Constellations*; and in peer-reviewed journals such as *Architectural Theory Review,* the *Journal of Architecture* and *Architectural Design*. Ben is Senior Lecturer in Architectural History and Theory at the Bartlett School of Architecture, UCL, and has been Director of UCL's cross-disciplinary Urban Laboratory since 2011.

Max Colson
is an artist using photography, video and installation. His practice playfully considers the relationship between paranoia, the banal and hidden power in urban redevelopment. He was the Leverhulme Trust-funded Artist-in-Residence at UCL Urban Laboratory between 2014 and 2015. *Virtual Control: Security and the Urban Imagination*, his first solo exhibition, was hosted at the Royal Institute of British Architects (2015). His work has been featured in a broad range of publications across architecture, design and photography, including *Icon, Architecture Today* and *Hotshoe International*. He has exhibited in group shows in London (2015), Berlin (2014) and Holland (2015). He was selected as one of the UK winners of the Flash Forward Emerging Photographer competition (2013). He currently teaches on the MA in Communication Design at Central Saint Martins.

Kate Crawford, Sarah Bell, Felicity Davies, Charlotte Johnson, Sunyoung Joo, Sharon Hayward and Richard Lee
This chapter was edited by a team of authors brought together by the UCL Engineering Exchange and led by Sarah Bell at the Department of Civil, Environmental and Geomatic Engineering (CEGE). At the time of writing, Kate Crawford and Felicity Davies were researchers at CEGE; Charlotte Johnson was a Public Engagement Fellow based at The Bartlett; and Sunyoung Joo was a PhD candidate at the UCL Energy Institute.

Sharon Hayward is a coordinator of the London Tenants Federation (LTF). LTF is an umbrella organisation bringing together borough-wide and sub-regional federations and organisations of tenants of social housing providers. LTF provides a strong democratic and accountable regional tenant voice, focusing on the housing, planning and community related issues that exist in the specific context of London with its high land and property values, lack of genuine affordability, high levels of housing need and widening gap between rich and poor. LTF challenges negative stereotypes of social-housing tenants, widely and generally in its work and directly in some of its projects.

Richard Lee is a co-ordinator of Just Space, a London-wide network of voluntary and community groups working together to influence planning policy at the regional, borough and neighbourhood levels.

Juliet Davis
is a senior lecturer at Cardiff University. She convenes the M.Arch. in Architecture at the Welsh School of Architecture and teaches in urban design, planning and architectural history. She graduated from Cambridge University with a first-class BA degree and the top portfolio prize in architecture in 1995 and with a commendation for the Diploma in Architecture in 1999. She has been a qualified architect since 2000, working for Eric Parry Architects from 1999 to 2005. She graduated from an AHRC-funded PhD based at the London School of Economics (LSE) Cities Programme in 2012, where she was also an LSE fellow teaching in the design studio of the MSc in City Design and Social Science and a member of Professor Richard Sennett's Nylon Research Network. She is interested in processes and effects of urban change and particularly with how sustainable and regenerated futures are imagined and constructed.

Bernadette Devilat
is a qualified architect and Master in Architecture from the Pontifical Catholic University of Chile (PUC). She is co-founder of Devilat Lanuza Architects. She has been

studying reconstruction after earthquakes in Chilean heritage areas since the 2005 earthquake, when she co-founded Tarapacá Project, whose main work has been published and also exhibited in 2010 at the Expo Shanghai, Venice Architectural Biennale and Architecture Biennial of Chile. Her master's thesis has won awards in two national competitions and also exhibited at the Architectural Biennale of Chile in 2010. She taught in the Architectural Design Studio at PUC from 2009 to 2010 and, after the 2010 earthquake, worked in the Heritage Reconstruction Programme at the Ministry of Housing and Urban Development of Chile. She has published in journals and books and has delivered papers at different conferences and exhibitions. She is currently a PhD candidate at the Bartlett School of Architecture, UCL, with a Becas Chile scholarship.

Mădălina Diaconu
studied philosophy in Bucharest (PhD, 1996) and Vienna (PhD, 1998) and received her *habilitation* in philosophy from the University of Vienna (2005), where she has been lecturing since 2006 at the Institute for Philosophy and the Institute for Romance Studies. She conducted research at the Academy of Fine Arts in Vienna, the Austrian Academy of Sciences and the University of Vienna. She is a member of the editorial board of *Studia Phaenomenologica* and Polylog, and of the editorial advisory board for *The Senses and Society* and *Contemporary Aesthetics*. She has published on aesthetics, the phenomenology of perception and sensory design. She is co-editor of *Senses and the City: An Interdisciplinary Approach to Urban Sensescapes* (2011) and *Sensorisches Labor Wien: Urbane Haptik- Und Geruchsforschung* (2011). Her latest books are *Sinnesraum Stadt: Eine Multisensorische Anthropologie* (2012) and *Phänomenologie der Sinne* (2013).

Ger Duijzings
is Professor in Social Anthropology at the Graduate School for East and Southeast European Studies (Ludwig-Maximilians-Universität München and Universität Regensburg). Before moving to Germany, he was Reader in the Anthropology of Eastern Europe at the UCL School of Slavonic and East European Studies and Co-director of the UCL Urban Laboratory. He did extensive research on the conflicts in the former Yugoslavia and is currently studying urban transformations and social inequality in post-socialist Bucharest. He published two monographs: *Religion and the Politics of Identity in Kosovo* (2000) and *History and Memory in Eastern Bosnia: Backgrounds to the Fall of Srebrenica* (2002). He (co-)edited *The New Bosnian Mosaic: Identities, Memories and Moral Claims in a Post-War Society* (2007), *Cities Methodologies Bucharest* (2011) and *Global Villages: Rural and Urban Transformations in Contemporary Bulgaria* (2013).

Alexandre Apsan Frediani
is a lecturer in community-led development in the Global South and Co-director of the MSc in Social Development Practice at the Bartlett Development Planning Unit, UCL. Alexandre has a PhD in Planning, and his topics of interest include housing and informal settlement upgrading, participatory approaches to planning and urban design and the application of Amartya Sen's Capability Approach in the context of urban development. Some current activities include the implementation the Sierra Leone Urban Research Centre with colleagues from Njala University as well as investigating the role of occupations by social movements in inner-city area of São Paulo in enabling substantive citizenship with colleagues from University of Sheffield and Universidade Federal do ABC in Brazil. Alexandre is an associate of Architecture Sans Frontières UK, where he has been working in the Change by Design programme, focusing on the use of participatory design methodologies to bring about social change.

Fugitive Images
are Andrea Luka Zimmerman and David Roberts, a collaborative cultural activist producing agency with a particular interest in, and commitment to, the social organisation of urban space. For the three works cited, Fugitive Images collaborated with their neighbours on the Haggerston West Estate and local artists Anne Louise Buckley, Briony Campbell, Chantel Forrester, Elam Forrester, Jahcheyse Forrester, Lorna Forrester, Rosie Fowler, Taina Galis, Steve Hart, Therese Henningsen, Lasse Johansson, Gillian McIver, Lewis Osbourne, Eric Phillip, Adam Rosenthal, Georgia Sangster, Ruth-Marie Tunkara, Smart Urhiofe, Julie Vandemark, Julia Vandemark and Cathy Ward.

Matthew Gandy
is Professor of Geography at the University of Cambridge. He has taught at the University of Sussex and at UCL, where he was Director of the UCL Urban Laboratory from 2005 to 2011. He has been a visiting professor at several universities including Columbia University, New York; Humboldt University, Berlin; Newcastle University; Technical University, Berlin; University of California-Los Angeles; and University of the Arts, Berlin. His books and edited collections include *Urban Constellations* (2011), *The Acoustic City* (2014) and *The Fabric of Space: Water, Modernity, and the Urban Imagination* (2014), along with articles in *Architectural Design*, *New Left Review*, *Society and Space* and many other journals. He is currently researching the interface between cultural and scientific aspects to urban bio-diversity. His book *Moth* was published in 2016 as part of the Reaktion animal series.

Mohamad Hafeda
is an artist and a designer. He is a founding partner of Febrik, a collaborative platform for participatory art and design research works in Palestinian refugee camps in the Middle East and housing estates in London. Mohamad is a lecturer in architecture at Leeds Beckett University. He has a PhD degree in Architectural Design at the Bartlett School of Architecture, UCL. He is the Co-editor of *Narrating Beirut from its Borderlines* (2011) and Febrik's project *Creative Refuge* (2014). His work

has been exhibited at the Beirut Art Center and Cities Methodologies exhibition at UCL. Febrik collaborates with local NGOs and institutions; their projects include residencies and exhibitions at the Serpentine Galleries, South London Gallery, the Victoria and Albert Museum, the Mosaic Rooms and the Architecture Biennale Rotterdam.

Suzanne Hall
is an urban ethnographer and has practised as an architect in South Africa. She is an assistant professor in the Department of Sociology and a senior research associate at LSE Cities at the London School of Economics and Political Science. Suzi is currently a principal investigator on an Economic and Social Research Council grant on Super-Diverse Streets: Economies and Spaces of Urban Migration in UK Cities and is conducting comparative research across Birmingham, Bristol, Leicester, London and Manchester. Her research and teaching interests are foregrounded in everyday formations of global urbanisation, particularly urban migration and migrant economies, urban multiculture and civility, ethnography and visual methods. She is the author of *City, Street and Citizen: The Measure of the Ordinary* (2012) and has made a research-based film called *Ordinary Streets* with Sophie Yetton (2015).

Andrew Harris
is a senior lecturer in geography and urban studies at UCL, where he convenes the interdisciplinary Urban Studies MSc and is a co-director of the UCL Urban Laboratory. His research develops critical perspectives on the role of art, creativity and culture in recent processes of urban restructuring and on three-dimensional geographies of contemporary cities. He has published articles in various journals including *Urban Studies*, *Cities*, *International Journal of Urban and Regional Research*, *Progress in Human Geography* and *Transactions of the Institute of British Geographers*.

Laura Hirst
is a PhD researcher at the Global Development Institute at the University of Manchester, working collaboratively with the NGO Operation Florian to investigate risks, well-being and pathways towards community involvement in decentralised fire and rescue services in resource-poor urban settlements in the Global South. Prior to this she worked with the Homeless Peoples Federation, Philippines on community mapping and participatory planning projects in Davao City. She was previously a graduate teaching assistant on the MSc in Social Development Practice at the Development Planning Unit, UCL as well as administrator at the UCL Urban Laboratory.

Margareta Kern
is a visual artist, cultural campaigner and lecturer based in Cornwall and London. Kern works in photography, film, drawing and animation exploring gender, labour, migration and construction of political agencies and subjectivities. Kern holds BA in Fine Art from Goldsmiths College and an MA in Visual Anthropology and SE European Studies from UCL. Her work has been presented in gallery and educational contexts, including at Tate Modern, Photographers Gallery, Durham University, Whitechapel Gallery, Centre for Possible Studies, Impressions Gallery, Iniva, Whitstable Biennalle, Kunsthalle Budapest, Shedhalle Zurich, SC Gallery Zagreb, 54th October Salon Belgrade and many others. Kern is a recipient of several project grants from the Leverhulme Trust, Arts Council England, British Film Institute, National Media Museum and most recently an award from the Cultural Centre Belgrade for her project *To Whom Does the World Belong?*

Felipe Lanuza Rilling
is an architect. He trained at the University of Chile and has a Master in Architecture from the Catholic University of Chile. His interests are situated in the areas of architectural and urban design, history and theory, where he has worked as an educator and researcher while a practising architect. Through his investigations on the notion of absence in urban leftovers, he explores processes of design and representation as a way of prompting alternative understandings and interventions in the built environment. He develops these ideas at the Bartlett School of Architecture, UCL, where he pursues a PhD in Architectural Design. Felipe is also co-founder of the practice Devilat + Lanuza Architects and Senior Associate at Urban Transcripts.

Leah Lovett
is a UK-based artist and writer currently researching her PhD at the Slade, UCL, with support from the AHRC. Her project investigates the spatial politics of Brazilian theatre director Augusto Boal's Invisible Theatre as a way of opening up questions and possibilities for her own performance-based practice. Leah participated in Cities Methodologies between 2010 and 2012. Other performances and exhibitions include *Light Transmission*, Wellcome Collection, London (2015); *Contra Band*, Floating Cinema, London, CASA 24, Rio de Janeiro and online (2014); *Murmuration*, Hemispheic Encuentro, Montreal (2014); and *A Small Hiccup*, Grand Union, Birmingham and touring (2013). Publications include 'Crowd Control: Encountering Art's Audiences' in Outi Remes et al., *Performativity in the Gallery: Staging Interactive Encounters* (2014).

Anthony Luvera
is an artist, writer and educator based in London. His photographic work has been exhibited widely in galleries, public spaces and festivals including the British Museum, London Underground's Art on the Underground, National Portrait Gallery London, Belfast Exposed Photography, Australian Centre for Photography, Malmö Fotobiennal, PhotoIreland and Les Rencontres D'Arles Photographie. His writing appears regularly in a wide range of periodicals and peer-reviewed journals including *Photoworks*, *Source* and *Photographies*. He is Course Director of Photography at Coventry University, and he facilitates workshops and gives lectures for the public education programmes of the National Portrait Gallery,

The Photographers' Gallery, the Barbican Art Gallery, and community projects across the UK.

Mariana Mogilevich
is a historian of architecture and urbanism whose research focuses on the design and politics of the public realm. Her current projects include a study of the role of the psychological sciences in urban design and the book *The Invention of Public Space: Design and Politics in Lindsay's New York* (1965–1973). She was an inaugural Princeton–Mellon Fellow in Architecture, Urbanism and the Humanities at Princeton University and has taught architectural history and urban studies at Harvard Graduate School of Design, New York University and Princeton University. Her written work appears in journals including *Praxis* and *Future Anterior*, and the edited volumes *Use Matters: An Alternative History of Architecture*, *Summer in the City* and *The City Lost and Found*. Mariana holds a BA in Literature from Yale University and a PhD in the History of Architecture and Urbanism from Harvard University.

Caroline Newton
is an experienced socio-spatial practitioner. Her work focuses on the socio-spatial dimensions and sustainability of design and critical spatial practices. The core of her interests is the intertwinement of the notions of freedom, public sphere, city, architecture and democracy. Caroline is currently working on several pilot projects in which research by design is used as a tool for both redefining existing policies and simultaneously redeveloping contested urban spaces. Caroline is a guest professor at the Faculty of Architecture at the K.U. Leuven, where she is teaching Critical Urban Theory in the International Masters.

Chi Nguyen
is a Toronto-based communications designer working at the intersection of visual communication and spatial practice. She holds an MA in Communication Design from Central Saint Martins and a Bachelor in Architecture from Carleton University, with additional training in art, technology and new media design from OCAD University and the Copenhagen Institute of Interaction Design. Her academic research focuses on design, media and visual culture within the context of the built environment with a particular emphasis on exploring experimental forms of civic participation in urban discourse and alternative ways of communicating about, in and to the city. Her work has been exhibited at Somerset House and Lethaby Gallery in London and at the Glass Factory in Shenzhen, China. In her professional practice, Chi has led the branding and communications efforts of some of Canada's leading architecture studios.

ThienVinh Nguyen
is a Vietnamese-born, California-grown, PhD candidate in the Department of Geography at UCL. As a member of the UCL Urban Laboratory, she curated the 'Learning to Walk' programme for Cities Methodologies week in spring 2014. Her thesis explores the themes of urban possibilities, infrastructure and governance in the oil city of Sekondi-Takoradi, Ghana. She is an avid walker and forager.

Mircea Nicolae
has developed a body of work researching the economical and socio-political structure of Bucharest. Through anonymous interventions in public space, he reflects on the social consequences of consumption, urban legislation and architectural production. In his latest work, Nicolae investigates the urban identity of a city in constant cultural and economic shift either by bringing outside public space inside the museum or through means of serial photography produced with the help of a large format camera. Nicolae is based in Bucharest. He was awarded the Special Prize and the People's Choice Prize at the Future Generation Art Prize in 2010. Recent group shows include *Pink Caviar* at the Louisiana Museum of Modern Art, *Humlebaek and One Sixth of the Earth: Ecologies of Image* at Museo de Arte Contemporáneo de Castilla y León. In 2011, he exhibited at the 54th Venice Biennial.

Rastko Novaković
is an artist working with the moving image. Over the past decade he has completed forty pieces that range from one-minute to feature-length single-screen videos, a public art panorama, a site-specific outdoor cinema installation, documentaries, lyrical films, campaigning videos and documented performances. His current practice is a set of long-standing collaborations. He is active in London and Europe-wide housing campaigns and in the UK trade-union movement. His latest film *Concrete Heart Land* (2014), co-authored with Steven Ball, which traces the twelve-year story of the social cleansing of the Heygate Estate (South London), has been screening extensively throughout the UK. He holds an MA in Research Architecture from Goldsmiths College.

Hilary Powell
is an artist who is preoccupied with marginalised histories, places and processes – from a DIY Olympics staged on the sites set to become London 2012 to a participatory roller-skating animation illuminating Archway Tower. Recent projects include the public production line of a pop-up book charting a hidden A–Z history of the Lea Valley emerging from investigation of the pop-up book as a tool to examine simultaneous construction/ collapse during an AHRC Fellowship in the Creative and Performing Arts at the Bartlett School of Architecture, UCL. The book won the Birgit Skiold Award for Excellence at the London Art Book Fair and is in the collections of MoMA NY, the Victoria and Albert Museum and the Poetry Library. Her work around regeneration sites has taken her onto the demolition site and led to an ongoing fascination with the processes, materials and people at work, and she is now Artist-in-Residence with Maylarch Demolition.

Sophia Psarra
is Reader of Architecture and Spatial Design at the Bartlett School of Architecture, UCL, and Editor of the *Journal of Space Syntax*. She uses computer modeling

to analyse spatial layouts in relation to social, cultural, cognitive and organisational performance. This analysis is combined with empirical data of users' activity to provide a detailed account of how organic cities emerge through self-organising process and how buildings are legible and address the architectural and organisational intentions. A second aspect of her work relates to the relationship between space, exhibition narratives and visitors' exploration patterns. Her activities in these areas have resulted in creative installations, design projects and publications (e.g., *Architecture and Narrative: The Formation of Space and Cultural Meaning*, 2009). She has collaborated with leading cultural institutions on layout design, exhibition narratives and visitors' experience (The Museum of Modern Art, New York; The Natural History Museum, London). As a practising architect, she was part of a team that won first prizes in international architectural competitions (e.g., EUROPAN). Her work has been exhibited at the Venice Biennale, the George Pompidou Centre, NAI Rotterdam, and in London, Berlin, Milan and Athens.

Joanna Rajkowska
is an artist based in London and Nowogród, Poland. She is a PhD candidate in the Department of Art at Goldsmiths, University of London. Rajkowska works with objects, films, photography, installations, ephemeral actions and widely discussed interventions in public space. Her artwork has been presented in the UK, Germany, Poland, France, Switzerland, Brazil, Sweden, USA, Palestine and Turkey, among others. Her public projects include commissions by CCA Zamek Ujazdowski (*Oxygenator*, 2007), Trafo Gallery (*The Airways*, 2008), Museum of Modern Art in Warsaw (*Ravine*, 2009), The Showroom (*Chariot*, 2010), British Council (*Benjamin in Konya*, 2010), 7th Berlin Biennale (*Born in Berlin*, 2012), Royal Society of Arts, Citizen Power Peterborough programme's Arts and Social Change, Arts Council England (unrealised project, *The Peterborough Child*, 2012), Frieze Projects 2012 (*Forcing a Miracle*, 2012) and Institute for Contemporary Ideas and Art (*Carpet*, 2014).

Kieren Reed
is Head of Undergraduate Sculpture at the UCL Slade School of Fine Art. His practice encompasses sculpture, performance and installation, from studies in form to the production of architectural structures. Artworks are most often linked to a place, a site or a consideration of a space or situation. Reed has also worked in management positions within various arts organisations including West London Projects, the Pump House Gallery and the South London Gallery. He works individually and in collaboration with artist Abigail Hunt. Recent projects and commissions have included Herbert Read Gallery, Artsway, Tate, Whitstable Biennale, Ritter Zamet, Quay Arts, Camden Arts Centre, Ikon Gallery, The New Art Gallery Walsall, Gasworks and Studio Voltaire.

Jane Rendell
is an academic and writer. She trained and practised as an architectural designer before studying for her MSc and PhD in architectural history. Her interdisciplinary work, through which she has developed concepts of 'critical spatial practice' and 'site-writing', crosses architecture, art, feminism, history and psychoanalysis. Her books include *Site-Writing* (2010), *Art and Architecture* (2006) and *The Pursuit of Pleasure* (2002), and the co-edited collections *Pattern* (2007), *Critical Architecture* (2007), *Spatial Imagination* (2005), *The Unknown City* (2001), *Intersections* (2000), *Gender, Space, Architecture* (1999) and *Strangely Familiar* (1995). Recent texts have been commissioned by Jasmina Cibic, Apollonia Susteric and transparadiso, FRAC Centre, Orléans, and Hamburger Bahnhof, Berlin, and her new book concerning transitional spaces in architecture and psychoanalysis will be published in late 2016. She is Professor of Architecture and Art at the Bartlett School of Architecture, UCL.

David Roberts
is a doctoral student in Architectural Design at the Bartlett School of Architecture, UCL, a course tutor on the MSc in Urban Studies at UCL, part of the collaborative art practice Fugitive Images and part of the architecture collective Involve. He uses poetry and performance to explore the relation between people and place. He has exhibited, lectured and published work related to public housing, architecture, critical methodologies and site-specific practice. David's thesis, *Make Public: Performing Public Housing in Regenerating East London* explores the history and future of two East London housing estates undergoing regeneration: the Haggerston Estate, a 1935–8 London County Council neo-Georgian perimeter block demolished in 2014; and Balfron Tower, a 1965–7 Brutalist high-rise designed by Ernö Goldfinger facing refurbishment and privatisation in 2016.

Jennifer Robinson
is Professor of Human Geography at UCL and Visiting Professor at the African Centre for Cities, University of Cape Town. She has also worked at the University of KwaZulu-Natal, Durban, the London School of Economics and the Open University. Her book, *Ordinary Cities* (2006) developed a post-colonial critique of urban studies, arguing for urban theorising that draws on the experiences of a wider range of cities around the globe. This project has been taken forward in her call to reinvent comparative urbanism for global urban studies in her recent articles 'Cities in a World of Cities' (in the *International Journal of Urban and Regional Research*) and 'Thinking Cities through Elsewhere' (in *Progress in Human Geography*). Current projects include exploring transnational aspects of Johannesburg and London's policy-making processes and collaborative and community-based research comparing governance of large-scale urban developments in London, Johannesburg and Shanghai (with Phil Harrison and Fulong Wu). She has also published extensively on the history and contemporary politics of South African cities, including *The Power of Apartheid* (1996).

Rebecca Ross
experiments, as a conventional humanities researcher and as a designer, with the ways in which images, media and data are actively intertwined with conditions in neighborhoods and cities. A recent project *London Is Changing* was displayed on digital billboards around Central London during February and March 2015. Ross has published in the *Journal of Planning History*, *Urban Constellations* and *Camera Constructs*. She is Co-founder and Co-editor (with Ben Campkin) of the *Urban Pamphleteer*, is an adviser to the UCL Urban Laboratory and works on a consultancy basis with Camden Council. Originally from New York, she is currently MA Course Leader and Senior Lecturer in Graphic Communication Design at Central Saint Martins in London. She holds a PhD in Architectural and Urban History from Harvard (2012) and an MFA in Graphic Design from Yale (2002).

Simson&Volley
are a collaborative partnership established in 2008 between the artists Henrietta Simson and Jo Volley. The partnership allows the subsuming and exploration of shared interests, which include working with installation, projection and sound. Their work employs a wide range of materials and media, combining the traditional with the contemporary. They have contributed to Cities Methodologies from 2010 to 2014. Mel Gooding, the well-known and respected British art writer and critic, described Simson&Volley's collaboration as, 'a lovely dual-imagination at work between media, scales and dimensions, intellectually clear and uncluttered. A meeting of good and vibrant minds, not afraid of beauty as fact or idea.' Exhibitions and publications include *The Hearing Trumpet*, West Dean College, West Sussex; *Brittle Crazie Glasse*, Islington Mill, Salford; *Jerwood Drawing Prize*, UK touring exhibition and catalogue (2012); *The Voice and Nothing More*, Slade Research Centre, UCL (2010); *spaces/places/senses/places/senses/spaces*, Visual Arts Center, Portsmouth, Virginia, USA (2009).

Andrew Stevenson
is a film-maker, sound artist and researcher from Manchester. He is based at Manchester Metropolitan University, in the Department of Psychology. Andrew uses a range of researcher methods, including sensory ethnography, ethnographic film and soundscape composition. His research interests include space and place, migration, culture, inter-corporeality and friendship. He has published several articles investigating the sensory apprehension of urban space.

Giorgio Talocci
teaches Urban Design for Development and Critical Urbanism in the MSc Building and Urban Design in Development, at the Bartlett Development Planning Unit, UCL. He is currently researching the significance of 'urban voids' in the government of the city, with a particular focus on South-East Asian urban environments. He worked as a researcher and practitioner in Phnom Penh, Cambodia, and took part in several experiences of community-driven settlement upgrading in Turkey, Brazil, Philippines and Italy.

Johan Thom
lives in Pretoria and works as an artist and a senior lecturer in Fine Art at the Department of Visual Art in the University of Pretoria. He uses a variety of media including sculpture, video, performance, drawing, print-making and photography. His artworks have been exhibited across the world at venues such as the Venice Biennale (Italy), Iwalewa Haus (Bayreuth, Germany), the Goodman Gallery (South Africa) and elsewhere. He completed a PhD in Fine Art on a Commonwealth Scholarship at the UCL Slade School of Fine Art in 2014. His current research interests include materiality, evolutionary theory and art, the body, unruliness and the experiential.

Henrietta Williams
is a photographer and videographer. Her work often focuses on telling stories about the built environment and on security and surveillance within the UK, and she has been widely exhibited and published. She has been featured in the *Guardian*, *Evening Standard* and *Open Democracy* and on the BBC. As a videographer, Henrietta is regularly commissioned by the *Guardian* and the Architectural Association. Her work is also often published within the architecture press, in particular *Dezeen*, *ARCH+*, *Domus*, *BD* and *Blueprint*. Henrietta has recently begun a practice-based AHRC-funded PhD in Architectural Design at the Bartlett School of Architecture, UCL. She regularly lectures about her practice in the UK and internationally at institutions such as the Bauhaus, the Royal College of Art, King's College London and Cambridge University.

Stamatis Zografos
is a teaching fellow in architecture at the Bartlett School of Architecture, UCL and a practicing architect at Dexter Moren Associates in London. He is also the founder of Incandescent Square, an interdisciplinary platform for research and design. He studied architecture at University of Westminster and at Kingston University. He completed his MA degree in Cultural Studies at Goldsmiths University of London and his PhD degree at the same department. His research is interdisciplinary and focuses on architecture, memory and fire.

INDEX

Note: Page numbers in italic indicate a page with illustration only.

Published in 2016 by
I.B.Tauris & Co. Ltd
London • New York
www.ibtauris.com

ISBN: 978 1 78453 459 2
eISBN: 978 1 78672 166 2
ePDF: 978 1 78673 166 1

A full CIP record for this book is available from the British Library
A full CIP record is available from the Library of Congress

Library of Congress Catalog Card Number: available

Designed by Bandiera, Guglielmo Rossi
Printed and bound in Spain by Grafo S.A.

Page I quotation from Bertolt Brecht, 'Against George Lukács', *New Left Review* 0 (84), 39–53, 51.